WITCHCRAFT FOR TOMORROW

Doreen Valiente was one of the founders of modern Wicca and was initiated into four different branches of the Old Religion in Great Britain. She is the author of *An ABC of Witchcraft: Past and Present, Natural Magic, The Rebirth of Witchcraft* and *Witchcraft: A Tradition Renewed.* She made many television and radio appearances, discussing witchcraft and folklore and displaying items from her collection of witchcraft objects. Doreen Valiente died in 1999.

Also by Doreen Valiente

An ABC of Witchcraft
Natural Magic
The Rebirth of Witchcraft

Witchcraft for Tomorrow

by

DOREEN VALIENTE

ROBERT HALE

First published in 1978 by Robert Hale

Paperback edition 1993

This edition published by Robert Hale, an imprint of
The Crowood Press Ltd, Ramsbury, Marlborough Wiltshire SN8 2HR

enquiries@crowood.com

www.crowood.com

This impression 2021

British Library Cataloguing-in-Publication Data
A catalogue record for this book is available from the British Library.

ISBN 978 0 7090 5244 9

Printed and bound in India by Replika Press Pvt Ltd

CONTENTS

Illustrations

Line Figures

THE WITCH'S BALLAD

Oh, I have been beyond the town,
Where nightshade black and mandrake grow,
And I have heard and I have seen
What righteous folk would fear to know!

For I have heard, at still midnight,
Upon the hilltop far, forlorn,
With note that echoed through the dark,
The winding of the heathen horn.

And I have seen the fire aglow,
And glinting from the magic sword,
And with the inner eye beheld
The Hornéd One, the Sabbat's lord.

We drank the wine, and broke the bread,
And ate it in the Old One's name.
We linked our hands to make the ring,
And laughed and leaped the Sabbat game.

Oh, little do the townsfolk reck,
When dull they lie within their bed!
Beyond the streets, beneath the stars,
A merry round the witches tread!

And round and round the circle spun,
Until the gates swung wide ajar,
That bar the boundaries of earth
From faery realms that shine afar.

Oh, I have been and I have seen
In magic worlds of Otherwhere.
For all this world may praise or blame,
For ban or blessing nought I care.

For I have been beyond the town,
Where meadowsweet and roses grow,
And there such music did I hear
As worldly-righteous never know.

D.V.

For those seeking the Old Ways and Green Spirituality, The Pagan Federation – BM Box 7097, London, WC1N 3XX – Europe's oldest Pagan organization, can supply information, publications, events and contacts in all Pagan paths, including Wicca.

Introduction

This book is written as a contribution to the Aquarian Age. The concept of the new Age of Aquarius is discussed on all sides today; but how many people know just what it means?

Our planet earth has three kinds of motion: its rotation upon its axis every twenty-four hours, giving day and night; its orbit round the sun, giving the seasons of the year; and the slow circling of its axis, like the motion of a spinning top, which gives the apparent alterations of the poles of the heavens, and the shifting of the equinoctial point known to astronomers as the precession of the equinoxes.

This gives the Great Year, consisting of about 25,920 earthly years, during which the equinoctial point moves right around the Zodiac. The Great Year is reckoned to have twelve 'months', one to each zodiacal sign, each of which consists of about 2,160 earthly years. The equinoctial point is observed to move at the rate of about one degree in seventy-two years, the average span of a human life. This makes one 'day' of the Great Year, which has 360 'days', divided into twelve 'months' of thirty 'days' each, corresponding to the 360 degrees of the circle.

At the moment, the equinoctial point appears to be in the constellation Pisces; but it is moving backwards through the starry Zodiac towards Aquarius. (The Zodiac of the starry constellations, the sidereal Zodiac, must not be confused with the tropical Zodiac, the apparent yearly path of the sun, divided into twelve signs. In the latter, of course, the spring equinox is always the first degree of Aries.)

We are therefore in the last part of the Age of Pisces, when the characteristics of that sign, which have been imposed upon mankind in general for nearly 2,000 years, are giving place to those of the sign of Aquarius. All over the world, human society is in a state of flux. The forms of the old order are breaking down, so that those of the new order may be built up. The characteristics of Aquarius, the fixed sign of air, are very different from those of Pisces, the mutable sign of water.

Aquarius has two ruling planets, Saturn and Uranus. Taken
in its highest manifestation, Saturn stands for those things which
endure, which have their roots in the very ancient past: the
eternal verities, the ancient wisdom, the *Dharma* as it is called
in the east. Uranus, on the other hand, is the revolutionary, the
bringer in of what is new, strange, even bizarre. The influence
of these planets working together can be seen in our society today.

A great alteration in human attitudes and behaviour took place
within the decade of the sixties, much to the alarm of conven-
tionally minded people. It has been called the sexual revolution,
the swinging sixties, the advent of the permissive society, and so
on; though a lot of it is simply the frankness of Uranus bringing
out into the open what was always there anyway, but discreetly
hidden beneath a cloak of polite humbug.

This mutation in our society was heralded by a remarkable
astronomical event. On 5th February 1962 no less than seven
heavenly bodies were forgathered in the sign Aquarius. These
were the sun and moon, and all five of the planets visible to the
naked eye, namely Saturn, Jupiter, Mars, Venus and Mercury.
Astrologers all over the world discussed this phenomenon, and it
was generally agreed that it marked some sort of turning-point
in mundane affairs, especially as it occurred in the sign of the new
age. Looking back on the changes that have taken place since
1962, there seems little doubt that the Great Conjunction, as it
was called, did in fact herald a speeding-up of the Aquarian transition, even to a rather uncomfortable pace.

Our knowledge of astronomical influences is not sufficiently
exact for us to be able to pinpoint precisely the start of the
Aquarian Age. Each age lasts about 2,000 years, with transition
periods as one age fades into another. However, thanks to Mr
Francis King, whose books have done so much towards recover-
ing and preserving important traditions of the occultism of the
western world, we know the date for this event as calculated by
the hitherto secret astrological rules of the famous Order of the
Golden Dawn. The date thus arrived at is A.D. 2010.*

According to Louis Charpentier, in his book *The Mysteries of
Chartres Cathedral*, this date is independently confirmed by
astronomical observation. He quotes it at the beginning of Chapter
20 of that book, seemingly unaware of the identical calculation
arrived at by the Order of the Golden Dawn.

Other calculations give the date as A.D. 2160 or even later;
while others claim that the Aquarian Age has already com-

* See *Ritual Magic in England* (Neville Spearman, 1970).

menced. However, it seems apparent that too much of the old Piscean influence still lingers for the latter claim to be true. Pisces is, among other things, the sign of suffering and self-undoing, characteristics singularly widespread in the world today; while the universal brotherhood which is associated with Aquarius is widely aspired to, but seldom reached. Nevertheless, the pace of change seems too rapid and too drastic for the later date of A.D. 2160 to be accurate. Therefore, it may well be that the secret knowledge possessed by the Order of the Golden Dawn is once again proved to be a source of enlightenment to our modern world.

This is not, however, a book about astrology, but about witchcraft. Still, it is necessary to point out that the present-day revival of interest in witchcraft, magic and the occult generally, is all part of the onset of the Aquarian Age. One has to consider the picture as a whole, in order to discern its meaning.

The resurgence of the old religion of nature-worship and magic really began in 1951, when the last of the antiquated Witchcraft Acts in Britain was finally repealed. People considered this Act to be a ludicrous anachronism, used mainly to persecute Spiritualist mediums; and it was largely through the influence of the Spiritualist movement, now widely accepted as respectable, that the Act was finally swept away.

This change in the law made it possible for Mr Cecil H. Williamson to open the Museum of Magic and Witchcraft at Castletown, in the Isle of Man. It was at first called the Folklore Centre, and according to newspaper reports it was planned as an international centre for present-day practising witches. Articles about it appeared under such headlines as 'He Plans a Jamboree for the Witches of the World' and 'Calling all Covens'.

It was news to most people that practising witches still existed; but Mr Williamson was reported as saying that he knew at least a dozen witches in Britain, and that when the Centre was ready he intended to send out a call to a coven of witches that was active in the south of England. At certain times in the year, the coven observed the fertility rituals, dancing in the nude. One of the witches was a very attractive girl, but some of the others were quite old.

Later in 1951, Mr Williamson had been joined by Dr Gerald Brosseau Gardner, who was described as 'the resident witch'. One press report stated that he was a doctor of philosophy from Singapore and a doctor of literature from Toulouse, as well as being a member of the Southern Coven of British Witches.

The question of Gerald Gardner's right to the title of doctor has been raised in recent years. When I got to know him (and we became close friends for many years), I always understood that his degrees were purely honorary. He did not, however, hold a degree from the present University of Singapore, because I communicated with them after old Gerald's death, and asked them this question. The University authorities stated that the University was not even in existence at the time that Gerald Gardner was resident in Malaya, where he was employed in the Civil Service as a Customs officer, before the Second World War. Later, I also got in touch with the University of Toulouse. They informed me that they had never conferred any doctorate of literature upon Gerald Gardner.

Being passionately interested in the survival of the old religion, I wrote to the Isle of Man, and ultimately met Gerald Gardner at the house of a friend. He was a most remarkable character, an endearing and delightful person with a vast knowledge of folk-lore and magic of all kinds. He had set out much of his knowledge about witchcraft in the form of fiction, in his occult novel *High Magic's Aid*, which was published by Michael Houghton of London in 1949. Michael Houghton, also known as Michael Juste, was then the proprietor of the famous occult book store, the Atlantis Bookshop, near the British Museum. However, the time was not yet ripe, and this book had made no great impact.

Gerald Brosseau Gardner is still what is known as 'a controversial figure', both within witchcraft circles and outside them. He was a pioneer naturist, long before naturism (miscalled 'nudism') became generally accepted, and when publicly supporting this scandalous movement took a good deal of moral courage. He knew almost everyone in occult circles in the south of England, including that dangerous acquaintance, Aleister Crowley.

It has been stated by Francis King in his *Ritual Magic in England* that Aleister Crowley was paid by Gerald Gardner to write the rituals of Gardner's new witch cult; and this statement has been repeated without question by various other writers. It seems to me, however, to be highly questionable. The basic rituals of the 'Gardnerian' witch cult were published in the form of fiction in the novel mentioned above, *High Magic's Aid*, which as already stated appeared in 1949. (Faced with hostile newspaper publicity, old Gerald later found it politic to deny this; but I was initiated as a witch by Gerald Gardner in 1953, and the rituals used were practically identical with those in *High Magic's Aid*). Now, Gerald Gardner never met Aleister Crowley until the very last years of the latter's life, when he was a feeble old man living at a private hotel in Hastings, being kept alive by injections of drugs. Gardner and Crowley were introduced by the late Arnold

Crowther, according to Mr Crowther's own statement to me, which I have no reason to doubt.

If therefore, Crowley really invented these rituals in their entirety, they must be about the last thing he ever wrote. Was this enfeebled and practically dying man really capable of such a *tour de force*?

Moreover, Gerald had been initiated as a witch in the New Forest area of England in 1939, and taken part in coven rites against the threatened invasion of Hitler's forces in 1940. Independent corroboration of the existence of this coven, and the performance of these rites, was given to Francis King by Louis Wilkinson, who wrote novels under the pen-name of 'Louis Marlow', and was also a friend of Aleister Crowley. The survival of the New Forest coven, therefore, does not depend upon the word of Gerald Gardner. So what rituals were they using? And what is the truth about the part played by Aleister Crowley in the present-day revival of witchcraft?

In my previous book, *An A.B.C. of Witchcraft Past and Present*, I wrote that Aleister Crowley was not a witch, in spite of the fact that his name as 'The Great Beast', 'The Wickedest Man in the World', and so on, was dragged into every so-called exposure of witchcraft in the sensational press. I knew that in Gerald Gardner's book *Witchcraft Today* he speculates upon the origin of the witch rituals, and states that he had been told by Aleister Crowley that Crowley had been a member of the witch cult when he was a young man. Gerald told me personally that Crowley claimed this, but added that he had left of his own accord because 'he wouldn't be ordered about by women' (Crowley's contemptuous attitude to women is apparent throughout his writings). However, I always took this with a grain of salt, thinking it probably just a piece of 'one-up-manship' on Crowley's part.

Some new and curious information has, however, recently come to light, from a correspondent to the witches' news-sheet, *The Wiccan*, an occasional publication which circulates among British and American witch covens and sympathizers. This gentleman, a former resident of East Anglia, states that he is a member of an hereditary Essex coven, and that it was known to his associates that both Aleister Crowley and Allan Bennett in their younger days were pupils of the famous male witch of Canewdon, Essex, 'Old George' Pickingill. An early photograph still exists, according to him, of Pickingill and some of his pupils. Allan Bennett is easily recognizable in it, and the young man beside him strongly resembles the youthful Crowley.

The period of this contact was during the time that Crowley

and Allan Bennett were room-mates in London, engaged together in the study of magic. In this connection, the contributor to *The Wiccan* (whose name was not given in the published account, at his request) points to the passage in Aleister Crowley's *Confessions* about Allan Bennett's 'blasting rod' and its strange powers. He suggests that Bennett did not acquire this magical weapon either from the Order of the Golden Dawn or the Theosophical Society, and this certainly seems a thought-provoking point.

Moreover, we find preserved in Volume 1, No. 3 of Aleister Crowley's publication *The Equinox* an extraordinary ritual devised by Allan Bennett about this period, entitled *The Ritual for the Evocation unto Visible Appearance of the Great Spirit Taphthartharath*. Taphthartharath is the Spirit of Mercury, and Bennett hoped to persuade this entity to instruct him and three of his friends in the secrets of the magical art and of occult wisdom generally.

This ritual, while resembling the involved and highly dramatic rituals of the Order of the Golden Dawn, also contained features which are not found in Golden Dawn practice. Its focal point in the centre of the circle was 'a small brazen cauldron, heated over a lamp burning with spirit in which a snake has been preserved'. This cauldron was the receptacle for the 'Hell-broth', of which Bennett, as the 'Assistant Magus of Art', was in charge. Its purpose was to provide a material basis for the spirit to take visible appearance. Some letters of Allan Bennett's dealing with the planning of this ritual, and especially with the composition of the 'Hell-broth', are reproduced in *The Magicians of the Golden Dawn* by Ellic Howe. He gives his friend F. L. Gardner (no relation to old Gerald, as far as I know!) a list of substances to be obtained, and cautions him not to talk to anyone about the ritual except the other three persons who are to take part.

Now this ritual, which took place in May 1896, is evidently closely related to witch practices. There is nothing in the rituals of the Golden Dawn about cauldrons or hell-broths, and it looks rather as if this magical venture was an unofficial and even clandestine affair. What its result was, if any, does not seem to be on record.

Bennett's association with British witchcraft was interrupted when he emigrated to Ceylon, probably early in 1900. Here he ultimately became a Buddhist monk, and is best known in association with his work for Buddhism in the West. Eventually, however, he became somewhat dissatisfied with the Buddhist creed, returned to England and took up again the study of practical occultism. He died in 1923, according to Ithell Colquhoun's account of him in her book *Sword of Wisdom: MacGregor Mathers and the Golden Dawn.*

My East Anglian source (who has given his permission for this information to be reproduced here) says that Bennett introduced Crowley to George Pickingill, and that Crowley was admitted to one of George Pickingill's 'nine covens' in either 1899 or 1900. However, Crowley 'did not last long in the craft'; he soon made himself disliked and was expelled. The priestess of his coven described him as 'a dirty-minded, evilly-disposed, vicious little monster'!

Many years later, Crowley met Gerald Gardner, who as we have already seen was a member of a witch coven in the New Forest area of Hampshire. Crowley told Gerald of his experience long ago in the witch cult, and I am told that the two compared notes. Gerald was very anxious to recover all the information he could about the ancient rites; so he asked Crowley to write down the rituals his coven had used. Gerald wanted to compare these with the two sources of information he already had, namely the New Forest coven into which he had been initiated in 1939, and another associated coven into which he had also subsequently been received. Both these covens, I am told, were among the 'nine covens' that old George Pickingill had founded; but it seems that the passage of time had eroded their knowledge of the basic lore that had been communicated to them.

Such, I believe, is the real story behind the allegation that Aleister Crowley wrote the rituals for Gerald Gardner's covens. That these rituals contain phrases from Crowley's published works is however undoubtedly true. Gerald told me that the rituals he recorded were fragmentary. He had to augment them in order to make them workable; and he used some quotations from Crowley's works because he recognized the magical power and beauty inherent in Crowley's writing, though he had no great admiration for Crowley as a man.

It has been alleged that a *Book of Shadows* in Crowley's handwriting was formerly exhibited in Gerald's Museum of Witchcraft on the Isle of Man. I can only say that I never saw this on either of the two occasions when I stayed with Gerald and Donna Gardner on the island. The large, handwritten book depicted in *Witchcraft Today* is not in Crowley's handwriting, but Gerald's.

To return to that remarkable and little-known character, George Pickingill. He was born in Hockley, Essex, in 1816, and died in the village of Canewdon in 1909. Although he was merely a humble farm worker by profession, he could trace his ancestry back for many centuries, to Julia the Witch of Brandon, who was killed in 1071. According to my informant from Essex, each subsequent generation of the Pickingill family served as priests of the Old Religion. 'Old George' himself was held in awe in the village of Canewdon, because of his strange powers, and many countryside tales were told of him. Eric Maple has detailed some of these in his book *The Dark World of Witches*.

A newspaper obituary at the time of Pickingill's death claimed that England had produced only two outstanding magicians: George Pickingill and Merlin! During his lifetime, he was consulted by people from all over the country, and even from Europe and America. Two Master Masons, who were later to become founder members of the *Societas Rosicruciana in Anglia*, from which the Order of the Golden Dawn eventually emerged, were accepted pupils of George Pickingill. These two were Hargrave Jennings and W. J. Hughan. It may be noted that the avowed object of the S.R.I.A. was to enable Masons to study the antiquities of the craft, and also to gather information about 'those mysterious societies which had their existence in the dark ages of the world when might meant right, when every man's hand was against his brother, and when such combinations were necessary to protect the weak against the strong'.*

Quoting from the articles in *The Wiccan* that originally gave this information: 'A small coterie of Master Masons established a lengthy and productive relationship with George Pickingill from the 1850s onwards. These Freemasons entertained Rosicrucian fantasies, and sought personal verification that Masonic Crafters and Rosicrucian Crafters were siblings of the Old Religion. 'Old George' awed these Masonic 'Rosicrucians' with demonstrations of his mastery over various elementals. He was also to fascinate them by expounding 'the inner secrets of Masonry'. None of these learned Master Masons could comprehend how this non-Mason had penetrated their craft mysteries. It was reluctantly conceded that the witch cult may have possessed some secret arcane knowledge.'

My informant goes on to give a remarkable account of what he says is the real origin of the famous 'Cipher MS' which came into the possession of the S.R.I.A. and out of which the rituals of the Golden Dawn were elaborated. He says that Hargrave Jennings purchased certain allegedly Rosicrucian manuscripts from the estate of the late J. B. Ragon, a French occultist and writer of note who died in 1862. From these manuscripts, which gave details of a degree structure, rituals and so on, Hargrave

---

* From *Secret Rituals of the Golden Dawn* by R. G. Torrens

Jennings, with the assistance of George Pickingill, concocted the Cipher MS.

If this account is correct, then it solves one of the great puzzles connected with this abstruse subject; namely that, although the Cipher MS was supposed to be from a Continental source, it was decoded into English.

Hargrave Jennings had taken the precaution of obtaining a bill of sale when he purchased the Ragon manuscripts; and, if I understand my informant rightly, he later cunningly displayed this, together with the coded manuscript he himself had concocted, using a code taken from an old book in the British Museum. He informed his suitably impressed brethren of the S.R.I.A. that possession of this document conferred upon its owner or owners the dispensation to found a branch of the authentic Rosicrucian fraternity. My informant states: 'One need hardly add that Jennings omitted to mention that he had collaborated with England's most notorious witch to amend and modify the said authentic rituals!'

The subsequent history of the founding of the Order of the Golden Dawn, from the rituals elaborated from this mysterious Cipher MS, has been admirably detailed and documented by Ellic Howe in *The Magicians of the Golden Dawn*, to which I must refer the reader who wishes to pursue this subject, as it is not strictly relevant to my own. My informant describes the Golden Dawn as being 'founded on a series of ingenious fabrications'; but I think it only fair to add that these mystifications were not necessarily carried out with bad intent, and that the Order of the Golden Dawn made an enormous contribution to the serious study of occultism in England and America.

To return to the subject of George Pickingill's 'nine covens': these, says my informant, were founded in Norfolk, Essex, Hertfordshire, Sussex and Hampshire, at various intervals over a period of sixty years. In each case, a basic format of rites was used, but ' "Old George" was invariably amending the wording and introducing different concepts'. The basic hallmark of the Pickingill covens was that they were led by a priestess, who could and did conduct the rites. This concept is allegedly derived from Scandinavian and French sources. There was a good deal of Scandinavian settlement in East Anglia, as the place-names there testify; and later on there was an influx of French and Flemish immigrants, who brought their old secret customs with them.

The idea of covens led by a woman was not acceptable to some hereditary leaders of the witch cult. They were accustomed to covens led by a male Master or Magister as he was called, who admitted candidates of both sexes. Moreover, they preferred (very naturally, I think, in view of the English climate) to perform their rites wearing robes rather than in the state of ritual nudity. However, they recognized the hereditary tradition inherited by the Pickingill family; and both branches of the witch cult knew the succession of 'three rites' which have developed into the present-day 'three degrees'.

Another reason why leaders of the very secret and hereditary witch covens looked askance at George Pickingill was, I am told, that he openly campaigned for the overthrow of the Christian religion and the establishment generally. At the time when 'Old George' lived, this was a daring and foolhardy thing to do, especially for a man of humble station. 'God bless the Squire and his relations, and keep us in our proper stations' was practically an article of the Christian creed; and magistrates' courts, jail and transportation were available for those who flouted it, as the Tolpuddle Martyrs of Dorset found out when they tried to form a trade union. Other witch leaders had good grounds for thinking that discretion was the better part of valour, in those days.

So fierce was 'Old George' 's dislike of Christianity that he would even collaborate with avowed Satanists; and this was another objection held against his activities. Contrary to the picture of witchcraft drawn by the sensational Press, genuine witches do not indulge in 'devil-worship' or invoke Satan. They believe that their Old Religion is the aboriginal creed of western Europe, and far, far older than Christianity; whereas 'Satan' is part of Christian mythology and 'Satanists' are just mixed-up Christians.

For all of these reasons, therefore, the real importance of Old George Pickingill and the part he played in the present-day revival of witchcraft have not heretofore come to light. Curiously enough, some of the most active denigrators of present-day witchcraft have been practising occultists of other persuasions. One is irresistibly reminded of H. G. Wells' definition of righteous indignation as 'jealousy with a halo'!

A number of inadequate and distorted versions of the rituals used by Gerald Gardner and the covens he founded are now in circulation, as are various allegedly ancient versions of witchcraft rites. For instance, I once discovered in a bookshop an American paperback which purported to be the rituals handed down by word of mouth for generations, and now published by the express permission of a lady modestly describing herself as 'America's Witch Queen'. I purchased the book and opened it—and literally the first words upon which my eyes rested were those of my own poem, 'Invocation of the Horned God', which first appeared in the periodical *Pentagram*, over my name and copyright mark, in 1965! To add insult to injury, they had both curtailed and misquoted it; and repeated letters to the American publishers did not even produce the courtesy of a reply.

Well, I suppose one can really regard this sort of thing as a kind of back-handed compliment; and I must admit to being moved to a certain amount of girlish mirth when I perused another set of published rituals, this time allegedly copied down from someone's 'witch grandmother' who had initiated him as a boy. It contained a poem beginning 'Darksome night and shining moon . . .', which Gerald Gardner and I wrote between us, about 1954 or '55. And so help me, they had misquoted me again!

There need be no argument as to who wrote *Liber Umbrarum: The Book of Shadows*, as given in this present work. I did; but it is based upon old material, and upon what I have learned in my years of practice as a witch. I may also remark that I own Gerald Gardner's original *Book of Shadows*, which he gave to me. This is the book depicted in the original hardback edition of Gerald Gardner's *Witchcraft Today* (1954) in the photograph of a witch's altar prepared for an initiation ceremony, to be found facing page 96 of that edition.

It is the circulation of bowdlerized versions of witchcraft rituals, as mentioned above, that has been one of the motives inspiring me to write this book. For one thing, it irks me to see misquoted versions of material I wrote for Gerald Gardner being offered for sale, no matter under what pretext. For another, if we are going to have any rituals published at all, then let them at least be literate and workable. After all, times and circumstances have changed radically since the days when everything was supposed to be concealed under an oath of secrecy. Today, people all over the English-speaking world are forming, or trying to form, covens of the Old Religion. It is time that they were able to find guidance instead of what they so often are finding, namely, exploitation.

The exaggerated claims of some self-styled 'leading witches' may be a standing joke to experienced occultists; but the way in which sincere newcomers to this ancient path are being overawed and exploited by what is often sheer bluff, has ceased to be at all amusing. I am sick and tired of these self-appointed 'leaders', who sometimes even resort to threats against anyone who questions their pretended authority. So I have decided to write a book which will put witchcraft within the reach of all.

The purpose of the revival of the Old Religion of Wisecraft, and its coming out into the open, is to contribute towards that new philosophy of life that is coming in with the tide of the Aquarian Age; not to make money for individuals, nor to provide them with material for ego-trips.

This book, therefore is simply intended to aid those who want to worship the Old Gods and make magic in the old ways. The desire of people to do this has become so widespread that I feel it should no longer be denied. All kinds of propaganda have been used against present-day witches and their craft; but its promulgators have found their efforts counterproductive. Every time there is a big 'exposure of the evils of witchcraft' in the sensational Press, it is followed by sackfuls of letters from people wanting to know how they can join a coven!

Many people, I know, will question the idea of self-initiation, as given in this book. To them I will address one simple question: who initiated the first witch?

Of course it is better to receive initiation personally at the hands of an experienced and sincere teacher. This concept applies all over the world, from the eastern traditions of the relationship of *guru* (teacher) and *chela* (pupil), to Carlos Castaneda's story of his apprenticeship to the wise old Yaqui Indian, Don Juan, as told in his marvellous trilogy of books, *The Teachings of Don Juan, A Separate Reality*, and *Journey to Ixtlan*. But I sincerely believe that my book will give people a starting-point, from which they can proceed by practice instead of mere theory.

Once people have arrived at this point, they will naturally go on to contemplate the question: should they try to join a coven, form a coven of their own (as this book will help them to do), or work individually? I go more fully into this matter in the section entitled *Liber Umbrarum*. The decision is really up to the individual; but whichever way you decide, be sure of one thing. You have a right to be a pagan if you want to be. This right is guaranteed to you by the Universal Declaration of Human Rights, to which Britain is a signatory. So do not let anyone browbeat you out of it. Here is the relevant passage from the Universal Declaration of Human Rights, as published by the United Nations :

Article No. 18. Everyone has the right to freedom of thought, conscience and religion; this right includes freedom to change his religion or belief, and freedom, either alone or in community with others and in public or in private, to manifest his religion or belief in teaching, practice, worship and observance.

The Old Gods

The gods of the witches are the oldest gods of all. They are the same as those divinities that were real to the men of the Old Stone Age, who painted them upon the walls of their sacred caves.

Churchmen and other writers who denounced witchcraft and the witches' heathenish practices, have described in their books two deities whom, they say, the witches worshipped in place of the Christian god. These are a horned figure, part human and part beast, who sat enthroned at the Sabbats, dimly lighted by the flames of the ritual bonfire, while the witches danced around him; also, by his side, a beautiful naked girl, who was regarded as the Queen of the Sabbat, probably because she represented and impersonated Diana, the goddess of the moon, or her daughter Aradia. Both of these central figures of the worship who were actually human beings, masked in the case of the horned god-figure, sometimes led the wild and orgiastic dances at certain stated and traditional times of the year, seasonal festivals which were so old that no one could remember the beginning of them. Such are the central features of the witches' worship, attested to by innumerable hostile witnesses.

Both of these divinities, the horned god and the naked goddess, can be found among the cave paintings and carvings of our pre-historic ancestors in Western Europe. The horned god can also be found in the religious art of the pre-Aryan cities of the Indus Valley, Mohenjo-Daro and Harappa. The likeness is precise, even to the feature of a torch between the horns, so often described by old-time writers upon the abominations of witchcraft. The civilization of these ancient cities of India is believed to date back to the third millennium B.C.

The image of a horned head with a light between the horns survives in the secret Tantric worship of India to this day. In the *Mahanirvana Tantra*, which describes the worship of the supreme goddess, Adya Kali, by means of the *Panchatattva* ritual, which includes the offering of wine, meat, fish, grain and sexual intercourse within a consecrated circle, we are told how a male horned animal should be sacrificed to the goddess. The animal is decapitated with one sharp stroke of a sacrificial knife; then the severed head, with a light placed on it between the horns, is offered with these words: 'This head with the light upon it I offer to the *Devi* with obeisance.'*

Before we accuse the Tantrics of cruelty to animals, we should take into account the fact that they believe the sacrificial animal to be released by this act from the bondage of its life as a beast, and enabled to progress into a higher state of existence. A special prayer to this effect is said over the animal before it is killed. It may not be too fanciful to speculate that the sacrificed animal really represents the prehistoric horned deity of pre-Aryan India. Many commentators upon the scriptures called Tantras have suggested that they incorporate extremely ancient religious concepts, although in the form in which we possess them today they have been edited by Brahmins and Buddhists in accordance with their much later ideas.

Still further east. we find fearsome horned gods depicted in the art of Tibet, Nepal and adjacent territories, which although ostensibly Buddhist, evidently contains much older elements which have been adapted to fit into the Buddhist religion. The most notable of these deities, represented both in statues and in the gloriously coloured wall hangings called *tankas*, is Yamantaka, who is sometimes shown with the head of a bull and sometimes with the huge curving horns of the Tibetan yak. He is coupled with his female counterpart, called his *prajna* or 'wisdom', and surrounded by an aura of flames. In spite of his terrifying appearance, however, he is not regarded by the Buddhists as an evil being, but as one of the 'wrathful deities' who act as guardians of the Buddhist religion; he is also called 'The Destroyer of Death'.

A clue to his real origin and antiquity is given by the fact that Yamantaka was also worshipped and invoked by the followers of the pre-Buddhist *Bon* religion of Tibet; a religion of a much more primitive kind which was concerned with magic and with the spirits and gods of nature, and was probably derived from the ancient shamanism of the remote regions of Asia, such as northern Tibet and Mongolia. A description of an invocation of Yamantaka by *Bon* magician-priests is given by Idries Shah in his book *Oriental Magic*. In view of the Communist Chinese invasion of Tibet, one has to use the past tense in writing of Tibetan traditions; but it may well be that in some remote forest or mountain valley Yamantaka is secretly worshipped yet, even as the witches

* *Tantra of the Great Liberation* (*Mahanirvana Tantra*), trans. by Arthur Avalon (Dover Publications, Inc., New York, 1972).

after the coming of Christianity in Europe forgathered clandestinely to worship their old pagan gods.

In Europe, the best known version of the horned god is Pan. He was the deity of the farmers and shepherds of Arcadia, the most rural part of ancient Greece. Although older and more primitive than the sophisticated deities of Mount Olympus, he was much beloved by country folk as the bringer of fertility. He was the incarnation of the life-force of nature, and known as *Pamphage, Pangenetor*, 'All-devourer', 'All-Begetter'. Even so, Osiris of Egypt was the symbol of the returning life-force, and at the same time the god of death and what lies beyond. To the ancient pagans, life and death were two sides of the same coin.

When offended, Pan could be the inspirer of terror, and our word 'panic' is still derived from his name. Nature is majestic, awe-inspiring and sometimes terrible. The word *Pan* also meant 'all, everything'. Some representations of Pan show him as a universal god. Hence his body, part human and part beast. The spotted fawn skin that drapes his shoulders represents the stars of heaven. His shaggy hair symbolizes the woods and forests. His mighty hoofs are the strong rocks. His horns are rays of light; while the seven-reeded pipe upon which he plays the mystic melody of life, enchanting all who hear it, is emblematic of the rulership of the seven heavenly bodies, the sun and moon and the five visible planets. In eastern sacred art, a similar representation is made of the god Krishna, whose apparition in his universal form is vividly described in the *Bhagavad Gita*.

The witches of Thessaly in ancient Greece worshipped the god Pan. He was said to be the secret lover of the moon goddess Artemis, the Greek version of Diana. He summoned his worshippers naked to his moonlight rituals, even as the witches danced naked at their Sabbats centuries later.

The Romans inherited Pan from the Greeks, along with many of their other gods and goddesses; they named him Faunus or Silvanus. His people were the satyrs and wood-nymphs, the personifications of the hidden life of nature. The animal sacred to him was the goat, who later became the goat of the Sabbat. His lusty merriment and shamelessness were naturally obnoxious to the early Christians, to whom this world was fallen from grace and the abode of sin. Hence, he provided the model upon which the horned and tailed Satan was formed. By an evolution well-known to students of comparative religion, the god of the old faith became the devil of the new.

The Buddhists, as we have seen, were rather more subtle in dealing with the primitive horned gods of their countries. Instead of declaring them to be devils, they incorporated them into Buddhism as guardians of the faith.

The Celtic version of the god Pan was Cernunnos, meaning 'the Horned One'. This name is found upon an altar dedicated to him which is now in the Cluny Museum, Paris. This altar was found beneath what is now the site of Notre Dame Cathedral. Probably the shrine of the new religion was deliberately built upon what was already a pagan sacred place.

Other famous representations of Cernunnos are the statue group dating from Gallo-Roman times, now in the Museum of Reims, and that found on the splendid silver cauldron known as the Gundestrop Bowl, which came from a peat bog in Denmark, where it was found in 1891. The former, which is a group of statues evidently influenced by Roman ideas, shows Cernunnos with Apollo and Mercury; but he is the most important figure, and is shown in his characteristic attitude, sitting cross-legged, just as his ancient prototype from the Indus Valley is depicted. The figure on the Gundestrop Bowl is shown in a similar way, and surrounded by lively representations of various beasts, perhaps to show that he is a kind of ruling spirit of nature. This magnificent work of Celtic art (although found in Denmark) is now in the National Museum at Copenhagen. It dates from the second–first century B.C.

A strange and numinous cave drawing from Val Camonica, Italy is cruder and older than these, dating from the fourth–third century B.C. In this, Cernunnos is a towering figure, crowned with stags' horns and seemingly dressed in a long robe. He is appearing to his worshipper, a naked man who holds up his arms in invocation. Upon the arms of the god are two of the torc bracelets or necklaces which often appear upon other representations of him; they probably symbolize wealth. Beside him is the strange creature also depicted with him upon the Gundestrop Bowl: a horned serpent, perhaps a phallic symbol.

When Margaret Murray wrote about Cernunnos in her book *The God of the Witches* she stated that most of our knowledge of the horned god in the British Isles comes from the written records made by monks and priests, as the ordinary people who worshipped him were illiterate and left no records. Since that time, however, many representations of Cernunnos have been found in Britain. There need be no doubt that the Celtic horned god was worshipped and invoked in these islands, just as he was in Gaul and elsewhere in western Europe. Margaret Murray's explanation of witchcraft as the underground survival of the old pagan religion is to that extent supported by evidence.

From the old Stone Age to Celtic Britain; from Thessaly to Tibet; the evidence of ancient records shows the universality and endurance of the archetypal figure of the horned god, the active spirit of life. More could be adduced, for instance the primordial Egyptian god Khnum, who is shown with the head and horns of a ram, in the act of creating mankind by shaping a human being upon a potter's wheel; or the supreme god of ancient Egypt, Amoun, who is sometimes depicted as an actual ram, exalted upon a shrine or an altar and crowned with the attributes of royalty.

Why, however, should these two cult figures, the horned god and his consort, the goddess of the moon, have such importance that they, of all the pagan divinities, should survive as the deities of the witches?

The answer seems to me to lie in their primordial nature. Both the horned god and the naked goddess, the latter sometimes alone and sometimes in triple form, are both found, as stated above, in man's oldest sacred art in his most ancient sanctuaries, the caves of the Stone Age. The triple form of the goddess is related to the three phases of the moon, waxing, full and waning. Her relation to human fertility is a vital one, as the female menstrual cycle of twenty-eight days coincides with the duration of the lunar month, a fact which primitive man would undoubtedly have noted. Indeed, some archaeologists believe that markings found to have been made by early Stone Age men are observations and reckonings of lunar phases, man's first attempt at astronomy and the making of calendars.

The virility of the great horned beasts, the stag and the bison, upon which man in his hunting phase depended; the beauty and mystery of the light of the moon, the meter-out of time and ruler of the tides, both of water and of feminine life; these were fundamental, primitive things. The pagans, who worshipped the divine made manifest in nature, personified them as the first divinities known to us.

They saw, as the peoples of the East still do, the interplay of opposite yet complementary forces, without which no manifestation can take place. These fundamental powers are called in the ancient Chinese system known as the *I Ching* or *Book of Change*, the Yang and the Yin.* The Yang is the active, masculine power and the Yin the passive, feminine one.

* A considerable spread of interest in the *I Ching* can be found today in the western world, and a number of translations are available, of which one of the best is *The Book of Change*, by John Blofeld (George Allen and Unwin, Ltd., London, 1968).

According to this venerable treatise, which is certainly one of the oldest extant books in the world, all things arise from this basic polarity of Yang and Yin, and their consequent interplay; while their union forms the symbol know as *T'ai Chi,* the Absolute, the ultimate reality. This is depicted as a circle divided into two equal parts by a curving line through its centre; one part is dark and the other light.

The Hebrew Qabalah, which was believed by its translator S. L. MacGregor Mathers to derive ultimately from ancient Egypt, shows a fundamentally similar idea, with its twin pillars of Mercy and Severity, balanced by the middle pillar of Beauty or Harmony. The pillar of Mercy is crowned by Chokmah, the archetypal masculine principle; the pillar of Severity is crowned by Binah, the archetypal feminine; while the middle pillar bears the highest crown of all, the divine white brilliance of Kether, the first emanation.

The symbolism has been perpetuated in the Twin Pillars of Freemasonry, Jachin and Boaz, which are explained as standing on either side of the porch of King Solomon's temple. They actually represent that fundamental and divine polarity which underlies all manifested nature, the two opposites whose union constitutes the symbolical Great Work of alchemy. This polarity is also indicated in alchemical symbolism by the masculine sun and the feminine moon.

Symbolism is the natural language of the mind, as evidenced by the psychological importance of our dreams. The great pioneer of this study was Carl Gustav Jung, the psychologist who started out as a pupil of Freud, but soon outgrew the limitations of Freud's materialistic views. Jung discovered that humans not only have a personal unconscious mind, but that at still deeper levels they are in touch with the collective unconscious of the race, in which are to be found the images, full of numinous significance, that have been stored there ever since man emerged upon this planet.

Jung, however, may only have rediscovered what the hierophants of the ancient mystery cults already well knew. Indeed, this view is supported by the statement in *The Tibetan Book of the Dead,* the *Bardo Thodol,* which deals not only with afterdeath states but with other entries behind the veil of matter, and tells its students that everything they see, and all the deities, both peaceful and wrathful, whom they encounter, have arisen from their own minds.

In the collective unconscious of our race, therefore, dwell timelessly the images of the gods. They are the personifications of the forces of nature, and all are modifications of the primordial pair, the All-Father and All-Mother. In ancient Egypt, all the multifarious gods and goddesses were different forms of the highest god, Amoun, whose name means 'the Hidden One', and of his feminine consort and counterpart, Amounath. In the temples of India, the sacred symbol is the *lingam-yoni,* a formalized representation of the male phallus and the woman's vagina. This represents not only human sexuality, but the interplay of the life-force in all its forms.

In prehistoric Britain, the great Neolithic temples of Stonehenge and Avebury display the same symbolized polarity, but in a more subtle and austere form. At the oldest temple, that of Avebury, the massive stones are of alternate shapes, a tall phallic pillar and a broader, roughly lozenge-shaped stone, which convey the significance of male and female. Two of the largest of these are known locally as 'Adam and Eve'. At Stonehenge, we have the great circle, the receptive womb, while outside it in the avenue is the Hele Stone, a phallic menhir on the summit of which the dawning sun seems to rest at midsummer. A smaller version of this design is seen at the Rollright Stones in the Cotswolds, where the tall King's Stone stands outside a stone circle, and is associated with local legends of witchcraft and fertility magic.

An occult writer who realized the true significance of the ancient gods, and their archetypal role in the collective unconscious, is the late Dion Fortune (1891–1946). Frequently reiterated in her works is the sentence : 'All the gods are one god and all the goddesses are one goddess and there is one initiator.' The one initiator is one's own higher self, with which the personality becomes more and more integrated as the path of spiritual evolution is followed. This is what Buddha referred to when he told his disciples to 'take the Self as a lamp'.

Dion Fortune wrote a remarkable series of occult novels, of which two in particular, *The Goat-Foot God* and *The Sea Priestess,** are relevant to our subject, as the former deals with the powers of the horned god, and the latter with those of the moon goddess. In these books, the horned god is referred to as Pan and the moon goddess as Isis; but it is made clear that these deities are universal in character.

The esoteric lore contained in these novels (and there is a

* *The Goat-Foot God* was first published in 1936 and *The Sea Priestess* in 1938, in both cases by the Society of the Inner Light, London, which was Dion Fortune's own magical order. They have since been reprinted by the Aquarian Press, London.

great deal, for those who can read between the lines) is developed
from her treatise on the western esoteric tradition called *The
Mystical Qabalah*. In this book, Dion Fortune, who was an
initiate of that tradition, discusses the real nature of the gods as
'magical images', made not out of stone or wood, but shaped by
the thoughts of mankind out of the substance of the astral plane,
which is affected by the energies of the mind; hence it is sometimes referred to as 'mind-stuff', for want of a better name. She
quotes the lines of the poet Swinburne:

> For no thought of man made Gods to love and honour
> Ere the song within the silent soul began,
> Nor might earth in dream or deed take heaven upon her
> Till the word was clothed with speech by lips of man.

What the great psychologist Jung discovered by painstaking
research and observation, the poet before him had known in-
tuitively. The unknown authors of the *Tibetan Book of the Dead*
knew it long before. The gods and goddesses are personifications
of the powers of nature; or perhaps one should say, of super-
nature, the powers which govern and bring forth the life of our
world, both manifest and hidden. In other words, we live upon
a plane of forms, superior to which is a plane of forces, upon
which the gods move, because by personifying those forces to
ourselves as gods we can establish a relationship with them.

Moreover, when such a magical image has been built up and
strengthened over the course of centuries by worship and ritual,
it becomes powerful in itself, because it becomes ensouled by
that which it personifies. The form may have started as imagination, but when that which it personifies is real, imagination becomes in truth the image-making faculty. Every image of art
must first be perceived in the mind of the artist, in the imagination. A subjective thought-form conceived by one person may be
fleeting; but the thought-forms of a race are a different matter.
Moreover, as C. G. Jung has shown, some thought-forms, such
as the 'Great Mother', the 'Wise Old Man', and the 'Divine
Child', are so universal that he calls them archetypes, dwelling
as they do in the collective unconscious of mankind, and appearing in dreams and visions, including the visions of the artist.

Visions, either spontaneous or induced, have always played
an important part in religious experience. 'Where there is no
vision, the people perish'.* Spontaneous visions arise in the form

* *Proverbs*, 29. v. 18.

of significant dreams, or spiritual experiences, the latter sometimes manifesting such potency that they can change a person's entire life. Induced visions may come about by means of entering into a state of trance or ecstasy. Such states and the various techniques of inducing them have been a basic feature of all world religions, from the most primitive to the most sophisticated. In this connection, we may note the derivation of the word 'ecstasy'; it comes from the Greek *ekstasis,* with the significance of being temporarily outside oneself, to have broken the bonds of one's everyday world and entered into another state of being. The most ancient and primitive ecstatic is the shaman.

Shamanism seems most probably to have been the earliest form of religion throughout the world. It has been defined by Mircea Eliade in his authoritative book upon the subject as 'technique of ecstasy' (*Shamanism: Archaic Techniques of Ecstasy*). The shaman (a word which comes to us from the Russian language, but which seems to have originated in the dialects of northern Asia) may be either a man or a woman, though the latter has come to be called a shamaness. He or she communicates with spirits, both human and non-human, and performs all kinds of magic; but the distinguishing feature of shamanism is its 'magical flights' into other realms of being, from which information can be brought back to this world. The relationship between this idea and the supposed magical power of witches to fly, either upon the traditional broomstick or upon some other kind of staff, is fairly obvious.

The means by which these magical flights were achieved, and still are achieved by such contemporary shamans as Carlos Castaneda's teacher, Don Juan Matus, were very often some hallucinogenic drug derived from plants or fungi. The shamans of northern Asia used the fungus called Fly Agaric (*Amanita muscaria*), which grows throughout northern and western Europe, and in the British Isles. Today quite a lot has been written about 'magic mushrooms', and a good deal of research is being done into the effects of these and other natural hallucinogens. The result has been that researchers are beginning to take an entirely fresh look at the recorded descriptions of European witchcraft, with its witches' ointments and traditional knowledge of herbs, or 'wort-cunning' as it was called.

Another means by which shamanistic ecstasy is induced is wild and rhythmic dancing, the kind of dancing which was notoriously a feature of the witches' Sabbat. While in a state of ecstasy, the shaman 'meets the gods'; that is, he enters into the world beyond the veil of matter, whether that world be called the astral plane or the collective unconscious.

With this in mind, we can take another look at that famous passage from the early canon laws of the Christian Church, found in collections of such laws dating back to the tenth century A.D. :

'Some wicked women, perverted by the Devil, seduced by the illusions and phantasms of demons, believe and profess themselves in the hours of the night to ride upon certain beasts with Diana, the goddess of pagans, or with Herodias, and an innumerable multitude of women, and in the silence of the dead of night to traverse great spaces of earth, and to obey her commands as of their mistress, and to be summoned to her service on certain nights.'*

Other accounts from ancient writers tell of fantastic Sabbats, during which the horned and hoofed Devil himself appeared, surrounded by eldritch apparitions of all kinds. This, indeed, became a favourite subject for the artist, and some painters, notably Hans Baldung, David Teniers, Frans Francken and Goya, specialized in depicting it; while in his *Night on the Bare Mountain* the composer Moussorgsky essayed the same task in music, with considerable success.

Such visionary Sabbats must be distinguished from the accounts of actual gatherings, which are much more sober, and contain nothing that could not be accounted for naturally, given the fact that the principal actor, the supposed 'Devil', was in fact a man dressed in a horned mask and a costume of animal skins, just like the masked dancer who was drawn by some artist of the old Stone Age in the Caverne des Trois Frères at Ariège, France.

There are a good many accounts also of early investigators who tested the confessions of witches to having attended wild and fantastic gatherings, to which they claimed to be conveyed through the air and later returned in the same way to their homes. Such accounts always tell the same story, namely that the witch was observed to anoint herself with some mysterious unguent, stripping naked for the purpose, then lying entranced for some time in a deep sleep, from which she eventually awoke to recount her adventures at the Sabbat. Sometimes, we are told, a rather simple-minded witch actually refused to believe the testimony of the observers that she had not really been flying through the air at all. (I use the pronoun 'she' for convenience, though such stories are also told of male witches).

One would think in the face of all this evidence, that the

* Translation quoted from Gerald B. Gardner, *The Meaning of Witchcraft.*

witch-hunters would have realized it was the witches' ointment, and not Satan, that conveyed witches in apparent flight, especially as the actual ingredients of such ointments were given, notably by Giovanni Battista Porta in his book *Magiae Naturalis*. However, the fanaticism of these men was such that they denied the possibility of the ointments having such an effect, and insisted on attributing everything to the interference of Satan in human affairs. This point is noted, with apparent approval, by the bigoted Montague Summers, in his *History of Witchcraft and Demonology*.

Times have changed, however, since Montague Summers wrote his admittedly scholarly but utterly biased book. There is, for instance, an extremely interesting symposium entitled *Hallucinogens and Shamanism*, edited by Michael J. Harner, which contains a section entitled 'The Role of Hallucinogenic Plants in European Witchcraft', written by Mr Harner himself, who is Associate Professor of Anthropology on the Graduate Faculty of the New School for Social Research. Mr Harner notes that the traditional plants alleged by Porta and others to enter into the composition of the witches' unguents are those of the *Solanaceae*, an order of plants which includes, beside humble and well-known things such as the potato, the tomato and the tobacco plant, such dangerous and hallucinogenic herbs as thorn apple (*Datura stramonium*), henbane (*Hyoscyamus niger*), mandrake (*Mandragora*) and deadly nightshade or belladonna (*Atropa belladonna*). He states that varieties of these plants are found throughout both Europe and the Americas, and that they are used in shamanistic practices by primitive people to this day.

A particularly interesting fact noted by Mr Harner and his fellow scholars is that people using hallucinogenic plants, either in the form of brews or unguents, for the purpose of 'taking a trip', tend to see the same or similar things in their visions, depending upon the cultural *milieu* in which they live. In other words, people taking such a drug will be strongly influenced in the visions and experiences they seem to have, by their previously held ideas and beliefs, and the nature of the circumstances in which the drug is taken, the immediate environment and so on.

Thus, South American Indians who believed in their tribal pagan gods might see these gods in their shamanistic trances; while other Indians who had been 'missionized', that is exposed to the influence of Christian missionaries, saw Christian symbols intermingled with pagan ones.

Certain visions, however, seem to be characteristic of certain drugs. In this connection, Mr Harner notes the experience of Dr

Will-Erich Peukert, of the University of Gottingen, Germany, who in recent years experimented with a seventeenth-century recipe for the witches' salve, or 'flying ointment', and actually experienced a trance lasting twenty-four hours, during which he seemed to be participating in the weird orgies of the legendary Sabbat. The recipe contained belladonna, henbane and thorn-apple.

Another characteristic recorded from many places and the statements of many witnesses, is the sensation during the shamanistic use of hallucinogenic drugs, of the soul or mind separating itself from the physical body and flying through space, to witness scenes either at a distance upon earth, or in some other dimension. This is all rather puzzling to anthropologists; especially when simple Indians who had never seen a white man's city or an automobile, claimed to visit such a city in trance and asked what were those strange things that travelled so fast along the roads? To the occultist who is familiar with the concept of astral projection, that is, the ability of the astral body to separate itself from the physical and to travel into other dimensions of being, an explanation in these terms will naturally suggest itself.

Mr Harner comments that scholars as well as present-day members of witches' covens, have generally failed to comprehend the great importance of hallucinogenic plants in the European witchcraft of former times. However, to my own knowledge this is not true of all present-day covens; but those who possess practical information on such matters generally prefer absolute secrecy. They derive their knowledge from old traditional sources, rather than from those present-day witches who seek publicity in the mass media; and they point to the fact that these hallucinogenic substances are dangerous to meddle with, both plants and fungi. They do not want the responsibility for encouraging foolhardy people to experiments that could have fatal results. I would like to make the point here also, that unless a person has specialized knowledge or guidance with regard to these things, practical experiment with them is most unwise.

I have already referred to Francis King's story, derived from his friend Louis Wilkinson, of the surviving New Forest coven into which Gerald Gardner was originally initiated, as given in Mr King's book *Ritual Magic in England*. Mr King states that this coven made use of the fungus called fly agaric (*Amanita muscaria*) as an hallucinogen, taking it by mouth in very small doses. They also used an ointment, but this was simply a greasy substance to protect their naked bodies from the cold while taking part in outdoor ritual. Mr King says it consisted mostly of 'bears' fat';

but I respectfully beg leave to doubt this. Surely, there are no bears in the New Forest? It seems more likely to me that 'boars' fat' is intended; in other words, ordinary hogs' lard, which was the usual basis for apothecaries' ointments. Benzoin was generally added to it, to improve its smell and make it keep better.

The use of fly agaric brings the practice of this coven right into line with the ancient shamanism of northern Asia, the area from which the very word 'shaman' derives. Fly agaric also seems to have a traditional connection with the world of Faery. Nearly every book of fairy stories will be found to contain somewhere in its pages a picture of this brightly-coloured fungus, with its red, white-spotted cap. It is not as common as it would have been centuries ago, owing to the increasing urbanization of the countryside; but it can still be found growing wild, especially under birch trees.

The world of Faery is the world of the souls of the pagan dead, of nature spirits, and of the pagan gods. This is made abundantly clear in the Celtic mythology of the British Isles, and of Europe generally. It is also the world of the Little People, those shadowy races who preceded the Celtic invaders and colonizers. They were dark and small in stature, though not so tiny nor non-human that they could not intermarry with the newcomers. They were the mysterious and sometimes dangerous Little People, with their aboriginal heritage of magic.

As one culture succeeded another, the gods and goddesses who were personifications of the primordial powers were still worshipped, albeit with differing rites, simply because these powers *are* primordial : life, fertility, death and what lies beyond. The Christian church built its sanctuaries upon pagan sacred places. Its central festival, Easter, took its name from Eostre or Ostara, the pagan goddess of spring. The Druidic mistletoe still decks our homes at Christmas. The Celtic Eve of Samhain became the Eve of All Saints, or Hallowe'en. Folklore can give dozens of such instances, where what was once the religion of the country has become, literally, the lore of the common folk.

The worship of the old gods has never died; it has merely either gone underground or changed its form. They who would once have been its priests and priestesses, the Christian church in Anglo-Saxon times began to call witches.

2

Witch Ethics

Some determined Christian opponents of witchcraft will, no doubt, consider the heading of this chapter to be a contradiction in terms. How, they will demand, can witches, who are devoted to evil and the worship of Satan, have ethics?

Such a question can, of course, only be asked by those who are determined to identify witchcraft with Satanism. Satanism, however, by its very nature, can only be an offshoot of Christianity; because before you can worship Satan you have to believe in him. Before you can celebrate a Black Mass, the essential act of which is to defile the sacred host, you have to believe in the real Mass. And if you believe in the real Mass, you are a Christian!

Satanism, in so far as it is genuine and not either a literary invention or an excuse for an orgy, seems most probably to have arisen from the oppressiveness of the Church, in either Roman Catholic or puritanically Protestant countries, which engendered a spirit of revolt. This expressed itself in practical forms, such as the formation of the notorious Hellfire Clubs in England, or the enthronement of the 'Goddess of Reason' (impersonated by a pretty actress) upon the altar of the Cathedral of Notre Dame in revolutionary France.

Sometimes the expression of this spirit of revolt took on much darker hues. When it shaded into real black magic, an aberrant mind might conceive the idea of deliberately committing evil deeds, and even ritual murder, in order to propitiate that evil power which some religious people believed to be everywhere, counterbalancing and apparently as potent as the power of good.

This ghastly belief, however, is really nothing to do with the old religion of witchcraft. Nor is it really very much to do with Christianity, or at any rate with the Christianity that Jesus taught. To ascribe to Satan a power co-equal with that of God, to divide the universe between dual contending forces, is to go back to the ideas and beliefs of Zoroaster, the religious teacher of ancient Persia who flourished about 650–600 B.C. He preached a religion which interpreted the world as an age-long struggle between good and evil, the principle of good being called Ormuzd and that of evil Ahriman.

Because of the Persian conquest of the Jews, the faith of the followers of Zoroaster had a strong influence upon the later Jewish religion, and thus indirectly upon Christianity. Out of Persia also came Mithraism, which was very influential throughout the Roman Empire in the first three centuries of the Christian era. Its background was the dualistic faith of Zoroaster, and many scholars believe that ideas derived from it became incorporated into Christianity during the latter religion's formative years.

I cannot profess to be a theologian; but it seems to me that Christians who believe in a personal, superhuman Satan have got themselves into a logical impasse with regard to their own religion. For either God cannot prevent the mischief of Satan, in which case He is not omnipotent; or else He could do so if He wished, but will not, in which case He is not benevolent. Fortunately, being a pagan witch, I am not called upon to solve this problem.

I prefer to look back to the ancient roots of our race, and consider the teaching of the pagan mysteries upon the deep questions of the significance of human life and how it should be lived.

Although Druidism, the ancient faith of Britain in pre-Roman times, is generally regarded as a barbarous religion, its ideas were nevertheless somewhat more enlightened upon the question of human destiny and the afterlife than is generally realized. They were certainly more so than those of the hellfire-and-damnation type of Christianity. As the following quotation will show, the beliefs of the Druids have much in common with the age-old *Dharma* of the east, with its teachings about *Karma* and reincarnation :

The transmigration of souls. The Bardic dogma on this head was, that the soul commenced its course in the lowest water animalcule, and passed at death to other bodies of a superior order, successively, and in regular gradation, until it entered that of man. Humanity is a state of liberty, where man can attach himself to either good or evil, as he pleases. If his good qualities preponderate over his evil qualities at the time of his death, his soul passes into Gwynvyd, or a state of bliss, where good necessarily prevails, and from whence it is impossible to fall. But if his evil qualities predominate, his soul descends in Abred into an animal corresponding in character to the disposition he exhibited just before he died. It will then rise as before, until it again arrives at the point of liberty, where it will have another chance of clinging

to the good. But if it fails, it must fall again; and this may happen
for ages and ages, until at last its attachment to good preponder-
ates. It was believed, however, that man could not be guilty twice
of the same sin; his experience in Abred whilst undergoing punishment for any particular sin, would prevent him from loving that
sin a second time; hence the adage, *'Nid eir i Annon ond unwaith'*.

The views of the Gaulish Druids, as far as they are expressed by
Caesar, do not appear to differ from the above. 'They wish to
inculcate this idea, that souls do not die, but pass after death from
one body to another.' The only thing that may be *supposed* to
be different is the passing from one body to another, which, in
the original Latin, seems as if it meant from one human body to
another human body, *'ab aliis ad alios'*. But in reality there is no
inconsistency between the two systems, even in this respect; for,
though the soul of a good man was considered in general as
entering an angelic body in the circle of Gwynvyd, and the soul
of a wicked man as entering the body of a beast, a reptile, or a
bird, in Abred, yet, it was thought that occasionally the good soul
returned from Gwynvyd to inhabit a human body, and that the
soul of one punished by death, against his will, for an injurious
evil, passed to another human body. There is no doubt that this,
with the Cymry, as well as with the Gauls, acted as a strong incentive to bravery, especially as they considered that to suffer in
behalf of truth and justice was one of the greatest virtues, and was
sure to bring the soul to everlasting bliss.*

Many questions are raised by this quotation from a book too
long forgotten, of which I am fortunate to possess a photographed copy. An immediate one, of course, is how on earth the
Druids knew of the existence of such minute forms of life as
water animalcules? They are recorded as being very interested
in astronomy as well. Do the sciences of microscopy and telescopy
go back much, much further than we have supposed? At the time
when *Barddas* was published, such a suggestion would have been
laughed to scorn. Today, Erich Von Daniken has published in
his books *Chariots of the Gods* and *In Search of Ancient Gods*
photographs of crystal lenses found in ancient tombs and now in
the British Museum. One came from Helwan, Egypt, another
from Assyria. I do not by any means endorse all of Mr Von
Daniken's conclusions; but—there are the lenses!
    Things like this lead us to conclude that the secrets of ancient

* Rev. J. Williams Ab Ithel, *Barddas; or a Collection of Original
Documents, Illustrative of the Theology, Wisdom and Usages of the
Bardo-Druidic System of the Isle of Britain*, (Welsh MSS Society, 1862).

fraternities of initiates may have been very real indeed, apart
from their metaphysical teachings. Also, that they seem to have
been of world-wide distribution and curious similarity, allowing
for local differences of outlook. Reincarnation, for instance, was
believed in literally from Tibet to Cornwall, in various forms of
the same basic idea. It was accepted by many of the early
Christians, until the Council of Constantinople in A.D. 553 declared it to be a heresy.

Gerald Gardner, who initiated me into witchcraft, was a strong
believer in reincarnation and the working-out of *karma*, and
most witches I have met accept this belief also. In general, however, believers in reincarnation today do not think that a human
soul can regress into an animal body. I would not like to be certain about it. Indeed, there would be real justice in some of our
more callous scientists being reborn as monkeys, rabbits or guinea-
pigs, destined for the experimental laboratory; or in some of our
hearty blood-sports enthusiasts coming back as foxes and hares.
Moreover, if a person insists in this life upon living at the level
of a beast, why should they not be reborn at that level? After
all, it was their choice.

However, we should recognize the fact that *karma* does not
in itself involve our ideas of reward and punishment; the carrot
dangled in front of the donkey to make him go, and the stick
applied to his posterior if he refuses. Our ideas of justice are
necessarily limited, 'for here we see as through a glass darkly'.
Karma is simply a Sanskrit word meaning 'action', without any
implications of reward or punishment as we envisage them, but
rather the idea that every action must bring forth its appropriate reaction, somewhere and somewhen, as a law of nature, not
something being handed out by a sort of heavenly magistrate
sitting up in the sky.

Later in British history, the Anglo-Saxons embodied the idea
of destiny or fate, the western equivalent of *karma* in a sense, in
the mysterious goddess whom they called Wyrd. She was originally conceived of in triple form, and is evidently analogous to the
Three Fates of classical myth. The Romans called the Fates the
Parcae, a word which seems to be linked with the verb *parere*,
meaning 'to bring forth', in the sense of 'giving birth to'. The
Greeks called them the *Moirai*, from the word *moira*, meaning 'a part' and they were said to refer to the three 'parts' or
phases of the moon. These are the waxing moon, the full moon
and the waning moon, symbolized as a young maiden, a beautiful mature woman and an old crone. The Scandinavian people
of the further north knew the Fates as the *Nornir*, or the
Three Norns, who dwelt at the foot of the World Tree Yggdrasill

and preserved it with water from their magic well.

Originally, the triple goddess of fate was supreme even over the highest of other gods, because she embodied the lingering idea of the Great Mother and the ancient days of matriarchy, the archaic form of human society. Later she was incorporated into Christianity as being another word for providence or destiny; hence the old phrase, 'to dree one's weird', meaning to work out one's destiny.

From being hidden and almost forgotten down the years, the idea of the triple goddess of fate emerged again from the shadows, thanks to the genius of Shakespeare. She is the original of the three witches in *Macbeth* :

> The Weird Sisters, hand in hand,
> Posters of the sea and land,
> Thus do go about, about.
> Thrice to thine, and thrice to mine,
> And thrice again, to make up nine.
> Peace, the charm's wound up.

These are evidently not merely three old women, but supernatural beings, 'posters of the sea and land', who can vanish and appear at will. It is generally agreed by Shakespearian scholars that some of the later appearances of the witches in the play, where they are represented as doing the commonplace misdeeds, such as killing swine, causing tempests at sea and so on, which were attributed to witches in the popular superstitions of the day, are probably interpolations into the text by a later and inferior hand, perhaps that of Thomas Middleton. Even so, they show the witches as worshipping, not the Devil as the witch-persecutors alleged, but Hecate, the ancient Greek goddess of witchcraft.

The moon was the measurer. She measured out time, by means of man's earliest astronomical observations. She measured also the ebb and flow of the tides, and the mysterious alternations of female fertility and barrenness. Once in a lunar month, she ran her course through the twelve signs of the zodiac, in each of which she had a different influence. In the swiftness of her observed motion, she also forms astrological aspects to the sun and planets which astrologers believe to affect the events of every day, and which are accordingly listed in popular magazines still. The almanac gives the days of new moon and full moon, which old-fashioned gardeners and farmers believed to be important in finding the right time to plant crops.

Mystery and romance, as well as fate, are attributed to the moon; nor does she shine any less brightly because in our own day man has essayed the great adventure of walking upon her surface. The full of the moon is still the high tide of psychic power, and witches still hold their Esbats, or monthly meetings, at that time, as they did in centuries past. It is therefore entirely natural for them to believe in the ancient idea of fate, destiny or *karma*, ruled over by the triple goddess of birth, life and death.

As Gerald Gardner says in his book *The Meaning of Witchcraft*, witches in general are inclined to accept the morality of the legendary Good King Pausol, 'Do what you like so long as you harm no one'. This idea has been put into a rhymed couplet called the Wiccan Rede:

> Eight words the Wiccan Rede fulfil:
> An it harm none, do what ye will.

This can be expressed in more modern English as follows:

> Eight words the Witches' Creed fulfil:
> If it harms none, do what you will.

This quite honestly seems to me to be the only moral code that really makes sense. If everyone lived by it, would not the world be a very different place? If morality were not enforced by fear, by a string of Thou-shalt-nots; but if, instead, people had a *positive* morality, as an incentive to a happier way of living?

It is curious how people seem to accept morality as a system of not doing things, rather than doing them. If a person is, for instance, a non-smoker, a teetotaller, a vegetarian, they are regarded—in some circles at any rate—as being 'good'. Well, Hitler was all of these things! Outwardly, he was very 'respectable' sexually as well; the world did not know about Eva Braun until the grisly marriage ceremony in the Berlin bunker. And even in those circumstances, the man who had soaked the soil of Europe in blood, and committed and encouraged every sort of crime against humanity, was concerned that he should pay his debt to 'respectability' by being lawfully wedded to his mistress!

It is notable that the enemies of human liberty, be they Fascist or Communist, are always very concerned with moral policing, as well as with political repression. With what tender care do they guard their subjects from 'decadence', by censorship of all

kinds and by the earnest promotion of a puritanical moral code!
In sexual matters, that is; when it comes to tyrannical cruelty,
oppression and mass murder, these moral puritans become very
easy-going indeed.

The eminent psychologist, Wilhelm Reich, himself a refugee
from Fascism, has most cogent things to say in explanation of
this apparent paradox, in his book *The Function of the Orgasm.*
He points out the great need of humanity to free itself from
false teaching, imposed as the instrument of oppression throughout the centuries, and achieve a normal, happy expression of
sexual love. People are beginning to listen to Reich in our day.
The man himself died in an American federal penitentiary; a
fact which future historians will rank with the murder of Socrates
and the imprisonment of Galileo. But his voice could not be
silenced, because in spite of appearances he was not saying
something new, but something very old; something, in fact, primordial, which breathes from the earth and blows in the wind.

We think today that we have a permissive society. In fact,
what we really have is a state of affairs in which some taboos
have been relaxed, because it has been found financially profit-
able to do so. What is being permitted is not sexual satisfaction,
but sexual exploitation. Very large numbers of people are just
as unsatisfied as ever, because their ideas and attitudes have
not basically changed. They are 'uptight', armoured against life,
fearful of their own freedom.

Sexual freedom does not mean freedom to spend one's money
to watch some ugly pornographic film; it means freedom to enjoy sex. Unfortunately, most people are so battered and damaged
by our so-called civilization, founded as it is on humbug and
greed, that they are no longer capable of realizing what natural
sexual fulfilment is.

There are signs, however, that younger people in particular
are rejecting the double standards of morality that are part of
the patriarchal Judeo-Christian religious outlook; and this re-
jection is expressing itself in many ways, as the old aeon draws
to its close. People are seeking for new knowledge, new standards,
a new outlook on life all together; while at the same time, what
Wilhelm Reich called 'the emotional plague' rages throughout
our neurotic world, bringing violence and misery along with it.
Any organized religion or political system that is anti-sex is anti-
life.

The words of the Wiccan Rede will inevitably be compared
with the famous dictum of Aleister Crowley: 'Do what thou
wilt shall be the whole of the law. Love is the law, love under

will.' Crowley, a strange genius who regarded himself as the
Logos of the Aeon of Horus, or the new age, obtained this saying
from his inspired writing *Liber Legis*, or the Book of the Law,
which he claimed to have received from a 'preterhuman intelligence' as the result of a magical ceremony in Cairo in 1904. The
full text will be found in *The Magical Record of the Beast 666*
by Aleister Crowley.

In practice, however, Crowley was just as much imbued with
the mental attitudes of the old aeon as anyone else. As Gerald
Gardner commented in *The Meaning of Witchcraft*, Crowley's
pupils and followers soon found out that for them what Aleister
Crowley willed was the whole of the law! Anyone showing signs
of thinking for themselves, or differing from the views of the
master, soon found themselves consigned to outer darkness.
(Incidentally, old Gerald's quoted comment shows that he was
by no means the unqualified admirer of Crowley that he has been
represented to be. He admired Crowley as a poet, but had no
illusions about him as a man.) Moreover, Crowley was a male
chauvinist pig of the crudest kind. This appears plainly in his
book *Liber Aleph: The Book of Wisdom or Folly*, a series of letters to his magical son, Frater Achad, which were never published in his lifetime but have been recently issued in the USA.
In this writing, Crowley declares that in the nature of woman
there is no truth, nor possibility of truth; and that although 'in a
certain sort' women could obtain the experiences of vision, trance
and so on, yet nevertheless woman has no capacity for advancement in magic. The limit of her aspiration, says Crowley, is to be
obedient to the right man, so that she may have better luck next
time in the round of rebirth, and be born in a masculine body!

These views did not, however, prevent Crowley from occasionally dressing himself up as a woman, with wig and make-
up, and parading about as 'Alys Cusack', in which guise he
sought to 'seduce' his male pupils. I have heard of a psychological phenomenon called 'penis-envy'; I am beginning to suspect that the possible origin of male chauvinist piggery is 'vagina-
envy'.

To be fair to Crowley, however, by 'Do what thou wilt' he did
not mean merely 'Do as you like', but that people should find
out what their true will really is and then do that and nothing
else. He said that if everyone did that, there would be no trouble
in the world, because people's true wills were in harmony with
each other and with the course of nature. The will to crime, for
instance, was a false will, born of a dis-ease of the spirit. Because
of centuries of repression, people have lost the knowledge of their

original nature. Their true will is the essential motion of their being, the orbit of that star which the Book of the Law declares every man and every woman to be.

This is really a very profound teaching. Crowley's remarks upon how the true will may declare itself by the images appearing in dreams and fantasies, are reminiscent of the present-day teachings of the Jungian school of psychology. We should not let the posturing of Crowley as 'the Master Therion', or his prejudices and crudities, blind us to the splendour of his poetry and prose or the stimulation of thought and understanding to be found in his writings.

This teaching of Crowley's, embodied in the dictum quoted above, 'Do what thou wilt', is by no means new, and was not invented by him. Long ago, Saint Augustine said, 'Love and do what you will'. The initiate of ancient Egypt declared : 'There is no part of me that is not of the gods'. The pagan Greeks originated the saying : 'To the pure all things are pure'. The implication is that when one has reached a high stage of spiritual development and evolution one has passed beyond the comparatively petty rules of religion and society at some particular time and place, and may indeed do what one wills, because one's true will is then knowable, and must of its own nature be right. The *Upanishads* or sacred scriptures of ancient India tell us that the knower of Brahma is beyond both good and evil.

Such a teaching has even acquired for itself a theological name: antinomianism. As Sir John Woodroffe has pointed out in his book *Shakti and Shakta*, it is particularly associated in the history of religions with ideas of pantheism, the belief that God is all and all is God. As such, it is found both in east and west; a number of Christian heretics have taught it to their followers. We may quote as typical the doctrine of Amalric of Bena : 'To those constituted in love no sin is imputed'. Curiously enough, a number of these heretics celebrated an *Agape,* or love-feast, very similar to the witches' sabbat. They may even have had some relation with the witch cult itself, though they are generally believed to be derived from the Gnostics, meaning 'those who know', the mystics who were the inheritors of pagan philosophy which they cloaked in a Christian guise.

In the east, the Tantrics who follow the ancient scriptures called Tantras, among whom are to be found both Buddhists and Hindus, also have this doctrine in a more or less esoteric form. The Hindu Tantrics regard mankind as being naturally divided into three *Bhavas* or dispositions: namely, *Pashubhava* or animal disposition, corresponding to *Tamas guna,* the qualities of grossness and darkness; *Virabhava*, or heroic disposition, corresponding to *Rajas guna*, the qualities of activity, force and fieriness; and *Divyabhava*, or divine disposition, corresponding to *Sattva guna*, the qualities of balance, equilibrium, harmony and perfection. The *Pashu* is not permitted to take part in the secret rites, which include wine-drinking and sexual intercourse; these are reserved for those who are capable of understanding them correctly, from the point of view of an initiate. (*See* Chapter 11, for a further discussion of this important point.) By taking part in such rites, the men and women of *Virabhava*, who have the will to spiritual attainment, may arrive at the highest disposition, *Divyabhava*. They are then said to attain to the state of *Svechchachara*, which means, in effect, 'Do what thou wilt'. They are the achievers of *Mukhti*, or true liberation.

This is in complete contrast to the ideas of attainment by repression of the natural instincts and renunciation of all earthly pleasures. As the *Kulanarva Tantra* says: 'By what men fall, by that they rise.'

The Buddhist Tantrics are somewhat more puritanical in their outlook than the Hindus; nevertheless, there are similar beliefs to be found among them also. For instance, among the 'Precepts of the Gurus' given in *Tibetan Yoga and Secret Doctrines*, we find under the heading of 'The Ten Equal Things' a number of sayings with a general meaning strikingly similar to that of *Svechchachara*. They imply that once a person has attained to spiritual enlightenment, and become in their heart a true follower of the *Dharma*, the ancient wisdom-religion which was from the beginning of time, and of which all the Buddhas have been exponents, then it matters not whether that person observes conventional codes of conduct or no, and whether or not he or she takes part in worldly activities and pleasures. Having attained mastery of mind, such a person will act from non-attachment, and therefore will not err.

Such then, it seems to me, is the inner meaning of the teachings of both Aleister Crowley and the cult of the witches in this respect. Is it healthier and wiser than the string of Thou-shalt-nots, the morality of fear and repression? I can only ask people to think about it and judge for themselves.

Today, we have an urgent need to find a new way of living, a new outlook on life, because man has at last become capable, literally, of destroying not only himself, but all life on this planet. What Buddhism calls the three fires, greed, wrath and ignorance, could burn up the world.

With this new scientific capacity, however, has come a new

relevation of nature. For the first time, we have seen our earth as it looks from space, incredibly beautiful, like a great jewel, a cloud-wrapped mandala, a harmony of water, land and sky; a sight wondrous and awe-inspiring. We know, too, that matter and energy are interchangeable terms; that everything we see around us is energy, manifesting in such a way that we perceive it as the three-dimensional world. Occult philosophy of both east and west maintained this for ages; now science says it. What is this energy? What sustains it? What is its source? What, indeed, can it be, but the One Divine Life?

Our limited minds, through ignorance, have distorted this beauty. Our greed has polluted the earth, air and water of this planet. Our wrath has ravaged it with war. Now we are like a spaceship with its life-support systems breaking down and its crew fighting among themselves. Spaceship Earth is in deep trouble; when that happens, we need to get in touch with our base.

Our base is the Divine Life of the universe. Our means of keeping in touch with it cannot be through any man-made dogma, but through nature, which man did not make. Men's hands wrote all the holy books and sacred scriptures; only the book of nature was written by divinity.

We cannot put the clock back to the days of the old paganism; but we can build a new paganism, which will take account of humanity as it really is, with its dreams, its frailties and its needs. Perhaps by that means humanity can advance towards what it might be. Science tells us that at the present time we are only using about one-tenth of our brain capacity. What are the other nine-tenths for?

The things which today are regarded as paranormal phenomena, such as clairvoyance, telekinesis, telepathy and so on—will they one day become within everyone's capacity? And how will it affect our lives if we are able to find, not faith or belief, but proof positive, of our minds' continuance beyond physical death?

We shall certainly need a new ethical standard, when these things come to pass.

3

Witch Festivals

The four Greater Sabbats of the witches' year are Candlemas, May Eve, Lammas and Hallowe'en. The four Lesser Sabbats are the equinoxes and the solstices. These are the natural divisions of the year, and all of them were celebrated by our pagan Celtic ancestors in Druidic times.

No one knows how old the Greater Sabbats really are. It has been suggested that they are connected with the breeding seasons of animals, in which case their origins are exceedingly primitive.

The Greater Sabbats are sometimes referred to as fire festivals, because they were celebrated with bonfires. So also was the mid-summer festival at the summer solstice or so-called longest day. Midsummer celebrations are still held in Cornwall, and the old bonfires still blaze from hilltops. Sometimes today, however, such fires are described as being 'to burn the witches'; but originally they were the witch-fires of the old pagan religion.

Our winter solstice festival has its counterpart of the mid-summer bonfire in the traditional Yule Log, though few people today have a fireplace big enough to burn the huge log that was carried in for this purpose in the olden time.

Further details of the old Sabbats are given later in *Liber Umbrarum*; but we may notice here their particular connection with fire, in the shape of blazing bonfires, torchlight processions and so on. Many of these old customs have been noted by the Cornish antiquary, T. F. G. Dexter, in his now rare pamphlet *Fire Worship in Britain*. Mr Dexter traces the connection of these picturesque survivals, some of which have lasted well into the present century, with the old Celtic festivals. He notes that a number of place-names throughout the country preserve the memory of the spot where the bonfires used to be lighted, in the form of 'Tan Hill', 'Tain Hill', or some similar name. This is sometimes Christianized into 'St Anne's Hill'; but its real deriva-tion is from the old Celtic *tan* or *teine,* meaning 'fire'.

The ashes of the ritual bonfires used to be preserved and scattered over the fields, in the belief that they helped to fertilize the soil and produce better crops. This is another sidelight on the importance of fertility, the life-spirit, in the practices of the old paganism.

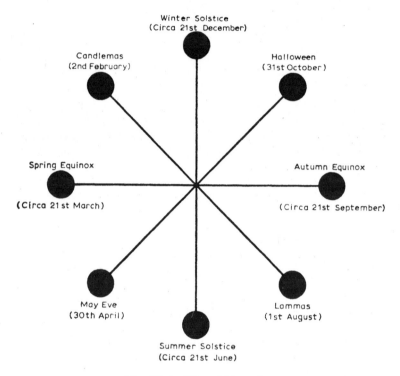

Winter Solstice
(Circa 21st December)

Candlemas
(2nd February)

Halloween
(31st October)

Spring Equinox

Autumn Equinox

(Circa 21st March)

(Circa 21st September)

May Eve
(30th April)

Lammas
(1st August)

Summer Solstice
(Circa 21st June)

The Eight Ritual Occasions

Fire, water, air and earth were the four elements of life to the ancient occult philosophers, because without them life could not manifest in this world. All were sacred; but fire was regarded as being peculiarly so because of its mysterious nature, its apparent closeness to pure energy. Hence the importance of candles, ever-burning lamps, and such practices as the keeping of a perpetual sacred flame in ancient sanctuaries. Many of these practices have been inherited by the Christian church, an instance of which may be seen in those churches which keep a small sanctuary lamp perpetually burning. The sacredness of fire probably goes back a very long way indeed into human pre-history, because the mastery of fire was one of primitive man's greatest discoveries, and helped to raise him above the level of the beasts.

Blazing bonfires are part of the traditional scene of the witches' Sabbat. In olden times, they served the practical purposes of giving light and warmth, as well as that of celebrating a ritual occasion. People brought their food to be cooked at them, having what today we would call a barbecue. They had probably come quite long distances to forgather at the Sabbat and intended to stay out most of the night, so they needed a hot meal. Moreover, the heat of the merry blaze encouraged them to throw off their clothes and take part in the naked dancing that the Sabbats were famous for. In olden days, when the countryside was much less populated than it is at present, such gatherings in remote parts were quite feasible. Among the vagrant classes of society, the 'rogues and vagabonds' outside the bounds of respectability, such merrymakings lingered on for a very long time. They were known as 'buff-balls', because those who took part in them were 'in the buff', or naked.

An interesting record of such a gathering is preserved in an old diary written by one John Manningham in the year 1602–3 : 'About some three years since there were certain rogues in Berkshire which usually frequented certain shipcoates every night. A justice having intelligence of their rabblement, proposing to apprehend them, went strong, and about midnight found them in the shipcoate, some six couple men and women dancing naked, the rest lying by them; divers of them taken and committed to prison.'

A 'shipcoate' is an old word for a sheep-pen. C. L'Estrange Ewen, who quotes this in his book *Witchcraft and Demonianism*, remarks that unfortunately no details of the depositions at the trial of these people seem to have been preserved, as the incident has every appearance of being a witch meeting. What gives it this appearance, of course, apart from the naked dancing, is the number of dancers involved : the traditional six couples. Six couples and a leader form the ideal combination for a working coven of thirteen.

My old friend, Gerald Gardner, told me an amusing story of a present-day witches' Sabbat (or at any rate, one that took place not very many years ago) in the Cheshire region, which was interrupted by the law, though with less unfortunate effects for the witches. It seems that a number of them met at a lonely crossroads on a heath, for the purpose of holding a Sabbat dance in the nude. It was such a remote spot that they thought it unlikely anyone would come by late at night, so they threw off their clothes and were dancing a merry round, when to their horror they saw the headlights of a lorry approaching. Fortunately, they were provided with black cloaks, so they hastily covered themselves and fled. Not, however, before the lorry driver had seen them; he looked out of his cab and then, rather to their surprise, increased his speed and drove on. After a breathless pause, two of the men volunteered to return to the spot and gather up any odd garments or witchcraft things that might have been left behind. They had just finished doing this when they saw the lorry returning. Hastily, the men dived behind some convenient bushes to watch developments.

This time the lorry stopped. They were able to see that the driver was accompanied by a very sceptical village policeman. In the still midnight air snatches of something like the following conversation carried to the ears of the cloaked and concealed listeners :

'But I tell you I *saw* them . . . they were *here* . . . dancing in a circle . . . witches.'

'Ho . . . well, they're not 'ere *now*, are they ?'

'Well . . . they've *disappeared*.'

'Ha . . . flown off on their broomsticks, no doubt,' (these words uttered with heavy sarcasm).

'Well . . .' (further description by the now embarrassed lorry-driver, followed by very decided utterance from the policeman).

'Now, look 'ere ! I don't want to hear any more about any naked witches. You just turn around and drive me back. And you mark my words, if you go telling any more yarns like this to the law, you'll find yourself in serious trouble !' (Exit policeman and lorry-driver, while the witches strive to stifle their laughter.)

This story was a standing joke with old Gerald and his Cheshire friends; but it is a good practical illustration of the value of the traditional black cloak as camouflage. In the past, such incidents have probably given rise to many tales of supernatural disappearances, whereas what really happened was that, as in this instance, the witches simply swathed themselves in their cloaks and melted into the shadows of the night. 'We just ran for the nearest hollow, threw ourselves down on the heath, and lay still,' they said afterwards. 'We knew the place well, so we knew where to run.'

Whether or not they had a bonfire burning, I do not know. The story did not mention one; but, even if they had, it would only have been a small one, suitable for what old Gerald used to call 'these lean-faced times'. The usual expedient in such cases is to have a good can of water handy, to douse the fire instantly. Once again, this could give the impression that the witch-fire had suddenly disappeared. One recalls those tales from ancient records, of how some traveller upon a lonely heath came within sight of the ungodly revels of the Sabbat, and how upon his making some pious Christian exclamation, the whole phantasmagoria (by the power of Satan, of course) was made suddenly to vanish!

Another expedient of witches in olden times was to impersonate the Wild Hunt, when they wanted to ride abroad by night. The story of the Wild Hunt is found in differing versions all over Europe. Sometimes it consists of a phantom cavalcade of wildly galloping riders, dressed in the costumes of an earlier age, and headed by some mythical figure or ancient hero. In the northern lands its leader was Woden or Odin; in the west country of Britain, King Arthur or King Herla; in the forest of Fontainebleau in France, Le Grand Veneur; in Windsor Forest, Herne the Hunter, whose ghostly appearances are still recorded even in our own day. Sometimes the Wild Hunt is an eerie visitation, as on Ditchling Beacon, the highest point of the South Downs, when on winter nights, as old Sussex people tell, the sound of the Wild Hunt, with its galloping horses, baying hounds and yelling hunters, approaches and rushes by, though nothing at all can be seen. To meet either manifestation is considered dangerous and ill-omened both to body and soul, so ordinary people would have given any mysterious cavalcade a wide berth if they met it after dark.

I remember in this connection that I once went to a small witch meeting in some woodlands quite near London. It was a full moon Esbat of about half a dozen people. We made our invocation, drank a toast to the Old Gods, and then danced in a circle. By the time the rite ended, we were all merry and exhilarated. It was a mild, clear night, with a silver moon shining through the trees. Somehow, instead of dispersing quietly, we continued to dance through the woods. I had brought along an old hunting horn, which the leader borrowed, and at the sound of this we laughed, leaped, shrilled the old cries and ran down the path between the trees, still attired in our hooded cloaks. Eventually, we came to a breathless halt at the edge of the woods, where lighted roads and civilization began. We looked at each other, and the leader said to us, 'You know what we've been doing? We've been playing the Wild Hunt!'

We realized that he was right. Some atavistic impulse seemed to have taken hold of us. It was a strange, uncanny experience, and one that I shall never forget.

The Esbat is the monthly meeting of the coven, held at every full moon. There are on an average thirteen full moons in a year, another instance of the witches' number thirteen. Indeed, this may be the oldest origin of the sacredness or magical nature of this number. The old pagan year was reckoned as consisting of thirteen months of twenty-eight days each, or thirteen lunations. This gave it a total of 364 days, to which one day had to be added to bring it in line with the solar year. Hence the expression 'a year and a day', which frequently occurs in fairy tales and legends. It is a relic of an older system of computing time.

The earliest version of the old English ballad, *Robin Hood and the Curtal Friar*, begins thus :

> But how many merry monthes be in the yeare?
> There are thirteen, I say;
> The mid-summer moon is the merryest of all,
> Next to the merry month of May.

A verse full of allusions to the festivals of witchcraft! Some versions of the story of Robin Hood tell us that he was the leader of a band of outlaws who, together with Maid Marian, numbered thirteen in all, which probably means that they were followers of the Old Religion.

When I visited Sherwood Forest a few years ago, I was shown the venerable tree called the Major Oak, widespreading and evidently of great antiquity. It is hollow within the massive trunk, to which access can be gained by means of a small opening. Local legends say that Robin Hood and his outlaws hid in the tree to escape pursuit; but there is another tradition, vague and less well-known, of young couples consummating their love within the hollow trunk of the oak, which is quite big enough for this purpose. This is probably a folk-memory of the old fertility rites of the forest, and ties up with the story of Robin Hood as a witch leader.

Old myths and legends often tell of significant companies of thirteen. There were, for instance, King Charlemagne and his twelve Paladins; the Danish hero Hrolf and his twelve Berserks; Romulus, the founder of Rome, and his twelve followers called *lictors*; some version of the story of King Arthur say that his Round Table consisted of twelve principal knights, namely Sir Galahad, Sir Bedivere, Sir Lamarok, Sir Gareth, Sir Gawaine, Sir Kay, Sir Geraint, Sir Percival, Sir Tristram, Sir Gaheris, Sir Bors and Sir Lancelot. There were many other knights of the Order; but these were the knights who actually sat with King Arthur at the famous Round Table, which was made by Merlin 'in token of the roundness of the world, for by the Round Table is the world signified by right'.

Another thirteen which figures in ancient British myth is the Thirteen Treasures of Britain, which Merlin took with him when he vanished into the Land of Faery. Perhaps a figure of speech for the lost knowledge of ancient times? A very strange story of a company of thirteen may be found in *Atlantis in Andalucia: A Study of Folk Memory,* by Mrs E. M. Wishaw. Various rather garbled versions of this story have appeared elsewhere, and as Mrs Wishaw's book is long out of print and hard to come by, I think it worth-while to put the facts straight, as they take the significance of thirteen back to Neolithic times.

Mrs Wishaw carried out extensive research into the archaeology and anthropology of Spain, which she believed to show traces of colonization from Atlantis in prehistoric times. In her book she tells the story of the Cave of the Bats, a Neolithic sepulchre which was first described by a Spanish savant, Don Manuel de Gongora, who wrote about it in 1868. The cave is a large natural cavern near the town of Albunol on the coast of the province of Granada. It takes its name from the great horde of bats which flew out of it when it was first discovered in 1851. For some time the cave was used as a shelter for wandering shepherds, after it had been cleared of centuries of bat droppings, which the local farmers utilized as manure. Then one day a visitor from the town, who had some archaeological knowledge, noticed that some great stones in the cavern had evidently been placed there as if to wall up something. The stones were removed and behind them another cave was found.

In the inner cavern thus revealed was found a remarkable royal burial of Neolithic times. Altogether fifty-eight skeletons were discovered, one of them wearing a splendid golden diadem which was eventually sent to the National Archaeological Museum in Madrid. But the most curious discovery was that of the skeleton of a woman, seated in an easy posture against the wall of an alcove, with the head leaned upon one hand as if she had fallen asleep there. Around her, carefully arranged in a semi-circle, were twelve other skeletons.

She was dressed in a tunic of skin and a necklace of sea-shells, with a boar's tusk pendant (the boar's tusk is still used as an amulet in our own day). Each of the twelve skeletons around her had a bag of finely-woven esparto grass beside it, but the contents had long since turned to black earth. However, among the many small objects found in the cave were the withered remains of a great many poppy heads, of the kind known as *Papaver ibericum,* from which the Romans used to obtain a very strong variety of opium.

None of the skeletons in the cave showed any sign of violence. It was as if they had all laid down and died of their own free will, in a drugged sleep. Then the cave had been sealed up from outside and the site marked by a great monolith some seven metres high, which Senor de Gongora observed a moderate distance away from the cave entrance. He regarded this as a landmark set up to the memory of this prehistoric king and his court, who had perhaps chosen to die together rather than yield to some long-forgotten invader.

However, in view of the similar discoveries of Sir Leonard Woolley in the tombs of ancient Chaldea, we know that sometimes when a monarch died his whole court followed him into the land of the shades, lying down in the tomb and swallowing a fatal draught of some opiate poison. The discovery in the Cave of the Bats may have been a Neolithic version of the same amazing custom; amazing, that is, to us in the scorn that it showed of the fear of death. All the king's people had accompanied him in his journey into the other world, including the priestess and her coven.

Some anthropologists now believe that observation of the moon and its phases and lunations goes back not only to Neolithic times but even earlier. Dr Alexander Marshack, in particular, has suggested that some of the markings found in caves used by men of the Old Stone Age were the beginnings of a lunar calendar. So the sacredness of the thirteen lunar months may, indeed, go back literally to the beginnings of recorded time.

Witches of the present day take note of the waxing and waning of the moon to assist their spells. The waxing moon is the time to invoke for the things you want, while the waning moon is the time to banish those things you wish to get rid of. The waning moon was also used as the time to put curses on people, on those rare occasions when it was felt that such conduct was justified in self-defence. Hence, the old word 'wanion', meaning a curse put on in the waning moon.

The full moon is the high tide of psychic power, and recognized as such in other religions besides the pagan faith of the witches. The Buddhists, for instance, honour the full moon of May, the Wesak Moon as it is called, because at that time Prince Gautama, seated all night in meditation beneath a tree, achieved enlightenment and became the Buddha. Many pictures of the Hindu god Shiva represent him as a yogi, seated in meditation by the light of the full moon.

Sometimes, however, the influence of the full moon is believed to be dangerously unsettling upon people of disturbed mind. The old word 'lunatic' actually means someone influenced by Luna, the moon. The belief that the moon has a subtle effect upon the human mind is a very old one, which consequently fell into disrepute with the arrival of the scientific rationalism of the nineteenth century. Nevertheless, it has received some confirmation in our own day, now that scientists are becoming somewhat less materialistic than they were, and more willing to investigate the subtle forces that affect human life.

The tiny electrical currents which flow along the nerves, when measured with a micro-voltameter, have been found to exhibit violent fluctuations when such tests were carried out at the times of new moon and full moon. The more excitable or unstable the person being tested was, the greater this effect seemed to be. The pioneer of this research has been Dr Leonard J. Ravity, a neurologist of Duke University, Illinois. This may be the reason why crime figures, especially those of crimes of a violent or bizarre nature, tend to increase at the time of the full moon.

Independent research by scientists in America and Australia, who have been concerned with collecting and studying weather statistics, has indicated the truth of another old belief. The idea that the moon affected the weather, though firmly believed in by country folk, has been dismissed with ridicule by the more sophisticated. However, the collected weather data show that there often *is* a rainy period two or three days after the new moon and the full moon, just as the old weather lore said.

The effect of the moon upon the tides of the sea is well known. It will be seen that these observed influences of the moon as described above, correspond with them. That is, the high and strongly flowing tides, called spring tides, occur just after the new moon and the full moon. The lower and weaker tides, called neap tides, occur just after the other phases of the moon, the first quarter and last quarter.

We may then summarize these important lunar tides as follows :

> Waxing moon : the time of construction, invoking.
> Full moon : the time of integration, perfecting.
> Waning moon : the time of destruction, banishing.

This may well be the real inner meaning of the *tryfoss* or *triskelion,* the emblem consisting of three radiating curves or legs, which occurs so frequently in ancient Celtic art and in the arms of the Isle of Man. It is the ever-returning cycle of lunations, the three phases of the moon. The Scandinavian people also revered it, regarding it as a sign of life and light.

There are also four tides or cycles in the solar year, commencing at the equinoxes and solstices. These bear some resemblance to the quarters of the lunar month, though upon a larger scale, so to speak. Of these, the tides which commence at the two equinoxes, those of spring and autumn, are strongly flowing, like the spring tides. Hence occult orders and those who practise magic make use of these occasions for the purpose of launching an idea or a thought, sending it out upon the flowing cosmic tide. The tides of the solstices, at midsummer and midwinter, are quieter and more gentle, rather like the neap tides. Hence these are more often occasions of holidaying and rejoicing, as at the festivals of Midsummer and Yule.

Now, the Great Sabbats take place about midway in each quarter of the year, *between* the equinoxes and the solstices. So it will be seen that the Lesser Sabbats are the *releasing* of the new cosmic tide at each quarter of the year, and the Greater Sabbats are its culmination, mid-point or perfection.

These festivals of immemorial age have been found to be marked upon the very landscape of Britain itself. Alignments radiating from stone circles, or through other mark-points, indicate the place of sunrise or sunset, either at the equinoxes and solstices or at the beginning of May and November. A former Astronomer Royal, Sir Norman Lockyer, observed this at Stonehenge at the beginning of this century. Then in the 1920s Alfred Watkins of Hereford made his now famous discovery of the system of ancient alignments all over Britain, which he called 'leys'. His work has been enlarged upon in our own day by John Michell and Paul Screeton.

In Paul Screeton's book *Quicksilver Heritage* he notes that in all there are eight days in the year at which observations of such astronomical alignments may have been made, namely the equinoxes, solstices and half-quarter days. These are, in fact, the eight ritual occasions of the witches.

4

Witch Signs and Symbols

Witches make use of a number of signs and symbols, many of which are held in common with the practice of ceremonial magic. Others derive from ancient religions. In fact, most magical signs probably take their origin from pre-Christian religions, although they have been used all over the world for so many centuries that no-one knows where they actually originated. An example of this is the swastika, made notorious in our own day by Hitler and his Nazis, yet before that revered as a good-luck sign by our Anglo-Saxon ancestors and venerated from China to Mexico. It has for long been a sacred sign of the Buddhist religion, and its name is derived from Sanskrit words meaning 'well being'. Hitler adopted it because he regarded it as a purely Aryan symbol; but its use is so ancient and widespread that one might as well call it Atlantean or even Lemurian as Aryan.

I do not know of any witches who use the swastika as a magical sign; but some modern witches have adopted another almost equally time-honoured sign, the ankh cross. This derives from ancient Egypt, where it is found in use from the most archaic period. To the Egyptians it meant 'life', being the union of the masculine and feminine principles. The looped part of the cross represents the feminine principle, while the T-shaped part represents the masculine.

Worshipping as they do the god and goddess of life, it is not difficult to see why witches of the present day find this sign appropriate, as also do other groups of pagans and nature-worshippers.

However, its use by witches is not as traditional as that of the pentagram, or five-pointed star. This, too, goes back a very long way. It was the badge of the followers of Pythagoras, perhaps because its proportions contain that mathematical secret known as the 'golden section', which is still used by artists and architects. The meaning ascribed to it by witches, however, is a simpler one. They see in it the emblem of magic, the four elements of the material world being ruled over by the power of mind, represented by the topmost point of the star. Reversed, that is with the point downwards, the pentagram shows the face of the goat-god, which Satanists take as a symbol of the devil, though actually it only means spirit hidden in matter. Both the pentagram and the six-pointed star were much used by ceremonial magicians in medieval times. These signs frequently occur in the books of magic called grimoires, which in olden days were very secret, because to be found in possession of a copy of one of them was to be revealed as a practitioner of forbidden arts. Grimoires such as *The Key of Solomon* or *The Goetia* are often wrongly regarded as witchcraft books. Actually, however, the practice of ceremonial magic as described in the grimoires differs from that of witchcraft in important respects. It is not pagan, but rather Christian or Jewish, often in a manner seemingly quite devout. It seems probable that many of its secret practitioners were clerics of one kind or another, who would indignantly deny being witches.

The essence of ceremonial magic of this kind is the evocation and binding of spirits by the power of the sacred names of God, which are derived from the Hebrew Cabbala. This, in turn, derived its words of power from even more ancient sources; possibly in many instances from Egypt, that immemorial home of magic.

Along with the use of the words of power goes the tradition of the protection of the magic circle; though the circles drawn by ceremonial magicians are usually much more elaborate than those used by the witch. The ideas of the witch cult generally seem to be simpler and more primitive than those of ceremonial magicians, probably because the cult was carried on by the common people of the countryside. The ceremonial magician had to be literate; he had to have some working knowledge of the languages in which all learned men of Europe in times past were versed, namely Latin, Hebrew and Greek, because these were the languages of his magical books. The witch, on the other hand, did not even need to be able to read or write so long as he or she had a good memory for the traditions handed down.

Gerald Gardner, in his occult novel *High Magic's Aid*, tells the story of a working partnership between a ceremonial magician and a witch, in a tale placed in the thirteenth century. In many instances, something like this story probably did take place, with practitioners of the secret arts helping and protecting each other and possibly borrowing from each other also.

Certainly witches and ceremonial magicians both make use of the magical circle, as noted above, and also of consecrated weapons, such as a magical sword or knife which is used to draw the circle and to command spirits. However, the ceremonial magicians derive the magical signs of the pentagram or five-pointed star and the hexagram or six-pointed star from King Solomon, the great traditional master of magic. Both of these signs are referred to as the Seal of Solomon, and it is not clear which of them really deserves this appellation, although it is most frequently given to the six-pointed star, which is also the symbol of the Jewish religion.

Witches, on the other hand, say that King Solomon may well have used these signs, but that they are actually even older than Solomon, and no one knows how old they really are. In fact, the pentagram goes back to Ur of the Chaldees and the hexagram is also found in India, where it often appears as the basis of the meditational diagrams known as *yantras*.

The pentagram is sometimes called the endless knot, because it can be drawn all in one line without removing the pen from the paper. In this connection, there is an interesting and little known explanation of it which seems peculiarly relevant to our times.

The topmost point of the pentagram is regarded as representing Deity, the divine source of life. From this point a line is traced to the lowest left-hand angle of the figure. This represents life descending from its divine source into the lowest and simplest forms of living matter. The line is then continued up and across to the upper angle on the right. This represents the ascent of life from primitive forms, by the process of evolution, to its highest physical form on this planet, the human being.

The line then continues across the figure to the upper angle on the left. This represents man's earthly progress, his achievements on the material plane, as he becomes cleverer, richer, more powerful, building himself great empires and civilizations. However, in his progress in this way he sooner or later reaches the danger point and begins to fall. To show this, the line goes down and across from this angle to the lowest angle on the right-hand side. This is the story of all man's empires; but because the human spirit is one with its divine source, it must and will strive upwards to find that source again. Hence the line of the pentagram rises up again from the lowest level to rejoin the topmost point from whence it issued.

Sometimes both the pentagram and the hexagram are shown enclosed in a circle. This is the sign of infinity and eternity, without beginning and without end.

The pentagram is known as the star of the microcosm, or little universe, because it bears some resemblance when drawn in the upright position, with one point uppermost, to a human figure standing with arms and legs outstretched. The old occult philosophers taught that man is himself a little universe, containing by analogy all that is in the great universe, the macrocosm. It is interesting to note that this teaching appears in the occult philosophy of both east and west. It is as well known to the Tantrics of India as it was to medieval magicians.

The hexagram is the star of the macrocosm, consisting as it does of two interlaced triangles, one pointing upwards and one downwards. These represent the two great forces of polarity, positive and negative, masculine and feminine, Yang and Yin, god and goddess of life, which bring all things into manifestation. The upward-pointing triangle is the triangle of the male element, fire; the downward-pointing triangle is the triangle of the female element, water. This symbolism too is found in the east. Each equilateral triangle consists of three angles of sixty degrees each, so that the sum total of all the angles makes 360 degrees, the perfect circle.

These beautiful and symmetrical figures, besides being magical signs, are in themselves harmonious and pleasing to the eye. Hence they are often found in architecture, though there is good reason to believe that the masons of ancient times knew well the inner meaning of such figures and did not use them merely for decoration.

Remarkably interesting decorations can often be found in our older cathedrals and churches, which seems to indicate a period when a good deal of the lingering faith of paganism intermingled with the new creed of Christianity. The old nature god of the witches himself frequently appears in the form of the foliate mask, or 'the green man' as he is sometimes called.

The foliate mask is the representation of a man's face, often with pointed ears and sometimes with horns, surrounded by green leaves which actually seem to be growing out of the face itself. Often leafy branches are seen coming out from the figure's mouth, as if he were breathing them forth. He is the life-force of nature, the power that clothes the spring woodlands with green, the continual renewal.

A good place to look for examples of the foliate mask is among the roof bosses of old churches; but he is also found in wood carvings and even in stained glass windows and among the decorations of illuminated manuscripts. He may be outside or inside a church or a cathedral, peering puckishly down from the top of a pillar or peeping up from the little seats known as misericords. The latter, incidentally, often contain all sorts of quaint and freakish scenes which show a robust and rather pagan sense of humour in the craftsmen who carved them. For instance, there are quite a number of examples, in this and other places in sacred edifices, of a fox wearing a monk's cowl standing up in a pulpit and preaching to a congregation of geese!

An even more explicitly pagan figure is the fertility goddess found carved on certain very old Irish churches, from whence she derives her Irish name of Shiela-na-Gig, which may be roughly translated as 'the merry Shiela'. This is the name given to certain crude and curious carvings, showing a nude woman with her genitals deliberately emphasized, in such a way that it seems a very strange thing to display upon a Christian church. Nevertheless, examples of these carvings can be found in British churches also, notably at Kilpeck in Herefordshire and at Whittlesford near Cambridge.

These Shiela-na-Gig figures are strikingly similar to those venerated by the Tantrics of India, as part of their worship of the Universal Mother, *Mahadevi*. When the Arts Council of Great Britain organized a splendid exhibition of Tantric art at the Hayward Gallery, London in 1971, among the exhibits were several figures strongly reminiscent of the Shiela-na-Gig. In particular, there was a photograph of an eleventh-century carving from a temple in Hyderabad, showing the goddesses as genetrix of all things, displaying her *yoni* or female parts for worship; and a similar carving from north-eastern India, dating from about A.D. 600.

It is tempting to deduce from this, and from the horned god figures of prehistoric India referred to in Chapter 1, that the faith of the Tantrics and that of our own pagan ancestors, which survived as the witch cult, had a common origin. Perhaps, however, one should not be too insistent in seeking such an origin, because the answer may really lie not in migration of tribes from some common centre so much as in the collective unconscious of mankind and the images which arise from it.

After all, what more potent images of the life force are there to our consciousness than those of sex and generation? I remember in a radio interview once being asked, wasn't there a lot of *sex* in witchcraft? I pointed out that there was a lot of sex in human life. Witches are not responsible for this fact, so those who object to it must direct their complaint to a higher power.

While upon the subject of old churches, we may note that the best place to look for something curious or equivocal in such an edifice is upon the north side. This is because the north side

was anciently believed to be 'the Devil's side'. Few graves are
to be found there, because this is not where the good people were
buried. Those who died by their own hand, or somehow in bad
odour with the Church, were buried upon the north side. The
north door of a church was known as 'the Devil's door', and one
frequently finds that such doors or the remains of them exist in old
churches, but have been blocked up.

The witch belief is that this was done because the pagans in
the congregation, who had to attend church by law, or at any
rate by prudence, used to forgather around the north door of
the church, deliberately choosing their place there as being the
place of pagan things. Eventually the north doors were closed up
and filled in with masonry, to discourage this practice.

Many of the curious signs which may be found engraved
upon the walls or pillars of ancient sacred edifices are masons'
marks, the signatures of the craftsmen who built our churches
and cathedrals; but I have seen others in such places which are
not masons' marks, though usually referred to as such in the
official guidebook. They are magical or pagan emblems. For
instance, I once found a small, deeply engraved version of the
eight-rayed figure which illustrates Chapter 3, the emblem of
the eight ritual occasions, on a pillar on the north side of an old
Sussex church. The pentagram is sometimes found also.

These things were not put there to deface or desecrate the
church. On the contrary, it is usually the church which has been
deliberately built upon the site of a pagan sacred place. The older
the church is, the more likely this is to be true. Innumerable instances of it could be given. The oldest church in my home town
of Brighton stands on a hill which was once crowned by a stone
circle. The church is dedicated to St Nicholas, who may be a
substitute for a pagan god, 'Old Nick', turned by the new
religion into another name for the Devil.

At Knowlton in Dorset the ruins of a twelfth-century Christian
church actually stand within the earth circle which once surrounded a pagan sanctuary. This is referred to by Jacquetta
Hawkes in her book *A Guide to the Prehistoric and Roman
Monuments in England and Wales*. She comments upon its
strange and haunted atmosphere. One of the most numinous
places in Britain, Glastonbury Tor, is crowned by the solitary
remaining tower of a church dedicated to St Michael; but the
Tor itself was sacred long before Joseph of Arimathea and his
twelve companions came to Britain and built the first Christian
church here, as local legends record that they did.

Another persistent legend declares that the site of what is now

St Paul's Cathedral in London once held a temple of Diana the moon goddess. The relic known as London Stone, still carefully preserved behind an iron grille in the wall of what is now the Bank of China in Cannon Street, which lies on the line between the Cathedral and Tower Hill, is reputed to have been an altar from this ancient temple. It has been suggested that Britain's capital city derives its name from this sanctuary. It began as *Lan Dian*, a Celtic name meaning 'temple of Diana'; this was Latinized into *Londinium*, which was eventually shortened into London.

To return to the subject of witchcraft signs, there is one which has not only survived into our own day, but even experienced a remarkable revival, though its real significance has been little realized. This is the sign known as the witch's foot in centuries past; but today it may be seen worn by many young people as a symbol of nuclear disarmament.

In the past this symbol was thought to come from the shape of a bird's foot, supposedly an attribute of female demons and, in particular, of the witch goddess who according to European legend, sometimes led the Wild Hunt on windy moonlit nights. This mysterious divinity had a variety of names in different countries, such as Holda, Frau Holle, Abundia or Dame Habonde, Nicneven in Scotland, Aradia or Herodias, and Bensozia (the latter meaning 'the good neighbour', an old synonym for one of the fairy race). Her distant ancestress is Lilith, the moon goddess of ancient Sumeria, who is depicted with bird's feet, probably because of her affinity to her sacred bird, the owl.

There is a faint trace of an old belief among witches that in days long ago people who were secretly members of the witch cult used to mark this sign somehow upon the soles of their shoes. In this way, walking upon soft ground, they would leave a trail of signs sufficiently plain to be followed, if they wished others of the faith to do so for any reason. This, too, might have something to do with the symbol being called the witch's foot.

This old sign had been almost lost in oblivion until it reappeared with its modern significance. Today, so the story goes, it signifies the letters 'N.D.', the initials of the words 'Nuclear Disarmament' as signalled by the semaphore system. The idea of it was allegedly conceived by the late Bertrand Russell in February 1958 and it soon became very popular. But it is precisely the same as the symbol which appears in Rudolf Koch's *Book of Signs*, where it is called 'The crow's foot, or witch's foot'.

It seems certain that in the days of persecution, the witches must have used signs and tokens as passwords of recognition.

The word *Toledo* is said to have been one such, from the school of sorcery which was supposed to exist in that city when it was under Moorish rule. To mention this word was a sign that you were interested in the forbidden and so-called black arts. No doubt in practice every coven had its own signs and passwords.

Two signs in general use which were made by the hands, were the *Mano Cornuta* and the *Mano in Fica,* or the sign of horns and the sign of the fig. The sign of horns was made by holding up the hand with the first and little fingers outstretched and the rest, including the thumb, folded into the palm of the hand. It signified the horns of the horned god. The other, the sign of the fig, was made by clenching the fingers and showing the thumb thrust between the first and second fingers. It signified the female genitals, for which 'the fig' is still a slang term in Spanish and Italian.

Both of these signs were supposed to be efficacious against the evil eye, perhaps because they opposed one witchcraft to another. Little amulets in the shape of hands making these signs are still very popular in Latin countries, where belief in the evil eye lingers tenaciously. But the actual hand signs were used by witches, sometimes for purposes of recognition. They bear some resemblance to the *mudras* of the east.

Another means of recognition was the so-called 'token of the Sabbat', which resembled a small coin or medal with some magical emblem imprinted upon it. A whole hoard of these was found in the River Seine in France, where they had probably been thrown at some alarm of danger. Some of them are depicted in *Two Essays on the Worship of Priapus* by Richard Payne Knight and Thomas Wright. The tokens are made of lead, a substance easily cast into moulds and hence popular for the making of such things in olden times. They show upon one side an equal-armed cross in a circle, the pre-Christian or Celtic cross, while upon the other side appears either a phallus or a stylized representation of the female genitals.

Not long ago I saw advertised for sale in an English magazine an alleged example of a 'witch's coin', which I took to mean a token of the Sabbat. A high price was demanded; but whether it was obtained, or whether the object was indeed authentic, I do not know.

A witch sign that was used in olden times in the county of Sussex, and perhaps elsewhere, was the number thirteen written in Roman numerals, thus: XIII.

Among the Sussex witchcraft objects in my collection are an old pewter candlestick with the 'XIII' marking on it, and two very old horn spoons, probably once used to stir some witch's brew, that bear the same marking. In the latter case, to the casual eye the 'XIII' could appear to be just a rough attempt at decoration; but the initiate would recognize it for what it was.

Once, when I was giving a lecture on witchcraft, I showed these things among other objects. In the questions and discussion that followed, a gentleman in the audience told me that he lived in an old house in Sussex where the same marking was cut into an old oak beam in one of the upper rooms. He had often wondered, he said, what significance it had—now he knew! Possibly the room had once been used for witch meetings.

Some present-day witches have adopted as a kind of password an old East Anglian greeting: 'Flags, flax, fodder and frig!' This means the basic things that make a happy life. 'Flags' means flagstones, the stones that build a house. 'Flax' is what linen is spun from, hence it means clothing. 'Fodder' is evidently food, enough to eat. 'Frig' is the name of the Anglo-Saxon goddess Frigga who was the goddess of love, though it degenerated in vulgar speech into another name for sexual intercourse; but in the old saying it simply means sexual love without any obscene connotation. So 'Flags, flax, fodder and frig' simply means a secure home, enough to wear, enough to eat, and someone to love you. A good basic blessing!

If people in the world were content with these four things, instead of spending their lives trying to grab more and more of everything, how different life might be.

5

The Magic Circle

The magic circle is a fundamental requirement of all kinds of occult ceremonial, and one of the most ancient. The magicians of Babylonia and Assyria used magic circles in their rites. Descriptions of their workings have come down to us, together with the name they gave to the magic circle, *usurtu*.

They seem to have had a very similar idea of magical practice to that which prevailed in medieval Europe, namely, that mankind was surrounded by a vast assembly of spirits, many of whom were dangerous demons; but that these could be controlled by the power of divine names and images. The Assyrian magician used powdered lime or flour to outline his circle, and set little images of his gods within it to form a kind of spiritual fortress, exactly as the European magician of the Middle Ages conceived his circle to be.

Instead of using images, however, the ceremonial magicians who followed the traditions of such adepts as Cornelius Agrippa (1486–1535) and Peter of Abano (1250–1316) inscribed around their circles divine names such as the Tetragrammaton, the four-lettered name of God found in the Old Testament. Other names were supplied by the Hebrew Qabalah or Cabbala, the secret tradition of Israel, which was much studied by European occultists, ostensibly for the purpose of converting the Jews, but actually for the magical secrets it contains.

For instance, the Cabbalistic word AGLA, often regarded as a word of magical power, is the initial letters of a sentence in the Hebrew language: *Ateh gibor leolam Adonai*, 'Thou are mighty for ever, O Lord'. Other magical words were derived from Gnostic sources in the Greek-speaking Egyptian city, Alexandria. Although pre-Christian in origin, they were adapted to Christian use and applied to the Christian God; such words, for instance, as PRINEUMATON or ATHANATOS often featuring in the figures of magical circles given in old books of magic. The name of the Archangel Michael, too, was used, as he was believed to be the leader of the heavenly host which fought against the powers of evil. Interspersed among the words of power were potent symbols such as the pentagram, the hexagram, and the equal-armed cross.

Why, however, should the figure of a circle be supposed capable of acting as a spiritual fortress in this manner? The answer seems to lie in the fact that the circle was believed to be the most perfect geometrical figure. This belief gave early astronomers a good deal of trouble, because they thought that the heavenly bodies could not possibly move in anything but a circular path, otherwise God's heaven could not be perfect. Only reluctantly did they abandon this idea when practical observation with telescopes showed them that the orbits of the planets were elliptical.

A primeval symbol of the infinite is the figure of a serpent with its tail in its mouth, known as the *Ouroboros*. The eminent psychologist Carl Gustav Jung, in his exploration of the archetypal images dwelling in man's collective unconscious, has recognized this as meaning the first undifferentiated state of things, containing the potentialities of all within itself. The ouroboric serpent may give us a clue to the meaning of the magic circle and its origin in the mind of man.

In drawing the magic circle, man, in a sense, creates and defines his own little universe. This idea is significantly developed by Israel Regardie in his book *The Tree of Life: A Study in Magic*. This book, written by a modern exponent of the western magical tradition, takes a much more sophisticated view of the function of the magical circle than that shown in the concept of the medieval magician defying the demons from within the safety of its consecrated round. The magic circle is that which limits the magician to the attainment of a specific end. He no longer wanders aimlessly. He is oriented, both figuratively and literally, between the four cardinal points, at which candles traditionally burn and from which sometimes incense arises. Plans of magical circles in old books and manuscripts often show a place for a censer of incense at each of the four quarters of the circle, north, south, east and west. A cross divides the centre of the circle, with sometimes the Greek letter *Alpha* inscribed in the east and *Omega* in the west, signifying the beginning and the end; another analogy to the figure of the serpent *Ouroboros*.

The circle also signifies man's own aura, the field of force which surrounds his physical body. In the case of a spiritually developed person, this aura is said to extend to a considerable distance, with strength to repel evil influences and magical power to bring to its owner that which he needs or rightfully desires.

It will be seen that the magical circle, with its emphasis on the cardinal points, essentially resembles the circled cross which is the most primitive form of mandala, an oriental word made familiar to us by the work of Carl Gustav Jung. Jung found the mandala to be a figure of great importance among the archetypes of the collective unconscious which he studied, signifying among other things balance and harmony. It is a word evidently related to the Arabic *Al-mandal,* 'the circle'.

The circled cross, or Celtic cross as it has come to be called, is a pre-Christian form of cross frequently found in the British Isles. Many circled crosses are, of course, Christian, but they often show subtle influences of older things. Cornwall can show many examples of the Celtic cross, as can Scotland, Ireland and Wales. But it is a remarkable fact that the megalithic standing stones of Callanish, on the Isle of Lewis in the Outer Hebrides, were originally erected to trace out on the ground the image of a circled cross approached by a long avenue of stones, the whole making a similar outline to that of the Celtic crosses referred to above. Many of the stones of the avenue have now disappeared; but archaeologists have found within the circle a chambered cairn dating back to around 2000 B.C. The plan of the Callanish stones is depicted in *Mysterious Britain* by Janet and Colin Bord.

It is at least a curious coincidence that the present-day village of Avebury as seen from the air looks very like a circled cross, with the four roads of the modern village meeting within the circle of the ancient earthwork. Actually, this was the town plan upon which many very old cities were built, namely a circular wall enclosing the city, with gates at the four cardinal points and main roads leading to a central open space, which was the market place and general gathering point. In other words, the city itself was a mandala. There is a close parallel between the magic circle of western occultism, oriented to the four cardinal points, with the stations of the four elements regarded as being situated at these points, and the beautiful mandalas of Tibetan art. A mandala can be very simple or almost infinitely complicated; but essentially it is a harmonious and balanced figure. Its simplest form, as we have seen, is the Celtic circled cross; but much more complicated mandalas than this have been evolved by the art of both east and west, showing the mandala to be a universal symbol. The great rose windows of medieval cathedrals are also mandalas; so, too, is the Chinese symbol of the *Pa Kua,* or eight directions, with the eight trigrams arranged around it from which all the figures of the *I Ching,* the ancient Chinese system of divination, are formed. The mariner's compass, with its complicated 'rose' of all the different points of the horizon, is a mandala. The astrologer's figure of a horoscope, with the earth in the centre surrounded by the twelve houses of heaven, is likewise a mandala, showing the arrangement of the planets and zodiacal signs for a particular time and place. All these, in a sense, are magic circles, be they large or small; because, of course, if you want to draw a harmonious geometrical figure, the easiest way to do it is to start with a circle.

The most famous magical circle of the island of Britain is Stonehenge. Archaeologists today tell us that Stonehenge was built in three stages. The earliest part of it is the great earth circle that encloses the stone structure at its centre. According to the latest evidence of the revised system of radio-carbon dating, this circle was constructed about 2775 B.C. The orientation of Stonehenge to the sunrise at the summer solstice is well-known. It is still a thrilling moment to see the midsummer dawn in this way, as the sun rises above the phallic monolith called the Friar's Heel, or the Hele Stone, and its rays strike into the feminine womb-shape of the so-called 'horseshoe' of the great trilithons, making the *hieros gamos*, the Sacred Marriage of heaven and earth.

Not so well known are the mysterious alignments which connect Stonehenge with Glastonbury and with the site of Salisbury Cathedral, to name only two of the leys which were discovered by Alfred Watkins of Hereford in the 1920s and written about in our own day by John Michell in his now famous book *The View Over Atlantis*.

One of these alignments had been previously noted by Sir Norman Lockyer, the astronomer. If a straight line is drawn from Stonehenge through the centre of the earthworks of Old Sarum, it runs directly to the site on which Salisbury Cathedral now stands; either a remarkable coincidence or a sign that the cathedral occupies, as such buildings usually did, a site of ancient sanctity. The other alignment runs from Glastonbury, the Avalon of Celtic myth, through the axis of the ruined abbey, along an old road called Dod Lane which runs past Chalice Hill, over Gare Hill and eventually on to Stonehenge.

The whole question of these alignments is still being investigated; but enough has been discovered to compel us to realize that a whole lost civilization, radically different from our own, employing a technology of a potent but different type from our own, lies hidden within the British landscape. To this lost civilization John Mitchell gave the figurative name of 'Atlantis'. No review of the Old Religion of Western Europe to which we give the name of witchcraft, can be complete without taking these discoveries into account, because they are deeply concerned with the hidden forces of nature, the powers which true magic sets out to contact.

We will return to the study of the leys in a later chapter; but here we will simply ask the question, what *is* the power of magic that is raised and contained within the magic circle? This mysterious power has been given all sorts of names, all over the world and in all ages. The Kahunas, or native magicians of the South Sea Islands, call it *mana*. The Hindu yogis call it *prana*. Bulwer Lytton, in his magical romance *The Coming Race,* named it *Vril*. (Lytton, incidentally, was a practising occultist and a member of a magical society.) Baron Von Reichenbach conducted many experiments in the early nineteenth century to demonstrate the existence of a similar force which he called *odyle*. Paracelsus and Mesmer also wrote of the existence of a mysterious force, to which the latter attributed the operations of what is now called hypnotism. Mesmer regarded it as a sort of invisible fluid, or all-pervading medium.

The famous French occultist, Eliphas Lévi, regarded this force as 'the Great Magical Agent', to which most of the operations of magic were indebted for their success. No one, however, seemed to be able to give any very clear definition of it; or perhaps, as its great potency was constantly stressed, their discretion as occultists did not permit them to do so.

Today we would call it a 'borderline energy'; that is, an energy somewhere between the physical plane and the metaphysical, or normally invisible realms. The person who has perhaps come closest to discovering its secrets in our own day is Wilhelm Reich, the psychologist who experimented with what he called orgone energy. According to his writings, this energy, which radiates from living matter and permeates everything, seems very like the *odyle, vril,* and so on, of the ancient writers.

In this connection, we may well wonder about that weird symbol, the so-called Hand of Glory. Most people know the story from the *Ingoldsby Legends,* of the thieves who enlisted the aid of a witch to concoct this horrible charm, made from the hand of a hanged man stolen from the gibbet. Five wicks of human hair were affixed to the thumb and fingers, greased with the fat of a black cat, while incantations of evil magic were recited, so that when this infernal light was kindled the criminals who carried it could rob with impunity, because everyone in the house would be cast into a death-like trance.

This fictional story has quite a number of parallels from folklore; but curiously enough, the Hand of Glory appears in old pictures of the witches' Sabbat, where it is certainly not being used as a robbers' charm. For instance, the hand with its flame-tipped fingers is shown in an old engraving by Jaspar Isaac, dating from 1614. It stands upon the mantelpiece of the witches' kitchen, where frightful imps of all shapes and sizes are disporting themselves. The two most famous seventeenth-century painters of witch scenes, Frans Francken and David Teniers, also depict the Hand of Glory in just the same situation.

Now, as Gerald Gardner pointed out, many of these old pictures actually depict the garbled popular beliefs of their day about witches and what they did. So the real Hand of Glory was a witch symbol; what of? When we read Baron Von Reichenbach's account of how his 'sensitives' could see the flames of odylic force streaming from the fingers of the human hand in a dark room, surely we can guess. The Hand of Glory was the symbol of this mysterious force, but the truth about it was kept secret. Hence the wild legends which grew up among the common people, who believed it to be some potent talisman of evil.

In the early days of Spiritualism, the operation of this force, sometimes called 'animal magnetism' because it was alleged to emanate from living things, just like the power inherit in magnets, was considered very important in the production of phenomena. In the description of the formation of a Spiritualist circle given by a pioneer French Spiritualist, Baron De Guldenstubbe, we are told that the ideal number of people to form such a circle is six of positive and magnetic nature, six of negative or sensitive nature, and a medium. Generally, though not always, men were regarded as 'positive' and women as 'negative'; in other words, the six couples and a leader of the old witch coven, though I doubt if the good Baron realized this!

It was often recommended also in early Spiritualist writings, that the medium should sit with his or her back to the north. This again harks back to the old witch belief that the north is the place of power. Streams which ran from north to south were believed to have magical properties, and their water was used for preference in spells. The Pole Star in the northern hemisphere is the pivot of the heavens, round which the rest of the stars appear to revolve. The fantastic displays of the *Aurora Borealis* or Northern Lights were believed to be an emanation of this mysterious power of the north, the place behind the north wind where dead heroes of Celtic myth dwelt in 'Spiral Castle', which has many different names in Druidic lore.

Other ancient tales speak of Hyperborea (meaning 'the land

beyond the north wind'), which was the original cradle of the human race, a land now hidden beneath eternal ice and snow. The phenomena of magnetism were known from a very early date, and probably regarded as an occult secret, because we read of statues in ancient temples being caused by magnetic means to hang suspended in the air, which no doubt struck awe into the ignorant populace. Hence it may well have been realized that the earth itself is a gigantic magnet, with the flow of power running through it between north and south.

It has been this belief which caused the rule of the orienting of the magical circle to the cardinal points. Old churches and cathedrals are also oriented, the high altar being at the east and the font at the west. One of the most carefully oriented buildings in the world is the Great Pyramid, which faces north, south, east and west with a precision rarely equalled in modern architecture.

The relationship of the circle of Stonehenge to the sunrise at the summer solstice has already been mentioned and is usually vaguely attributed to 'sun-worship'; but what of a similar, though much less well-known phenomenon in the great French cathedral of Chartres? Here a certain window in the western aisle of the south transept is so arranged that when the sun is shining at noon on the day of the summer solstice, a ray will strike and reflect from a piece of gilded metal set in a certain flagstone. This stone is whiter than its neighbours, and set in a different fashion, while in the window above a clear space has evidently been left for the ray of light to shine through. It was this curious circumstance which first attracted the attention of Louis Charpentier and led him to write his book *The Mysteries of Chartres Cathedral.*

Charpentier expresses his belief that the orientation of churches and cathedrals springs from the ancient knowledge of the mysterious forces of earth which he calls 'telluric currents', which were symbolized by the figure of the winged serpent or dragon, the *Wouivre*. These forces could be beneficent or malevolent, according to how they were used; hence, perhaps, the real meaning behind the extensive dragon-lore of our world, which extends from the proud dragon which is the crest of Wales, through the many stories of dragon-slaying saints and heroes, to the glittering monsters which appear so often in the art and legend of the Far East. There are currents of the earth and also of the sky; all around us invisible forces move, of which, as yet, we know very little.

It will be seen that all this is far removed from the vulgar idea of magic as of something that consists of conjuring demons or taking part in orgies. Again and again we are brought back to the definition of magic as given by S. L. MacGregor Mathers, the Chief of the Order of the Golden Dawn; namely, that magic is the science of the control of the secret forces of nature.

With this in mind, we may get a better idea of what witches mean when they talk about 'raising the Cone of Power'. The traditional ritual nudity has for its purpose the free flow of power from the naked bodies of the participants. In ancient Greece and Rome also, those who took part in magical ceremonies were either naked or clad in loose flowing garments. Those who are trained to see the human aura are able to perceive it best surrounding the unclothed body. Hence, when a circle of naked or loosely robed dancers gyrates in a witchcraft ceremony, the power flowing from their bodies rises upwards towards the centre of the circle, forming a cone-shape which is called the Cone of Power. This is directable by the concentrated will of those present to carry out the object of the ceremony, by bearing its influence from the physical to the more subtle planes of the universe, where the power of will and imagination can, in turn, affect the physical again and influence material events.

Gerald Gardner used to tell me that he believed these effects to be brought about, not by direct action upon matter, but by influencing people's minds. Thus, when the witches raised the Cone of Power against Hitler's invasion, they sought to reach the minds of the German High Command and persuade them that the invasion could not succeed, or alternatively to muddle and stultify their thinking so that the plans for the invasion fell through. Generally, old Gerald said, there was someone somewhere whose actions would vitally affect whatever it was that the witch ceremony was trying to bring about. This person's mind would be acted upon, without their knowledge, so that they would behave in one way rather than another, and thus the desired result would happen.

This may be the *modus operandi* of magic; but we know today that the apparent opposites of matter and energy, of force and form, are not really opposites at all, but different manifestations of each other. Matter and energy are interchangeable terms. So is it really impossible that material effects can be brought about by the power of thought?

The old alchemists who actually worked with metals, trying to find the philosopher's stone or medicine of metals and the elixir of life, would not have agreed with this limitation of magical power to the realms of thought. They believed that

actual transmutation could be effected by the prayers and ceremonies which usually accompanied their efforts. Another instance which springs to mind of an actual physical effect apparently brought about by magic is the rain-making magic of
certain tribes of American Indians. I have been told by friends
in USA that this really works, though no white person knows the
secret of it.

Dancing in a circle is perhaps the most primitive and universal
magical rite. We have a cave painting of it from Cogul in north-
eastern Spain, dating from the days of the Aurignacian cultures
of the Old Stone Age. It shows a group of women dancing round
a naked man, who is depicted with garters tied round his legs
just below the knee. Not only is the traditional witches' garter
displayed in this fantastically ancient picture, but the dancing
women are wearing another well-known attribute of witches,
namely pointed hats or caps. There are nine women forming
the circle of dancers, while all around are drawn and painted
the figures of the great beasts upon whom the people of this
hunting culture depend for their food.

One wonders whether this coven met in the cave within which
this wall painting was found. Some present-day witches still believe that caves are a very potent place to work in, if one can
find one that is safe from intruders and has a sufficiently level
floor. One is in natural surroundings, while at the same time
sheltered from wind and rain. Moreover, the power is concentrated, not only by the magical circle but also by the rocky walls
themselves, full of the earth-force in a way that a room in a
house is not.

Another form of natural magic circle is the so-called 'fairy
ring' of darker grass often found upon fields and hills which are
covered with turf. In Sussex these are called 'hag-tracks', because they were believed to be made by the dancing feet of
witches who had gathered there to cast their spells. Actually, the
fairy ring is caused by a kind of fungus, which spreads outwards
from a centre to make an almost circular patch of grass which is
noticeably of a different colour from its surroundings. Old Sussex
people used to stand within a fairy ring at the full moon and
make a wish, with their eyes fixed upon the silver orb of the
moon's disc as she rose in the summer twilight. Witches, too,
would seek out a fairy ring as a basis for their circle; but they
would not neglect to draw the circle in the usual way also. They
just regarded the fairy ring as a propitious place in which to
work.

Connected with the practice of dancing the magical round is

undoubtedly the mysterious and widespread pattern of the maze. The earliest examples of this are not merely puzzles constructed for amusement, though many of these were built later as a feature of formal gardens, such as that at Hampton Court in Surrey. The earlier mazes definitely had a magical and religious significance, as is shown by their presence on the floors of some old churches and cathedrals, another example of an old pagan idea being incorporated into a Christian building. The magical maze was sometimes drawn as a square, though more frequently as a circle. It conformed to a very definite pattern, known in the British Isles as Troy Town or *Caer Droia*, from the old story that it commemorated the winding walls of Troy and recalled the legendary origin of the British race from Brutus, the son of Aeneas, who came here with his followers as refugees when Troy fell to the Greeks.

These mazes of the Troy Town pattern were cut in the turf in times long past. They are the 'quaint mazes in the wanton green' that Shakespeare refers to in *A Midsummer Night's Dream*, and were part of the traditional country sports associated with Easter and May Day. People used to dance their way through the maze to the centre and out again, because you cannot actually lose your way in this kind of maze if you just keep going; you will inevitably thread your way through the labyrinth, going first deosil and then widdershins, round and round, until you return to where you entered. Such a rite is, in fact, a form of dancing out the magical circle.

Examples of these turf-cut mazes, or the remains of them, may still be found in Britain. Eight all together are known to be in existence. Many more are recorded that have since been destroyed in various ways, though fortunately plans of them have usually been preserved, showing that some were more complicated than others, while still keeping the essential feature of being able to be danced through. Place-names which preserve the indication that a maze once existed here are Troy Town, sometimes corrupted to Drayton; Mizmaze; Julian's Bower (from a supposed connection with a Trojan prince called Julius); and Shepherd's Race, from the May Games once played within the maze.

Earlier still than the merry mazes of the May Games is the Troy Town maze pattern carved upon a rock face in Rocky Valley near Tintagel in Cornwall. This is believed to date back to about 1500 B.C., and it is identical with the maze depicted upon coins of the old Cretan capital of Knossos, home of the fabled Labyrinth and its fearsome dweller, the Minotaur.

Moreover, the same pattern occurs upon Etruscan wine jars,

upon Danish runic crosses, in religious carvings and pictures from India, and perhaps most remarkable of all, among the Hopi Indians of North America, who call it the 'Mother Earth' symbol. In these cases it is not merely a similar pattern which recurs, but the *same* pattern, which is a fairly complicated one.

Is this drawing of such vast antiquity that it was brought to North America when the land bridge between that country and Asia was still in existence? Or did it spread both east and west from some common centre now lost when the waves of ocean drowned Atlantis? The question is valid, because the distribution of the Troy Town maze pattern is a fact. Pictured examples of it can be found in *The Mystic Spiral* by Jill Purce.

Dancing out the maze requires concentration and can develop into a mystical experience, as the mind is withdrawn from the ordinary world into another realm, a place between the worlds where the laws of this world are temporarily suspended. To concentrate upon the pictured maze pattern is to be reminded of those whirling spiral devices used by some psychologists to induce hypnosis. Perhaps, like so many other things, this is merely a re-discovery of an ancient technique.

It may be significant that the rock-carved maze near Tintagel (itself a place much associated with the legends of King Arthur) is in the neighbourhood of Bossinney, where an ancient tumulus called Bossinney Mound has a wonderful legend attached to it.

The story goes that King Arthur's Round Table is still miraculously preserved here, though hidden by a magical veil from mortal eyes. After the last battle, when the mortally wounded King sailed away in the barge to Avalon, the Round Table was removed by unseen hands and buried in Bossinney Mound. Once a year, upon Midsummer Eve, the Table rises out of the mound and manifests itself again, shining with so great a light that it illuminates the whole world. But it is 'the light that never was on sea or land' that the Table spreads around it, a mystic illumination that is only visible to those whose interior sight, or Third Eye, is opened. Others will only see the dark, turf-covered mound.

Bossinney Mound is actually a Bronze Age barrow, and therefore much older even than the time of the Arthurian legends. So is this story perhaps a remote folk memory of the mysteries of the Old Religion that used to be celebrated here, connected with the treading of the maze and the opening of the Third Eye?

There is one last and rather amusing development, or perhaps one should say degeneration, of the magic circle, that may often be seen in the more old-fashioned streets of England. This takes the form of little semi-circles of white paint drawn on the pavement, around the edges of doors, the corners of buildings and anywhere else that the owner does not wish to be fouled by dogs. Whether or not these painted magical barriers (because that is what they really are) actually work or not, I cannot say. However, from their fairly frequent appearance and the fact that they seem to be repainted now and then, the belief in them has evidently survived.

6

Witch Tools

The typical weapon of Witchcraft is the athame, or ritual knife (pronounced ath-*ay*-me). Old books of magic give several variations of this word, such as 'arthany', 'arthame', and so on. Clark Ashton Smith introduces it as a tool of magic, with the spelling 'arthame', into one of his eerie fantasies, 'The Master of the Crabs', first published in 1947 in that classic source of such genre, the American magazine *Weird Tales*.

The origin of the word is at present unknown, though some present-day exponents of the near-eastern cult of Sufism have attributed it to the Arabic *adh-dhame*, meaning 'blood-letter', in the sense of it being a shedder of blood, which is just what the witches' athame is not. Hence this derivation does not seem very convincing.

Traditionally, the athame should have a black hilt, a circumstance which caused Gerald Gardner to think that it might be related to the Scottish Highlander's *skean-dhu*, which literally means 'black knife' and, in fact, usually has a hilt of this colour.

The famous medieval grimoire, *The Key of Solomon*, gives directions for making both the black-hilted knife and another with a white hilt, as well as a whole armoury of other magical weapons. The knife with the white hilt is to 'perform all the necessary operations of the art, except the circles', whereas the knife with the black hilt is specifically 'for making the circle, wherewith to strike terror and fear into the spirits'. Various unexplained sigils are given for engraving upon the handles of both knives. One of these sigils, upon the black-hilted knife, is certainly the symbol of the Eight Ritual Occasions, although this grimoire is not a treatise on witchcraft, but on ceremonial magic.

The idea of using a magical knife to banish evil is actually as old as the Roman writer Pliny. Lewis Spence, in his *Encyclopaedia of Occultism*, quotes Holland's translation in its quaint old-fashioned English : 'As touching the use of Yron and steele in Physicke, it serveth otherwise than for to launce, cut, and dismember withall; for take the knife or dagger, and make an

ymaginerie circle two or three times round with the point thereof
upon a young child or an elder bodie, and then goe round withall
about the partie as often, it is a singular preservative against all
poysons, sorceries, or enchantments.' This is very reminiscent of
the use of the athame by witches.

Like the Hand of Glory, the athame sometimes appears in old
paintings of witchcraft scenes by such masters as Francken and
Teniers. In David Teniers' picture, *The Departure for the Sabbat*, the black-hilted knife may be seen stuck upright in the floor
at the edge of the magical circle, while an old witch and a demon
confer over the preparation of a magic brew, and a young witch
is being anointed ready to fly up the capacious chimney on the
broomstick.

Gerald Gardner has been accused by various superficial critics
of taking the idea of the witches' athame straight from *The Key
of Solomon*. However, the reverse argument has at least as much
evidence to sustain it, and probably more; namely, that it was
The Key of Solomon, and similar books, which were written by
ceremonial magicians who borrowed the primitive practices of
witches and presented them in more elaborate and sophisticated
form.

A magical weapon is, after all, an expression of someone's
will and their capacity to carry out that will. A conductor's baton,
a bishop's crozier, a chairman's gavel, are in a sense magical
implements. In ancient times, we had processions of Bacchantes
or religious revellers carrying the *thyrsus*, or ivy-wreathed wand.
Today, we have processions of demonstrators carrying placards
and banners as emblematic expressions of their will and purpose.
At the solemnities of the Queen's coronation, magnificent symbolic swords were part of the ceremony, as well as the royal
sceptre itself, the magical wand of empire. The Mace which lies
on the Speaker's table in the Houses of Parliament has a purely
symbolic significance; and, in spite of Cromwell's command to
'take away that bauble', it still remains. What Cromwell and his
Puritans did not understand was that such 'baubles' have a significance which speaks to the unconscious mind of humanity,
which naturally thinks in symbols.

When man became a maker and user of tools, he lifted himself up from the beasts. He made himself an edged tool to cut, a
staff to walk with and to defend himself, a platter to eat from, a
horn or cup for his drink, and a length of twine or rawhide to
bind with. Today, witches use these elemental weapons or implements : the wand, the knife, the cup and the disk or pentacle,
together with the cord called the witches' garter. They are called

elemental weapons because they are attributed to the four elements of life : the wand for fire, the cup for water, the knife or dagger for air and the disk or pentacle for earth. The cord typifies that unseen quintessence or spirit which binds all together.

The elemental weapons appear also in the emblems of the Tarot cards, of great antiquity and unknown provenance : the wands, cups, swords and pentacles of the pack of seventy-eight cards, the forerunners of our playing-card pack, about which so much has been written in speculation and fantasy. The fact that the suit signs are shown in the hands of *The Juggler,* the first of the Tarot trumps, and are displayed upon his table, is an indication that they were realized to be the tools of magic.

In divination, the wands indicate energy and creative will, the cups relate to the emotions, the swords presage danger and the need to be on guard, while the pentacles (which are sometimes shown as coins) are the emblems of material wealth and property. The trump cards with their mysterious pictures are related to the forces of destiny, spiritual matters and occult powers.

These ideas can evidently be correlated with the magical uses of the weapons and implements. The wand is the expression of the magician's will and is used for invocations. It is an obvious phallic symbol, as the cup is a yonic or feminine one. The cup serves for magic brews or draughts of Sabbat wine, which affect the feelings and emotions. The sword or knife defends from hostile forces, drawing the magic circle for this purpose. The pentacle, with its engraved signs and sigils, is the materialization of certain cosmic powers and their expression in a material object.

There is no doubt that the Tarot is a magical book without words, a *mutus liber* or 'dumb book' like those used by the alchemists, full of strange and significant images. Most witches today own a pack of Tarot cards and use them not only for divination, but for meditation, as they were likewise used by the initiates of the Order of the Golden Dawn.

The wand is the magical weapon of invocation; but among witches it sometimes took the form of the riding-pole, upon which they performed the traditional jumping dance to make the crops grow tall. This dance was probably the origin of the idea that witches used broomsticks or staffs to fly through the air upon. We see a version of the spring jumping dance in the traditional skipping that used to be performed by adults as well as children in Sussex villages on Good Friday, in the belief that this helped to make the crops grow. The idea behind it was what the anthropologists call 'sympathetic magic', though witches describe it as 'showing the thing what to do', a concept which is basic to many witch rites.

Among Scottish witches, the riding pole was called a 'bune wand', the wand upon which they went 'abune' or above. It often took the form of a forked stick, perhaps as a reminiscence of the old god's horns.

To dance over the ground with a pole or staff between the legs is an obvious phallic gesture of the old fertility rites. Hence the end of the riding pole was often carved in the shape of a phallus. This, however, marked the staff as an obvious magical object, an adjunct of the Old Religion that it was dangerous to have leaning against one's cottage wall in the times of persecution. So the phallic riding pole had its carved end disguised with a bunch of twigs and became the witch's broomstick.

In the same way, the magical sword was not a safe thing to have in one's house, because in the old times a sword was a badge of rank. Only a 'gentleman' carried a sword, or a soldier in the service of the king or a feudal lord. The peasant's weapon was a quarterstaff. For a woman to have possessed a sword would have looked particularly suspicious. So the magical sword was replaced in general use by the athame, which was simply the old-fashioned kitchen knife, with a black wooden hilt; though; of course, the witch would have kept her athame separate and not used it for anything but magic. She would have written the magical signs on it in ink at the time of its consecration and then washed them off again, perhaps putting some small private mark on the knife that only she would recognize. (See further remarks on the magical weapons in *Liber Umbrarum*).

Why, however, was a sword or a knife considered to have a magical potency? The answer lies in the belief in the universal borderline energy, to which reference has already been made in the previous chapter. Call it 'astral light' or what you will, the old practitioners of magic aver that concentrations of it can be repelled and dispersed by the sharp point of an iron or steel implement. The wand *directs* the magical current; but because it lacks a sharp point and is generally made of wood, it cannot so effectively serve for defence and banishing. Hence to draw the circle the witch uses the athame.

Sometimes, of course, the master of a coven would have been a person of rank who was entitled to own a sword. In that case, he may well have been custodian of the coven sword, which would have been lent to the priestess to use on solemn occasions. Legend and romance have many stories of famous swords, which were given names, as in the case of King Arthur's sword Excalibur, as if they possessed a kind of personality and life of their own.

For instance, the favourite sword of El Cid was called Tizona; while the sword of Roland had a splendid name: Durandane. The idea of putting magical signs upon weapons is at least as old as the Northmen, who engraved their weapons with runes to make them more powerful:

> Runes of victory shalt thou know,
> If thou wilt have the victory,
> And cut them on thy sword-hilt.
> Some on the hilt rings,
> Some on the plates of the handle,
> And twice name the name of Tyr.

It took a good smith to forge a good sword, and the smith himself has been regarded all over the world as a natural magician. Many interesting details of this subject are given by Frederick W. Robins in his book *The Smith: The Traditions and Lore of an Ancient Craft*, which also quotes the lines from the old Norse poem, *The Edda*, as given above.

The idea of the ritual knife as a magical weapon of defence may go back to ancient Egypt. Among the magnificent treasures of King Tutankhamen's tomb were two daggers, one of which seems to have been intended for display rather than use, as its blade was made of gold. Perhaps it was a symbolic weapon, like the dress sword of army and naval officers. The other dagger, however, had a blade of iron so finely wrought that after thousands of years in the darkness of the tomb only a few spots of rust discoloured it. This would certainly have made a splendid magical weapon. Such may, indeed, have been the intention when it was buried with the young Pharaoh, because the ancient Egyptian *Book of the Dead* has many vignettes showing the soul of the deceased person defending himself against various hostile entities of the other world, which are pictured as huge serpents, crocodiles, etc., by holding up knives against them.

There seems to have been a very prevalent idea in ancient times, when grave-goods of all kinds were buried with the deceased, that a double or astral counterpart of the buried article went with the dead person into the other world. This was the primary object of the furnishings all over the world of those splendid tombs which have yielded such wonderful things to the spade of the archaeologist and, unfortunately, to the grave-robber also. Even today, people sometimes ask that a cherished possession shall be buried with them, though they must be aware that the actual material object cannot accompany them into the beyond.

The magical dagger is known in far-off Tibet, as well as in the western world. Among the Tibetans, such a weapon is called a *phurba*. It is used in very much the same way as the witches' athame, to serve as a magical means of defence and to command spirits and exorcize demons. The *phurba* has a curious triangular blade, while the hilt bears representations of divine beings. Another magical weapon of Tibet is the *dorje*, or sceptre, sometimes regarded as representing a thunderbolt, which serves a similar purpose to the magic wand of the west. Tibetan divinities are often pictured holding a *dorje* in one hand, symbolizing the male element, while the other hand holds a bell, which has a female significance.

Sometimes a particularly large and potent *phurba* is retained as the property of a monastery. Such a weapon may be centuries old, much revered and even feared for its demon-controlling powers. Although Tibet itself has now passed under the rule of Communist China, very similar traditions to those of Tibetan magic and religion are still to be found in the neighbouring countries such as Nepal, Sikkim and Bhutan. Here the magic of the *phurba* is still in demand for its power over demons.

The invasion of Tibet has resulted in many Tibetan refugees bringing their beliefs and practices within reach of the western world, often for the first time. Not long ago, I met a young Englishman who was a student of the occult, and who was using in his magical practice a present-day replica of a Tibetan *phurba*, cast in bronze. He claimed that it was very effective.

Cauldrons, too, have been given a magical significance in the east as well as the west. They were used by shamans to prepare magical brews, just as the witches did. Sometimes a shaman of the Altai regions of Siberia and Mongolia would have his favourite cauldron buried with him when he died. Such cauldrons were quite small, just big enough to heat over a small bonfire, like the 'gipsy-pots' which are the favourite cauldron of the present-day witch, much more practical than the huge cooking-pot usually depicted by artists painting witch scenes. I am sure the makers of such pictures can never have tried to get one of these enormous pots actually to boil over a bonfire!

The cauldron is a feminine symbol, as the broomstick is a masculine one. Moreover, it is reminiscent of the triple goddess of the moon, because of the three legs it usually stands on. It also involves the powers of the four elements, because it needs water to fill it, fire to heat it, the green herbs or other products of earth to cook in it, while the steam arises from it and spreads its aroma into the air.

In the case of the cauldron brew containing narcotic herbs, such steam may well have produced visions, as in the famous witch scene in Shakespeare's *Macbeth*. The wavering clouds of steam, upon which the flickering fire-light shone, would have served as a kind of glass of vision, with forms appearing and disappearing in them. Such an attempted breakthrough into the psychic world would have been dangerous for a person to essay alone, however, as they might fall into trance and be either burnt or scalded. The more experienced witches would keep their distance from the steaming brew, being less affected by the fumes than a newcomer.

Alternatively, the cauldron was used for simply decocting herbal remedies, the great stand-by of the white witch in olden times and often quite effective. They were certainly less dangerous than the orthodox medical practices of their day, which went in for bleeding, sticking on leeches and similar drastic things, while modern ideas of hygiene and antiseptics were unknown.

It will be noticed that the cauldron, the broomstick and the black-hilted knife are all things that might be found in any woman's kitchen in olden days. It was the magical imagination that turned them into witches' weapons. Similarly, the witches' garter was simply a piece of twine or cord, which was tied round the leg to support the hose that were worn by both men and women. Wealthy people might wear more elaborate garters, of course. It is supposed to be the loss of her garter while dancing that put a beautiful court lady into confusion, until the chivalrous King Edward III came to her assistance, picking up the lost garter and binding it round his own leg. Upon this circumstance the Most Noble Order of the Garter, still the senior order of chivalry in Britain, is supposed to be founded.

Margaret Murray's speculation that it was a witch garter that was thus revealed and that the King was a sympathizer with the Old Religion, is now well-known. She gives a number of curious particulars about the significance of the garter in her book *The God of the Witches*. The garters depicted as being worn by the man in the Stone Age witch-rite of the Cogul cave-painting have been already noted in Chapter 5.

Less well-known is the significance of the cord or rope in the practices and beliefs of the shamans of Siberia and the remoter parts of Asia generally. Here the cord represents the passage between heaven and earth, in the sense of being a kind of ladder by means of which the gods and spirits can descend to earth and the shaman can climb up to heaven. It is the emblem of the ecstatic journey, in which, although the shaman's entranced body remains upon earth, his soul penetrates into realms unseen; or as occultists would call it, he goes out upon the astral plane. It is this ability to explore the realms of the beyond and bring back knowledge from them that is the very essence of Shamanism.

As we have already seen, there is a good deal of similarity between the shaman and the witch. Once again, we come back to a kind of fundamental unity which seems to underlie the practice of magic all over the world and to go back to prehistoric times. Considering again the Cogul cave painting, we have to remember that the so-called 'garters' that the man in it is wearing can hardly have been actually and literally garters in the sense of being needed to keep up stockings, because people of those days had none. Probably it was simply a convenient way of carrying one's magic cords or thongs around, to have them tied upon one's body. Thus, the tradition of the cord and what it symbolized, judging from what we know of primitive Shamanism, continued through countless years.

Eventually, the time came when the witches had to disguise the cord, even as the athame was to outward seeming a kitchen knife and the magical staff a broomstick. So the cord became a garter; but it was a very special kind of garter. Some garters were badges of rank in the witch cult, like the one that the lady lost in the romantic story of King Edward III and the founding of the Order of the Garter, referred to above.

The tying or binding of a cord or garter is also connected with the 'binding' of a spell, the 'binding' of spirits and so on. Witches who cast spells by making knots and breathing upon them are referred to in the Koran; but the subject of magical knots is a vast one, from the elaborate knots of eastern talismans to the children's game of 'Cat's Cradle' which is found all over the world and sometimes has magical affinities.

7

Methods of Witch Divination

In the previous chapter mention was made of the uses of the witches' cauldron; but without touching upon its other traditional use, namely for the method of divination known as scrying.

Scrying is the old word for all kinds of clairvoyance involving the use of some object, such as a crystal ball, a vessel of water, a magic mirror and so on, in which the seer gazes and in which, or by the aid of which, visions appear. Such an instrument is called a speculum.

This practice goes back to the remotest antiquity and is found all over the world. At the same time, it is in use among all kinds of witch covens and magical societies at the present day.

The speculum used may be large or small, according to the personal taste of the practitioner who uses it. For his famous series of explorations into other dimensions which he recorded under the title of *The Vision and the Voice,* Aleister Crowley used a large golden-coloured topaz, set in a wooden cross of six squares painted vermilion, being reminiscent of the shape of the rose and cross emblem of the Rosicrucians. He held the cross in his hand and gazed into the stone. The use of a semi-precious stone is considered by some practitioners of magic to be particularly efficacious. Of course, real crystal or beryl, the original crystal-gazing ball, is itself a semi-precious stone and expensive accordingly. But experience teaches that all kinds of things can be used as a speculum, including things which are not costly at all, and people can still get results with them.

An example of quite a large object being used as a speculum is the magic mirror which Gerald Gardner used to display in his museum in the Isle of Man. Old Gerald used to tell the story of how he found this rather splendid magical object in a London junk shop, amongst a load of second-hand furniture. The shop was shut when Gerald noticed the mirror in its murky window, so he got there early next morning and waited on the doorstep for the shop to open in order to secure his prize, purchasing 'that old picture frame' for a few shillings. Covered in dust and cobwebs, it did, indeed, look like an old-fashioned round picture frame with unusual slightly convex glass. However, instead of containing a picture or a mirror surface, the glass had been coated inside with a dark greyish-black substance. The frame itself bore faded gilding and the names of the four archangels of the elements and the four cardinal points: Michael, Gabriel, Uriel and Raphael. It had probably been used as part of the furniture of a magical lodge.

It is part of the perennial charm of junk shops that one never knows what is going to turn up in them. Dion Fortune tells in one of her books how a magic wand was once found in a similar way, tied up with a bundle of old fire irons. However, a word of caution is necessary here. If you are fortunate enough to discover something like this, then it is wise to cleanse the object thoroughly and preferably do a banishing ritual over it also, before using it yourself, as it may have been associated with undesirable practices, or with things which may have been innocent enough in themselves but, nevertheless, antagonistic to your sort of magic. This is where the working use of the athame comes in.

As soon as you conveniently can, circle the object with the athame three times widdershins (i.e. anti-clockwise), saying over it: 'In the name of the Powers of Light, Life and Love, may all evil and hostile influences depart hence—NOW!' Point the athame at the object and will it to be cleansed. Picture a ray of silvery-blue light jetting from the point of the athame and dispelling and breaking up anything undesirable that lingers there. Then give the object a good cleaning. Other suggestions for cleansing the aura of an object which has come into your possession and whose history is unknown or suspect are given in *Liber Umbrarum*; but this simple, quick banishing ritual is useful generally in many ways. The tendency of widdershins movement is to banish, hence its use here. Some covens draw their magic circle widdershins; but personally I think this is rather too negative a way of drawing the magic circle for general working purposes. It is more suitable for specific banishing rites like this one.

My own favourite means of divination by scrying is to use the cauldron, though I have got results with the magic mirror and with a silver witch ball or a green glass fishing float (the hollow balls of thick dark glass, usually green, used in times past by fishermen to hold up and mark the position of their nets—now, alas, replaced by globes of plastic).

Again, the little gypsy-pot type of cauldron is the one to use. It is made of cast iron, so it is suitably black inside. Fill it about two-thirds full with water and the black interior of the cauldron will make an excellent speculum. Drop a silver coin into the water, to make a point upon which to concentrate. I have an old silver threepenny bit which I keep for this purpose; but any small silver or silver-coloured coin will do, so long as it is bright.

The faculty of scrying is a very individual thing, so really there are very few hard and fast rules. What provides good conditions for one person may not suit another. The right thing to do is what proves in practice to work. In general, however, a subdued light is the best. Some people like to arrange the light so that it shines on to the speculum and is reflected. Such reflections are called *points de repère*, because they tend to become the centre of a picture which forms itself, or appears to do so, upon the surface of the speculum. Others, myself included, prefer the surface to be dark, save for the appearance of the silver coin through the water, like a moon in the night sky.

There is, indeed, something very lunar about this kind of clairvoyance. You may find that you are better able to get results at the full of the moon, or at some particular phase of the moon; again, an individual matter which only experience can inform you of. Crystal, the semi-precious stone, is governed by the moon; so is water affected by the moon's tidal pull. Scrying in vessels of water is one of the oldest and most widespread forms of divination. Sometimes rulers of ancient days owned costly chalices which were used for this purpose. Such was 'Jamsheed's seven-ringed cup' referred to in the *Rubaiyat* of Omar Khayyam. Such, too, seems to have been the silver cup owned by Joseph in Egypt 'in which my lord drinketh, and whereby indeed he divineth.'* However, the humble cauldron of the witch, or the gourd full of water of the South Sea Islands *kahuna*, serves the purpose just as well, if the scryer has the faculty developed.

The reason is that the vision does not in fact appear in the speculum, though it may seem to do so, but in the mind of the clairvoyant. My own experience is that after a period of concentration, the surface of the water or the magic mirror disappears, and a picture appears before the mind's eye, just as if it were suddenly projected upon a cinema screen. Sometimes there is a transition stage, when the picture, or some symbol, appears to be upon the surface of the speculum; but this is usually of short duration. The most vivid pictures appear when the speculum has vanished, or rather when I have ceased to be aware of it.

Such pictures may be actual representations of distant, past or future events; but they are more often symbolic. One has to

* *Genesis,* 44.

develop the intuition to discover what the symbols mean; and again, this is a matter of experience. The study of Jungian psychology can be helpful in this matter. I would particularly recommend the book *Man and his Symbols,* edited by Carl Gustav Jung.

There is no need to stare unblinkingly at the surface of the speculum. Indeed, it is better to gaze deeply into the water or the crystal, rather than to look at its surface. Just relax, allowing yourself to drift into a kind of borderland state. If other persons are present, they must be quiet and concentrate upon the purpose of what is being done. The best results are usually obtained after sunset rather than during the daylight hours. The candle-lit atmosphere of the magic circle is best; but if you happen to be scrying at some other time and place, then the room should be suitably darkened. The burning of some good incense or joss-sticks will always help.

The development of the faculty of scrying needs patience and practice; so if you see nothing the first time you attempt it, do not give up. What you are really doing is to awaken the faculties of your own inner mind. This is not going to happen all at once; nor will you always be able to perform automatically. Sometimes there will be disturbing psychic influences which will inhibit results. You must not be easily discouraged; nor must you fall into the trap of interpreting the vision to suit your own wishes or predilections. The symbol you see may be true; but your interpretation of it may be coloured by your own hopes or fears, if you let it.

The technique of scrying is very much the same, whether one uses an expensive crystal ball, a magic mirror, or whatever; so it is a question of finding the kind of speculum that suits one best. Incidentally, not everything sold as a 'crystal ball' is really crystal. Sometimes balls of glass are described in this way, as often antique dealers themselves do not know the difference. It is not easy for one without expert knowledge to distinguish between the two; but real crystal tends to be heavy and to be peculiarly ice-cold to the touch. Held against your cheek, it will feel colder than glass—to the expert, at any rate. The latest development, however, started in USA, is to make gazing balls of clear plastic. Thus modern technology catches up with ancient witchcraft!

The magic mirror is one in which the glass is backed, not with a mirror surface, but with some dark substance. I have seen many mirrors backed with good quality black enamel paint, and stated by their owners to give satisfactory results; but the traditional material for the backing of the magic mirror is Stockholm tar, the stuff the old wooden ships used to be tarred with. It is the black, aromatic residue left after turpentine has been distilled, hence it is sometimes called turpentine asphaltum.

Some mirrors are convex, others concave, while others may be simply a flat sheet of glass. In my opinion, the concave mirror is the best; that is, a round piece of glass like that which covers a clock face, only turned the other way over. Such a piece of glass may be obtained from a clock repairer, or perhaps from an old clock itself.

It should be well cleaned and then given three coats of black paint, or whatever pigment one decides to use. Make sure each coat of paint is dry before applying the next one. As the paint is applied to the back of the mirror, if you want your mirror to be concave then you must paint the convex side, and vice versa. When each coat of paint is dry, magnetize it by making passes with your hands over it before applying the next coat.

Then you must contrive to make a frame for your mirror, according to your own skill and ingenuity. A square wooden box of suitable size will do for this. Pad it inside with cotton wool or kapok, so that you can sink the mirror firmly into the padding. Then cut a square piece of thin wood or hardboard to fasten over it, with a round hole framing the mirror surface but at the same time holding it in place. Fix this in position with a good adhesive. Then make a lid for the box so that the mirror is protected from dust when not in use. Finish the box with a coat of paint, perhaps adding some magical sigils as you prefer.

A very good magic mirror was made for me by a friend in this way. The box is painted black, with magical sigils added in silver paint. The lid has a pair of small hinges to hold it in place. From its size and shape, I suspect that the box was a wooden cigar box.

In these days of plastic containers of all kinds, one may be lucky enough to find a round plastic container which is just the right size to take the mirror glass. The glass can be attached to the rim of the container with adhesive, and the container painted in some suitable colour and adorned with magical signs, according to your own taste. In this case, however, you will also need a square of black material to wrap the mirror up in when not in use, as the mirror's surface should not be exposed to the light. Apart from gathering dust, such exposure will destroy the mirror's sensitivity, especially if it is exposed to strong sunlight.

Gazing crystals or glass balls, too, should be kept wrapped up when not in use. The black wrapping cloth will come in useful as a background to the speculum when you are actually scrying.

In addition to magic mirrors of this kind, some witches also

use a small ordinary reflecting mirror for various magical practices. This is one of the secrets of old traditional witchcraft; but
I can give one instance of the way in which it is used. Such
mirrors, which are, of course, kept for this purpose and not used
for anything else, are small, just enough to reflect the witch's
face and no more. They are mounted in a wooden frame, usually
hand-carved in some curious design, according to the skill of the
artist.

The witch places the mirror in front of her in a dim light,
usually with a candle on either side of it. It should be just light
enough to reflect the face of the person looking into the mirror.
She sets some incense burning, then looks into the mirror, concentrating upon some wish that she desires to come true. (I use
the pronoun 'she', though, of course, a witch may be either a
woman or a man).

The instructions given in a manuscript book from which I
quote are as follows : 'Concentrate your eyes upon the reflected
image of your eyes. Then close your eyes and be still. Develop
the image of the wish in your mind. When you have visualized
it clearly, open your eyes. Concentrate hard upon the eyes imaged
in the mirror. Try to see through them into space beyond.
Whisper the wish three times. Make another offering of incense,
to close the ritual.'

I am told that the use of a mirror in this way is a potent adjunct
to magical practice, provided the user has firm faith and belief
in what they are doing and provided also that the wish is something within their sphere of possibility. One can, indeed, use a
mirror in this way to build up one's self-confidence, by talking
to one's own mirrored image as if one were talking to another
person.

Another aid to witchcraft practice is the witch ball, the an-
cestor of those shining globes used to decorate the Christmas
tree, though, of course, the large witch balls seen in antique
shops are made of much heavier and more durable glass. In
olden days, they were hung in the windows of houses to reflect
the glance of the evil eye back upon the ill wisher. The older ones
are of bright reflecting silver colour; some are made to hang in a
window, while others were intended to stand upon some piece of
furniture in the dark corner of a room. Later, other colours were
introduced, usually bright blue, green or gold. Witch balls are
a very attractive antique, and one often finds that shopkeepers
are reluctant to part with them, because they seem to think a
witch ball is something lucky to hang in their shop, though
they no longer remember the real reason for its presence.

Witches use witch balls, especially the silver ones, for scrying as well as for magical protection. They say that if the ball is gazed at in a dim light with this purpose in mind, eventually the miniature scene reflected in its mirror surface will change into another scene, according to the clairvoyant faculty of the scryer. From personal experience, I can recall instances of this myself, sometimes even when one has been just idly looking at a witch ball in a relaxed way, thinking of nothing in particular.

I have not made any extensive use of the witch ball as a speculum; but I can give here a little rune which is meant to be spoken over the ball as one looks at it. Like most charms, it should be repeated at least three times:

> Round of silver shining bright,
> As the moon at still midnight,
> When the witching hour has struck,
> Shadows show of life and luck.
> By this rune be now enchanted,
> And the second sight be granted.

Mention has been made previously of the hollow glass balls which used to be used by fishermen to keep their nets afloat. These often turn up in antique shops and are sometimes erroneously referred to as witch balls, though their actual use was something much more prosaic. However, from my own experience, these make excellent specula for scrying purposes. The best ones are those which are made of glass of a deep, glossy green colour. They can easily be mounted upon a stand in order to use them for scrying.

Witches in old seaport towns used to prefer these fishing float balls even to a ball of crystal, because the latter was a dangerous thing to have in one's possession in the times of persecution. It could only have one possible use, namely for magic, whereas the glass fishing float was quite a common object that could be in anyone's cottage.

There used to be a belief in the days of medieval magic that the results obtained by the crystal ball were really caused by a demon, who had been bound to the crystal by magical ceremonies. According to the witch persecutors, therefore, it was not the clairvoyant faculties of the witch that produced the visions, but the demon who caused them to appear in the speculum. Hence, anyone who practised scrying could be accused of trafficking with evil spirits, which was a capital offence. No wonder witches used their ingenuity to find scrying instruments in things of common use, such as cauldrons and fishing floats.

Apart from scrying, there are many methods of divination used by witches, such as interpreting dreams, observing omens, and so on, which would be impossible to treat of in full detail here. Some witches practised the better-known occult arts, such as astrology and palmistry, which they held in common with other occultists. These arts were, indeed, more or less respectable in olden time, because they were part of that system of occult philosophy which was accepted and practised even by churchmen. Only in later days did they fall into disrepute. Hence, there is no lack of books upon these subjects; so I have preferred here to deal with some of those methods of divination specifically associated with the craft of witches.

One of these, of which little, if anything, has been written before, is lithomancy, or divination by stones. This type of divination is particularly associated with witchcraft, to such an extent that it has given the French their word for 'witch', namely, *sorcier* (male witch) and *sorcière* (female witch), being one who practises *sortilège*, literally the casting of *sorts* or lots, for purposes of divination.

There are a number of different ways of doing this. I will give details here of the one I know and which I have tried with good results. It requires thirteen stones, the typical witches' number, namely seven stones for the seven planets, plus a life stone, a luck stone, a love stone, a home stone, a news stone and a magic stone.

The witch must collect these stones herself, at an appropriate time. If she knows something of astrology, she will choose a day in the waxing moon when that luminary is well aspected by the appropriate planets. Otherwise, one of the Great Sabbats may be chosen, if an opportunity to collect stones arises. At least, let the finding of the stones take place in the increase of the moon.

A sea beach is a good place to look, as, of course, the stones do not need to be large. They should be roughly about the size of dice, as they are going to be cast in a similar way. There should not be too much disparity of shape or size between the stones, or this will affect the casting of them. Today, it is not difficult to find shops which sell semi-precious stones which have been smoothed by the 'tumbling' process, quite sufficiently to make them suitable for this purpose; so, if you cannot find enough of the right sort of stones to make up your own set, you can augment them by stones purchased at the appropriate time.

The essential point is that the stones should appeal to you personally as being right for that particular purpose. They do not have to be semi-precious. Any stone which is curiously marked or beautifully coloured in such a way as to suggest the thing it symbolizes will do.

My own set of stones consists of a mixture of stones which I have found and those which I have bought. If I describe it, the reader may get an idea of what such a set of stones ought to be, though there is no need for him or her to imitate it slavishly. Rather, one's set of divining stones should be individual to oneself, satisfying one's own idea of what is right in this way and appealing to one's own inner mind.

With this proviso, here is my own set of divining stones. Firstly, the stones of the seven planets: for the Sun, a piece of golden crocidolite or tiger's-eye; for the Moon, a piece of cloudy white quartz with silvery streaks in it; for Mars, a piece of bloodstone; for Mercury, a piece of what I think is a kind of agate, a variegated stone mainly of a lavender colour, streaked and spotted; for Jupiter, a piece of dark blue crocidolite with a lightning-like effect in it as it catches the light; for Venus, a piece of very smooth light green stone, probably aventurine; for Saturn, a highly polished piece of completely black stone.

Now the other six stones. Of these, two are stones which I have found. One of them, the magic stone, is quite unusual. It is a very tiny specimen of the fossils known as 'shepherds' crowns', actually a fossil sea-urchin. Although so small, it is beautifully marked with a five-rayed star, making it a most appropriate magic stone.

The other stone found by myself is a fairly small but very smooth pebble with a round hole neatly through its centre. Such 'holey stones' have been lucky since time immemorial, hence this is an obvious choice for the luck stone.

The life stone is a bright red piece of cornelian, anciently spelt 'carnelian', meaning 'flesh-like stone'. Red is the colour of life, hence its frequent use in magic.

The news stone is a multi-coloured pebble, similar to the one used to represent Mercury, though darker in colour. Its different coloured spots and streaks show that news may be good or bad.

The home stone is a piece of blue and green moss agate, a stone associated with earth, as the streaks and veins of green within it look like tiny growing plants.

Lastly, the love stone is a piece of rose quartz, a stone whose beautiful rose colour is naturally associated with love and sentiment. Curiously enough, this piece is roughly in the shape of a heart.

I keep the stones in a little draw-string bag made of soft suède leather. For casting them, I spread out a piece of black fur fabric upon the floor, or upon a table, rather a modern innovation, I know, but really there is no reason why one should not use modern things in witch rites if they answer the purpose. In olden days, the stones would have been cast upon an animal's skin, or simply upon the earth floor of the witch's cottage, though a skin or thick cloth protects them from accidental chipping. The divination is made from the way in which the stones relate to each other as they fall. The diviner must be guided by intuition, as well as by some knowledge of what the different planets govern in astrology.

More details about astrological influences may be obtained from any standard book about astrology. Here, as a few generalized indications, it may be said that the Sun is a good influence, bringing light and cheerfulness into a situation; the Moon indicates journeys by water, also feminine matters and motherhood, together with psychic things; Mars brings strife and struggle, though also energy to meet them; Mercury governs communications, writing, travel and the gaining of knowledge; Jupiter brings good luck, expansiveness and the gain of money; Venus is the planet of love, beauty and artistic things; while Saturn indicates restriction, slowness and sometimes misfortune.

With regard to the other stones, the luck stone, the love stone and the news stone have the obvious meaning of their names. Where the magic stone falls shows the most important part of the divination, the ruling factor. The life stone is the personal life of the one who is the subject of the divination; it may relate to physical or mental health. The home stone relates to one's actual home surroundings; it can also indicate one's personal property or real estate.

As said above, one has to use one's personal judgement to interpret the fall of the stones. If, for instance, the news stone fell close to the home stone, with the Venus stone nearby, one could divine that a love letter was on its way. If the love stone lay beside the magic stone, then this would be really important to the person who received it. And so on; the permutations of the different stones and their meanings are practically endless, because naturally they have to be interpreted in accordance with the individual for whom the divination is being done. As with all forms of divination, practice brings facility and skill.

The actual procedure of divination is as follows. The stones are thrown within a circle made by the cord, the witches' garter, coiled round upon the cloth or skin which is laid out smoothly upon the floor or a table. The words of an old Welsh charm are used when casting the stones: ADA ADA IO ADA DIA. It is pronounced like this: '*Ah-da, ah-da, ee-o ah-da dee-a.*' Exactly what it means frankly I do not know; but it is a traditional divination rune or formula of words of power, probably Celtic in origin.

Light a candle and stand it by the circle. The room should be dimly lit, or darkened if it is day-time. Also have some incense burning, an incense-cone or a joss-stick. Take your athame and place it by the circle, on the right if you are right-handed. Have your divination stones ready in their little bag, or 'wise-woman's wallet' as it used to be called ('wiseman's wallet' in the case of a male witch).

When you have everything neatly laid out, take up your athame and consecrate the circle with it, circling three times round the small circle which you have outlined with your cord, pointing the athame and concentrating just as if you were making the big working circle. You may kneel upon the floor if you have laid your divination circle there, or be seated at your table. Of course, this kind of divination may be done within the standard-size magic circle of the coven, or one may use it oneself in private, like most other kinds of divination; but as usual, if other people are present they must be quiet and concentrate in order to aid its success.

As you consecrate the circle with your athame, repeat these words :

> Witches' garter, bind the spell.
> Thirteen stones, the truth foretell.
> Earth and water, wind and flame,
> Magic in the Old One's name !

Then lay your athame aside and take out the stones. Hold them in your hands and warm them, concentrating upon the object of your divination. Shake them from one hand to another, as the words of the spell are recited three times : ADA ADA IO ADA DIA. When you are ready, cast the stones at random into the circle. You must make a completely random cast; do not deliberately distribute them in any way. Then look carefully at the way they lie, consider and interpret them.

You may throw the stones three times at a sitting, but no more. This will allow for a general reading and two questions. To answer a question 'Yes' or 'No', a slightly different procedure is followed.

In this case, you use just three stones, one for affirmative, one for negative and one for the indicator, laying the rest of the stones aside. You use the magic stone for the indicator. If you are asking the question, 'Shall I follow such and such a course of action?', then you use the Jupiter stone for affirmative and the Saturn stone for negative. In astrology, Jupiter is the Great Fortune and Saturn the Great Infortune, in other words the indicators of good luck or bad luck, so they are appropriate for this particular type of question. In other cases, use the Sun stone, the positive influence, for 'Yes' and the Saturn stone, the negative influence, for 'No'.

Shake the three stones together using the rune ADA ADA IO ADA DIA, as before. Then cast them into the circle. The answer will be told by which of the stones lies nearest to the indicator stone. If both are about equidistant, the answer is doubtful. The question is not yet formed, will not arise, or this is not the time to ask it. This placing can also indicate that the question is frivolous or insincere.

This is really quite a simple method of divination, but it can tell a good deal if you really concentrate on it and take time and trouble over it. It is especially useful for ordinary, down to earth matters.

If, however, you seek for guidance upon matters of a higher plane, clairvoyance by one of the various methods of scrying will be more suitable. Alternatively, you can make use of the Tarot cards, which have the advantage of being able to give insight into affairs of either the most mundane or the most metaphysical kind. The Tarot is part of the general heritage of magic and mysticism and may be studied in that context. I need only say here that personally I accept the interpretation of the Tarot cards as given by the Order of the Golden Dawn, as being the most fruitful for study. It may be found in detail in the compendium of the Order's teachings edited by Dr Israel Regardie, entitled *The Golden Dawn.*

8

Witches' Attire

The name of this chapter may seem to be a contradiction in terms; because the traditional attire of witches is generally believed to be nudity. When Gerald Gardner first revealed the present-day practice of witchcraft in his book *Witchcraft Today*, his statements about the communal nakedness of witchcraft rites provoked a good deal of shock and scandal, or at any rate professed shock and scandal, among journalists of the popular Press. Today, however, times have changed. It is rather amusing to note that newspapers which formerly published articles attacking this 'evil cult' that was supposed to be sweeping the country, and solemnly warning people against it, now specialize in providing their readers with luscious portraits of nude young ladies.

Nor does anyone seem any the worse. Indeed, it is coming to be recognized that people who get indignant about human nakedness are not psychologically healthy or well-balanced. It is the prudes today who are on the defensive. In the issue of the *Daily Mirror* dated 14 June 1975, under the headline 'Nude's not rude —it can do you good!' appeared the views of a number of psychologists and psychiatrists who support the belief that nudity, particularly communal nudity, is healthy and beneficial both mentally and physically.

Naturists have always maintained this; and Gerald Gardner was a pioneer naturist, in the days when it was considered very shocking indeed to support those 'nudists' and their dreadful goings-on. It may well be, however, that Gerald Gardner's naturist beliefs coloured his ideas about witchcraft; because he maintained that witches *always* worked in the nude, and in the climate of the British Isles this is just not a practical possibility. Of course, one may work indoors, with modern central heating and so on. Probably the majority of witchcraft rites today take place indoors; but one misses the contact with living nature that is found in outdoor rites, a thrill that once known is never forgotten.

It is true that the Roman writer Pliny, dealing with the

magical practices of ancient Britain, says that the British women and girls performed religious rites in the nude; but there is reason to think that in former times our climate was somewhat milder than it is now.

However, when nude working is possible it is undoubtedly both pleasant and effective. It is true that one can in a sense cast off one's everyday self with one's everyday clothing. As the room in an ordinary house becomes a different place by the light of the candles round the magic circle, so the naked witch dancing by the light of those candles is a different person from the usual inhabitant of that room. As the witch saying has it; 'The circle of the coven is between the worlds', a borderland place where two worlds meet and where unusual things can happen.

Normal people enjoy being nude, if the surroundings are warm enough to prevent chills. And why shouldn't they? Now that the great blight of pseudo-morality is beginning to be lifted, as a result of the revolutionary social trends of the 1960s, why shouldn't people assert their right to enjoy sunshine and fresh air on our beaches, for instance, without having to fasten funny pieces of cloth around their bodies for fear of offending someone? Surely, if some people are offended by nudity, that is their problem?

If people appeared more often in the nude, they would take more pride in the health and strength of their bodies. One would not see so many flabby, round-shouldered victims of middle-age spread, for instance. There is no need for people, even in their sixties and beyond, to be afraid to be nude, if their bodies are healthy. People whose bodies are bronzed by exposure to sunshine and fresh air soon begin to look aesthetically pleasing at any age, when they straighten their backs and shed their surplus weight.

I wonder if one day we shall see the great primitive religious centres of our nation, such as Stonehenge and Avebury, once again alive with happy, naked people dancing in and out of the great stones in a wonderful round of air and sunlight and joy? Today, thanks to the books of Gerald Hawkins and Alexander Thom, we are beginning to look with new eyes at the work of our remote ancestors, seeing them not as savage numbskulls but as people with remarkable knowledge in the way in which these great monuments were made; even, perhaps, as people from whom we can learn forgotten spiritual truths. At the moment, such a vision of our ancient heritage of joy in nature and our own humanity is just a dream; but not, I think, one too fantastic to come true.

In the meantime, there has arisen of late years a mischievous prank known as 'streaking', being a means of defying the prudish by dashing naked through some public place and hopefully not getting caught. Recent warm summers have even brought out male streakers across such sacred precincts as English cricket grounds and Twickenham, the home of Rugby football, causing policemen to use their helmets as emergency screens before their captives and elderly persons to wonder aloud what the country was coming to.

It is curious to note that streaking is nothing new. Charles Godfrey Leland wrote of it in his book *Gypsy Sorcery and Fortune-Telling*. He says that forty years before this time of writing, which would make it about the 1850s, there was a craze for the more daring type of young girls to go out late at night and try to run naked round some public square or block of houses without being caught by the police. He connects this with the old witch belief in the magical efficacy of nakedness when casting a spell. According to him, there is an old witch ceremony to enable a girl to marry the man she loves, that requires her to go out naked when the moon is full and run around some enclosure, dwelling or group of trees without being seen. If she succeeds in doing this, the charm will work.

Unfortunately, Leland does not specify what the enclosure or group of trees ought to be; but my guess is that originally this was a stone circle or the remains of some sacred grove. So the custom of streaking may be really the lingering folk memory of a very ancient ritual. Like many other things, it has survived as a game or a prank long after its original significance has been forgotten.

Another relic of ancient beliefs connected with the Old Religion is the Lady Godiva procession, originally held at Coventry in Warwickshire and now often copied at other carnivals. A beautiful young girl is chosen to act the part of Lady Godiva, riding through the town mounted upon her white horse and clad in nothing but her flowing hair, though today a flesh-coloured bikini is sometimes added as well. Most people know the story of Lady Godiva's naked ride through the streets of Coventry, in order to persuade her hard-hearted husband, Earl Leofric, to remit the oppressive taxes that were burdening the people. Lord Tennyson wrote a noble Victorian poem about it. However, at the time when the historical Earl Leofric and his wife lived, Coventry was just a village. According to Domesday Book, written after Godiva's death, it consisted of about three hundred people, mostly serfs, who would have been liable only for feudal dues which were still being paid. What Godiva and her husband really did for Coventry was to found a monastery there, which raised the status of the place and helped it to grow into the prosperous city that it afterwards became.

Hence the ancient story of a naked lady riding on a white horse came to be told as a Christian legend about an actual bene-factress, instead of what it really was, namely the survival of the appearance of the naked goddess of the Old Religion in the person of her priestess. The commemorative ride took place annually at Coventry Fair, which was granted approval by King Henry III in 1217. It was held in summer, commencing on the day after Corpus Christi.

The nearby village of Southam also had a Godiva procession in olden days. This was an even more pagan event, because it featured two nude Godivas, one of whom was stained black. One is reminded of the Egyptian Isis and Nephthys, or the bright moon and the dark moon. According to Lewis Spence in his book *The Magic Arts in Celtic Britain,* there was also in the procession a man wearing a horned mask shaped like a bull's head; clearly enough the old horned god himself, who was the goddess's consort. One wonders, if the name Godiva really derived not from Godgifu, the wife of Earl Leofric, but from *Goda diva,* the goddess Goda?

The reason for ritual nudity once again connects with the belief in odic force or animal magnetism, the mysterious border-line energy referred to before. Wilhelm Reich believed that the energy he had discovered, orgone energy, was the basic pre-atomic energy which pervades everything. All other energies are modifications of this basic energy. So-called static electricity, according to Reich, is really more related to orgone than it is to the electricity we use for light and power.

It is well known that the human body generates electricity; but according to Reich, all living substances radiate orgone, which has beneficial effects when accumulated in the right way, unlike electricity, the effects of which may not be beneficial at all. Be that as it may, the effects of static electricity can easily be seen in a dark room, when sparks can be stroked from one's hair or from a cat's fur. The wearing of some nylon underclothes and then removing them in a dark room can cause a blue flash of static electricity to become visible. It is easy to say, 'Oh, that's just static electricity'; but what *is* static electricity? No one really knows. Such flashes produced from a woman's long hair in the darkness of a cave must have seemed strong proof to our distant ancestors of the force-field surrounding the human body.

I remember Naomi Mitchison bringing this fact into one of her stories about Stone Age people, which referred to a girl being chosen as a priestess because of her fiery hair.

'Letting one's hair down' was originally more than just a figure of speech. The Scottish witch Isabel Gowdie describes how the 'Devil' of her coven instructed her to recite spells : 'When we had learned all these words from the Devil, we all fell down upon our knees, with our hair down over our shoulders and eyes, and our hands lifted up, and our eyes steadfastly fixed upon the Devil, and said the foresaid words thrice over to the Devil.' Old spells to be performed by women often contain the instruction that they are to be carried out 'with hair loose and feet bare'. In ancient Greece and Rome, ritual nudity was regarded as essential for the practice of magic; alternatively, if complete nudity could not be attained, then the wearing of light, loose flowing robes was enjoined.

In our colder climate, such robes can be made of woollen material. Their basic design is similar to that of a monk's robe, or a hooded caftan. This design is popular among the members of magical orders also, because it recalls the figure of the ankh cross. The body of the robe, with the long loose sleeves, is the T-shaped part of the cross, while the oval-shaped hood represents the loop of the cross, the ancient Egyptian sign of life. Such robes are quite simple to make. They can be girdled in the middle with a belt or tie, according to one's fancy. This will hold a sheath for the athame. Sometimes a large pocket is incorporated in the design as well, or worn suspended from the girdle. This comes in useful for outdoor rites, to hold things needed in the ritual. Such a loose robe can be slipped on over one's top clothes, if one is working outdoors in very cold weather. A robe that opens right down the front is a bit more complicated to make, but easier to get on and off for outdoor work.

Sandals are the usual accompaniment of a robe; though, once again, in very cold weather, something more substantial may be needed outdoors. I once took part in a very successful outdoor Sabbat, when it was so cold that many of us were wearing heavy boots. Commonsense and practicality are the things to be guided by, in my opinion. One cannot work magic if one is half frozen.

As explained in *Liber Umbrarum*, the traditional black robe or cloak of the witches was to enable them to slip through the shadows without being seen, on the way to their meetings in olden days; but black has also the significance of being the emblem of night and secrecy. Earth brown is also a pleasant colour for a woollen robe, recalling our connection with Mother Earth and the powers of nature. Some covens have the Maiden or priestess attired in a scarlet cloak, the colour of life.

If you have a desire for more colourful robes in your own working, here is a list of the astrological significance of colours, according to the correspondence given by the Order of the Golden Dawn :

Red . . . Mars
Orange . . . Sun
Yellow . . . Mercury
Green . . . Venus
Blue . . . Moon
Indigo . . . Saturn
Violet . . . Jupiter

The brighter colours generally associated with witchcraft in the past have been scarlet, the colour of the life-blood, and green, the fairies' colour. Hence, probably, the belief that green is unlucky; because of its magical potency and its association with paganism, it became dangerous to meddle with. One recalls the lovely wanton Lady Greensleeves of the old English folk song. She may have been originally a form of the nature goddess herself.

There is an old English Morris dance tune called 'Green Garters' which, according to Margaret Murray, was the traditional accompaniment to the processional dance on May Day morning to the place where the Maypole had been erected and where the revels were held. An old version of this dance tune, associated with the Morris Dancers of Bampton, Oxfordshire, has some interesting words :

First for the stockings, and then for the shoes,
And then for the bonny green garters.
A pair for me and a pair for you,
And a pair for them that come arter.

'Arter', of course, is the dialect version of 'after'. This could be a veiled reference to the witch garter and the handing down of the old pagan tradition.

Another old folk song relates to the witches' Sabbat of Hallowe'en. It is quoted from *English Folk Rhymes*, by G. F. Northall.

Heyhow for Hallowe'en,
When all the witches are to be seen,
Some in black, and some in green,
Heyhow for Hallowe'en!

The Devil of the coven is often referred to in Scottish folk-lore as 'the Man in Black'. It seems that the male leader of a coven often dressed in black. Did the priestess, the Queen of the Sabbat or the Queen of Elphame, dress in green? She might well have done, on account of the relationship that existed between witchcraft and the world of Faerie, more especially in Scotland than elsewhere.

The whole question of the fairy world is one that would need a book in itself to be done justice to. There are fairy legends which seem to be dealing with the spirits of nature, a kind of parallel evolution which inhabits this world alongside mankind. Other stories seem to be derived from folk memories of the aboriginal races of Western Europe, who lived in turf-covered round houses and were shorter and darker than the Celts who took over the country from them. Still other stories regard the Land of Faerie as the other world, beyond the bounds of the physical plane, where pagan souls go when they die. The *Sluagh Sidhe* or fairy host of Ireland is said by some accounts to be made up of those who were too bad for heaven but too good for hell. In both Scotland and Italy, long after the coming of Christianity, the pagan goddess Diana was regarded as queen of the fairies. So much of the old paganism simply moved over into fairyland that the liking by witches of the fairies' colour, green, is quite explicable.

As stated in *Liber Umbrarum*, however naked the witch priestess may be, she should always wear a necklace in the circle. This tradition derives from the goddesses of the ancient world, who are usually depicted even when naked wearing jewellery of some kind. I own a quite delightful little statue from Egypt of the Ptolemaic period, around the time of Cleopatra. It portrays the goddess Isis in somewhat Hellenized Egyptian form, wearing nothing but a necklace, an elaborate headdress and a mischievous smile. The more grave and dignified statues of Diana of Ephesus, depicting her as the Great Mother, many-breasted, show her with a necklace made of acorns.

Jewellery looks particularly attractive upon an otherwise nude body, whereas to be simply bare may be rather stark. Perhaps this is the origin of the practice; but I think it more likely that the priestess's necklace is either symbolical, perhaps of the round of the zodiac through which the moon passes in a month, or else magical, consisting of talismans and amulets.

The witch priestess's other traditional ornament is a wide silver bracelet, the metal of the moon. This may be engraved with magical signs and sometimes inset with semi-precious stones, especially moonstones. Green chrysoprase, too, looks very effective set in silver, and I have seen it used in witch bracelets; once again, perhaps, because of its pure green colour, the green of nature and the fairy world.

The actual design of the bracelet varies from coven to coven. Nowadays, when many people are able to take up the craft of the silversmith as a hobby, some beautiful bracelets are being produced. However, if one really cannot afford silver, a brightly polished pewter bracelet would make a good substitute. Pewter is a popular handicraft material which lends itself to fine workmanship and the setting of semi-precious stones.

In the old days such precious regalia was handed down from mother to daughter, or from the old priestess to the young one. In times of danger it was buried, to be dug up again when the danger was past.

The 'grand array' of the Devil of the coven, which he used to wear upon the occasions of the Great Sabbats, consisted, as we have seen, of a horned helmet or headdress and a costume of animal skins. Sometimes the male coven leader still disguises himself in this way on some special ritual occasion. A long black robe with a horned mask is a favourite present-day version. Some covens like to keep up the old tradition of the rest of the coven wearing masks also. Although this derived from the days of persecution, when people who attended the Sabbats did so at peril of their lives, nevertheless there is something very potent and curious about the effect of a mask.

I remember when a grand meeting of Morris Men was held on the green lawns outside the Royal Pavilion at Brighton a few years ago. We were fortunate in having a splendid summer day and there were groups of dancers from all over England taking part. The pipe and tabor sounded their merry tunes, the bells rang, the handkerchiefs waved and the quarterstaffs clashed. Around the dancers circled the traditional beasts, the maskers with animal heads and costumes reminiscent of bulls and stags, hobby-horses and dragons. It was a very strange sensation, even in broad daylight on a crowded lawn, to have one of these horned, masked figures towering over one. How much more eerie must it have been by night on some lonely heath to see a figure like that, illuminated by the glow of a witches' bonfire! Even when one knew perfectly well that underneath the mask was a man, perhaps someone known for years, still there was a strangeness there, a presence that was something more than the person one knew. Masks used to be made of leather or velvet, and ranged from the simple black covering of the upper part of the face to elaborate animal and bird designs, sometimes horned or with two pheasants' feathers to simulate horns. When one put on a mask, one put on a magical personality; a fact known to primitive tribes all over the world. Actually, the word 'personality' derives from *persona*, a mask. Animal masks were also used by the mummers, the people who took part in traditional countryside plays at Christmas and other times of festival. The masked ball, or masquerade, was an opportunity for people to shed their ordinary, everyday selves and put on a new personality, just as they did at the witches' Sabbat.

If, therefore, you are clever at handicrafts you may care to try your skill at making masks and experimenting with their psychological effect. Today there are many new materials, such as fibreglass and papiermâché, out of which masks can be made. Alternatively, a theatrical costumier may be able to provide you with some exciting new faces and headdresses. Remember, the psychological effect may be a good deal more than just dressing up; you will be doing something which has its roots in our very primitive past. What it is capable of releasing from the deep levels of your unconscious mind may surprise and even alarm you.

We have seen how even in the Stone Age cave painting the witch dancers were depicted wearing pointed caps, perhaps to symbolize the cone of power. But what of the tall pointed hat that is the trademark of the witch in all our nursery picturebooks?

It seems that this may have been a pointed riding hat originally. It was called a *copataine* and was worn to protect the head in the case of falling off one's horse when riding over rough country. It was made of very stiff material, hence the sugar-loaf shape of the design. Probably a veil or a tie beneath the chin secured it to the head. The tallness of the hat has been exaggerated by generations of artists until it became the typical witch's hat of caricature.

Ladies of quality who rode on horseback on the Sabbat would have worn *copataines*. They were the headgear of the more upper-class, stylish type of witch. Perhaps in people's minds they became associated with midnight jaunts across moonlit countryside or down dark lanes, and so became the typical witch's hat.

And yet—in the native Mexican painting known as the Codex

Fejèrvàry-Mayer, there is a picture which looks very much like that of a witch, naked except for a pointed hat, riding upon a broomstick! Lewis Spence comments upon this in the article 'Witchcraft' in his *Encyclopaedia of Occultism.* There was a kind of witch cult in pre-Columbian Mexico. This painting raises curious questions as to its origin, and that of the witch hat.

Lewis Spence regards the presence of witch cults in both ancient Central America and ancient Europe as yet another piece of evidence for the existence of the sunken continent of Atlantis, from which the cult may have spread both east and west. He refers to this in a number of places, in his various books about Atlantis. Perhaps one day archaeologists will find definite evidence from the sea-bed which will place Atlantis in the Atlantic Ocean, where Plato said it was. Already interesting results have been forthcoming from diving carried out in the neighbourhood of Bimini in the region of the Bahamas. The remains of massive walls and pavements have been discovered and photographed. Perhaps in the not too distant future Atlantis will have ceased to be a myth, as Troy has ceased to be a myth.

At present, however, such views of the far distant past of our planet and of the origin of its cults, including witchcraft, must remain matters of opinion. What has now ceased to be a matter of opinion and become a matter of scientifically proven fact, is the aura which occultists have long claimed to surround all living things. This has an important bearing upon the subject already referred to more than once in this book, namely the force-field, *odyle*, 'animal magnetism', and so on, which is believed to be the agent of magic. I make no apology for reverting to this, because I believe it to be one of the most basic concepts of witchcraft and one of the least understood or explored; that is, until now.

The break-through has come with the Kirlian photography process, which has enabled the aura not only to be proven to exist, but to be studied in its actions and reactions. In the first chapter of Gerald Gardner's book *Witchcraft Today,* he discussed the question of ritual nudity and the aura, remarking that it would be interesting to study the effectiveness of having one team of witches in the traditional nude and another wearing bikinis. Now, since 1968, when Sheila Ostrander and Lynn Schroeder first brought Kirlian photography from Russia to the western world, we are able to do just that!

Briefly, Kirlian photography enables living things to be photographed in such a way that what science now calls their bioplasmic energy appears. This manifests itself as an aura surrounding them, causing pictures of the human hand, for instance, to bear a striking resemblance to the old 'Hand of Glory' when taken by this process. When the subject is healthy and normal, this aura appears regular and harmonious in form and a beautiful blue in colour. If the subject is injured, disturbed or ill, the colour changes to various shades of pink and crimson and the appearance of the auric halo becomes spiky and out of shape. What is still more remarkable and full of possibilities for the future in research and diagnosis, is the fact that illness can show up in the aura *before* it becomes manifest in the physical body.

Such things are no longer the optimistic claims of clairvoyants. They are proven laboratory facts, backed by money provided by the United States government for experiments in this new and exciting field of research.

The Kirlian photography process was discovered by a Russian experimenter called Semyon Kirlian, from Krasnodar in the USSR. He was interested in electricity and in trying to photograph its effects. One day, while attempting to photograph the spark patterns made by high-frequency electrical impulses, he found that he had photographed the aura of his hand. He continued to develop this new possibility, finding curiously enough that the Soviet government was more open-minded and willing to sanction and back further research than western authorities at first proved to be. Kirlian became famous for his new photographic technique; but it was practically unknown outside the Soviet Union until two American women freelance writers, Sheila Ostrander and Lynn Schroeder, came to Russia and discovered that these experiments were going on.

They published their findings in a book entitled *Psychic Discoveries Behind the Iron Curtain*. At first, however, orthodox science would have none of it. No one would build the experimental unit to the design that they had brought out of Russia. In the eyes of American science, all this stuff belonged in the realm of the occult and was therefore crazy. The first American-built Kirlian unit was made by a California insurance salesman who experimented with electronics as a hobby!

Within the last few years, however, things have changed dramatically. Major universities and medical centres, backed by government money, have started Kirlian photography research, while leading scientific equipment manufacturers are turning out Kirlian units. The break-through came when Dr Thelma Moss, a psychologist at the University of California's Los Angeles Neuropsychiatric Institute, began a serious examination of the claims made by Sheila Ostrander and Lynn Schroeder.

Among other experiments, Dr Moss duplicated the extraordinary 'phantom leaf' result obtained by the Russian researchers. She cut a leaf from a plant in half and then photographed one of the cut halves by the Kirlian process. In the developed film, not only the actual portion of leaf appeared, but also a phantom image of the missing portion.

Briefly, the Kirlian process consists of amplifying the aura, or bio-luminescence as it has been named, of the subject, by giving it a short charge of high-frequency electricity as it is being photographed. Naturally, special equipment and expert technique are needed to do this and the whole subject is still in the development stage. Already, however, Kirlian photography has been used to reveal the serial numbers which had been completely filed off a gun. The disturbances they made in the basic molecular structure of the gun's metal when they were originally engraved showed up on the film. This demonstrates that the Kirlian technique will work with non-living matter as well as with organic matter. This brings us back to the old occult claim that everything has an aura; moreover, that this aura carries within it the history of the thing itself, which can be perceived by the practice of psychometry. The relevance of radiesthesia, dowsing and pendulum divining is another aspect of these borderline energies which may eventually be considered in this connection also.

In this coming Aquarian Age, science and the occult are joining hands. In the meantime, how old Gerald would laugh to see his jocular suggestion become a practical possibility!

9

The Witches' Alphabets

Writing has always been a magical art. In Egypt Thoth, the god of esoteric wisdom, was regarded as the inventor of letters, the scribe of the gods. There was one writing in which sacred inscriptions were recorded, the hieroglyphic script, while another and simpler form of letters was used for more commonplace purposes. Similar conventions ruled in many other parts of the ancient world also.

Moreover, a number of ancient alphabets, as Robert Graves has shown in his book *The White Goddess,* contained various religious secrets. For instance, there might be a twenty-two lettered alphabet of which seven letters were vowels. This commemorates the fact that twenty-two divided by seven gives approximately the value of the mathematical term *Pi,* being the relationship of the diameter of a circle to its circumference.

The circle is the sign of infinity and eternity, while the diameter is emblematic of the finite and mortal. Hence this concept involved the relations between earth and the cosmos, between the macrocosm and the microcosm, or between the human and the divine.

The idea that letters are holy things and that written inscriptions hold sacred power survived into the present day in Tibet. Tibetan refugees have complained that the Communist Chinese invaders strewed the writings from pillaged shrines and monasteries upon the roads, so that the people could not come out of their houses, because in so doing they would have had to walk upon the sacred writings.

The Hebrew Cabbala is full of allusions to the mystic power of the letters of the Hebrew alphabet. The Cabbalistic treatise called the *Sepher Yetzirah,* or *Book of Formation,* says that God created the universe by means of the three forms of expression: numbers, letters and words. This treatise was first introduced to the non-Jewish world in 1552, in a Latin translation by William Postel. It divides the twenty-two letters of the Hebrew alphabet into three 'Mother' letters, corresponding to the elements of Fire,

Air and Water; seven 'Double' letters, corresponding to the seven planets; and twelve 'Simple' letters, corresponding to the signs of the Zodiac.

In addition to this classification of the Hebrew letters, each letter also corresponds to a number. The first ten letters correspond to the numbers one to ten, the next eight letters correspond to the succeeding numbers, twenty to ninety, while the last four letters continue to count in hundreds, from 100 to 400. Five final forms of the letters bring the correspondences up through 500 to 900. By this means every word written in Hebrew has a numerical equivalent. Thus the sacred four-lettered name of God, IHVH, translated as 'Jehovah' in the English Bible though its actual pronunciation is unknown, has the numerical equivalent of twenty-six. I = ten, H = five, V = six, H = five.

The same system of equating letters with numbers applies to the Greek alphabet also, and to Arabic. Hence there are said to be a Hebrew Cabbala, a Greek Cabbala and an Arabic Cabbala. (This word is sometimes spelt Kabbalah or Qabalah). A good deal of Cabbalistic lore appears in the Apocalypse, or Biblical *Book of Revelations*. For instance, it is probably the reason why Christ is described as 'the *Alpha* and the *Omega,* the beginning and the end', *Alpha* being the first letter of the Greek alphabet and *Omega* the last.

It is also the explanation of the famous text which refers to 'the number of the Beast . . . Six hundred, threescore and six'. The Apocalypse was written in Greek, so the reader who was initiated into the *Gnosis,* or secret occult wisdom, could compute the value of the number of a man's name or some other combination of words and find what ideas were associated with this number.

666 is a solar number, being the sum of the numbers one to thirty-six, which are arranged in the figure known as the Magical Square of the Sun. A magical square is a mathematical device whereby figures are arranged in a square in such a way that each column or row when added up gives the same number, in this case 111. There are seven such squares associated with the seven planets. The knowledge of them is an important part of talismanic magic. Hence 666 is not really either an 'evil' number or a 'good' number. It can be either, just as the number thirteen, much dreaded by some superstitious folk, may be either fortunate or otherwise. Numbers, like the planets and signs of astrology, denote natural forces, each of which has a positive and a negative side. A good astrologer will tell his clients that there is really no

such thing as a 'lucky' or 'unlucky' sign to be born under; each has its qualities and also its defects which are characteristic of it.

The knowledge of the correspondences between letters of the various alphabets and the numbers to which they correspond is known as gematria. The foregoing remarks have necessarily been a very brief sketch of a profound subject, one that is still intensely studied by occultists who work in the western tradition of magic, most of which is founded upon the Hebrew and Greek Cabbala. However, it may well be asked, what has this to do with the simple pagan and rural traditions of the old religion of witchcraft? We have already seen that countryside witches were often quite illiterate, like most of the common folk of olden days.

This is quite true; but, nevertheless, the old religion of witchcraft has its roots deep in the same soil as the rest of the western magical tradition. Indeed, in basic ideas, the magical traditions of the whole world are interrelated at their deepest levels. Moreover, at the deepest levels magic and religion are also closely entwined about each other and are concerned with the same great theme : the marriage of heaven and earth, the union of macrocosm and microcosm, the Great Work.

> The cabbalistic theology, representing the endless reasoning of countless generations of ingenious men, is the epitome of man's first efforts to grasp the problems connected with the cause and continuance of life, the inscrutable mystery which has baffled the understanding of all inquirers alike. They reasoned concerning all the phenomena of existence by their analogy to human creation, and it was supposed that the universal creation took place after the manner of human creation, and that the generative attributes of a man and a woman were those of God and the universe, and finally that all the bodily functions of a human being had their counterpart in the macrocosm or greater world.

The foregoing quotation is taken from a remarkable work entitled *The Canon: An Exposition of the Pagan Mystery Perpetuated in the Cabbala as the Rule of all the Arts*. It was first published in 1897. Nothing is known of its author, William Stirling, save that he was a Freemason, and that, unfortunately, he died by his own hand, perhaps as the result of the indifference with which this learned book, his life's work, was received. *The Canon* is an abstruse work, needing a certain amount of mathematical knowledge to appreciate it. In the days when it was first published, the idea that the peoples of ancient lands, including our own, possessed real mathematical and astronomical knowledge as well as mystical insight beyond that commonly possessed today, was laughed to scorn.

However, nowadays we are no longer quite so sure of anything as we were in 1897. When Professor Gerald S. Hawkins published his discovery that Stonehenge was not only a temple but an astronomical observatory and a means of computing eclipses, his ideas were at first called everything from 'meretricious persuasion' to 'moonshine'; but, as he has written in his later book *Beyond Stonehenge,* the 'acceptance gap' has closed or is closing. One of the most influential of Professor Hawkins's supporters has been the eminent astronomer, Sir Fred Hoyle; whereas one of the chief arguments advanced against Professor Hawkins was simply that the Ancient Britons just couldn't possibly have built such a structure as he describes.

The time has been ripe, therefore, for William Stirling's work to be republished for the benefit of a new generation of students. It has duly appeared with the assistance of the Research Into Lost Knowledge Organization and with a foreword by John Michell. It will be recognized from the quotation above that once again we are confronted with the very old idea of the universal principle of polarity, the Chinese Yang and Yin, the Great Father and Great Mother of the Cabbalists, or the God and the Goddess of the old religion of witchcraft.

In this way, I believe, and in no other should these or any other deities be conceived; but because people need to invoke and worship, and because they cannot invoke or worship an abstraction, all the pageantry of the imagination clothes the gods with the forms that have come to be associated with them in the human mind. As William Blake said: 'All deities reside in the human breast'.

William Blake himself, although a mystical Christian, was deeply interested in the ancient faith of these islands, which he associated, according to the ideas of his day, with Druidism. I remember the late Ross Nichols, Chosen Chief of a present-day Druidic Order, telling me how he had discovered a recorded fact relating to this. Apparently on one occasion, I believe when William Blake was resident at Felpham in Sussex, he was called upon to be witness in a court of law. Blake declined to take the usual oath, on the grounds that he was a Druid. The essential theme of *The Canon* could be summed up in another quotation from William Blake: 'The antiquities of every Nation under Heaven is no less sacred than that of the Jews. They are the same thing, as Jacob Bryant and all antiquaries have proved.'

Traditions claiming to be Bardic and Druidic were handed down in Wales, to emerge in the eighteenth century in the form of various neo-Druidic societies. It was with these that William

Blake was associated, and present-day Druids claim him as a former leading member of the order from which their various associations have sprung. Our knowledge of the actual Druids of Celtic Britain is unfortunately very limited, as they left no written records and all we know of them is contained in references from Greek and Roman writers. One of these references, however, is very pertinent to the present theme, because it tells us that the Druids of Britain and Gaul were acquainted with the Greek letters. William Stirling in *The Canon* quotes Julius Caesar's account of the Druids, which declares that they 'deemed it unlawful to commit their statutes to writing; though in other matters, whether public or private, they make use of Greek characters. They seem to me to follow this method for two reasons : to hide their mysteries from the knowledge of the vulgar : and to exercise the memory of their scholars . . . They likewise teach many things relating to the stars and their motions, the magnitude of the world and our earth'.

Now, one of the themes developed in *The Canon* is the way in which, by means of gematria, the Greeks bestowed upon their gods and goddesses names which were appropriate to their particular nature and function. The actual examples given by William Stirling are rather too abstruse for the present chapter; but a simple illustration may be seen in the name of the mysterious Gnostic god *Abraxas,* which by Greek Cabbala yields the number 365, the number of days in the year. Images of this god depict him with the head of a cockerel, the bird whose crowing greets the dawn; hence, he was a symbol of the power of the sun throughout the year. The name of the god Mithras, in its Greek spelling *Meithras,* also gives the number 365. The cult of the solar god Mithras was very popular throughout the Roman empire, especially among soldiers. It will no doubt be remembered how the remains of a Mithraic temple were found in fairly recent years, when some excavations were being carried out in London.

Bearing all this in mind, would it be possible to discover what were at least some of the actual names of the god and goddess of Ancient Britain? I believe that it would.

One of the names of the sun god of Ancient Britain was Belinus. This, in my view, is commemorated in a number of place-names which survive to this day; for instance, Billingsgate in London, Billingshurst in Sussex, and so on. If this name is given its Greek form, it will read as follows :

$$\text{ΒΕΛΗΝΟΣ} = 365$$

This is a very appropriate number for the name of the god worshipped by the priesthood who inherited Stonehenge, although we know today that the Druids did not build that splendid sanctuary, with all its astronomical alignments throughout the year. We know also that lunar as well as solar observations were connected with our megalithic monuments. Professor Alexander Thom called his second book upon the remains of prehistoric Britain *Megalithic Lunar Observatories.* So what of the moon goddess as well as the sun god? She would have been his necessary complement, the feminine aspect of nature, as Isis was to Osiris and Diana to Apollo.

We know the name of the goddess worshipped by Queen Boadicea. She was the goddess of the great forest of Southern Britain, which the Britons called *Coid Andred,* the Romans *Silva Anderida* and the Saxons *Andredsweald.* Today the name has been shortened to the Weald, an area of the south of England where remnants of the great forest still survive: Ashdown Forest, St Leonard's Forest and so on. She was the goddess of other forests also. According to the historian Dion Cassius, it was in 'the grove of Andate' that Boadicea sacrificed her women prisoners, probably somewhere in the region of what is now Epping Forest.

Dion Cassius's version of the story of Boadicea's rebellion is very circumstantial, and contains details not mentioned in the shorter and more matter-of-fact account by Tacitus; although Tacitus describes the strange omens that preceded the destruction of the Romanized cities of Londinium, Camulodunum and Verulamium (London, Colchester and St Albans). He gives two versions of the goddess's name, *Andraste* and *Andate.* Dion Cassius wrote in Greek and he spells Andate thus:

A N Δ A T H = 364

This is the number of days in the old Celtic *lunar* year, which consisted of thirteen twenty-eight-day months. I have indicated elsewhere in this book the probability that this is one of the factors in the sacredness of the number thirteen and its association with witchcraft. Here, therefore, we have an evident lunar significance in the Greek spelling of the name of Boadicea's goddess.

If the numbers of the names of the sun-god and the moon-goddess, Belēnos and Andatē, 365 and 364, be added together, they come to 729, which curiously enough is given by Aleister Crowley as the number of 'Baphomet', the androgynous god of the Knights Templars as drawn in the famous picture by Eliphas

Levi. Crowley received this number by psychic means, through the clairvoyance of his 'Scarlet Woman', Ahitha (Roddie Minor). Be that as it may, the number 729 is 9 × 9 × 9, the cube of 9.*

The number 9 is the trinity of trinities, a kind of universal solvent of numbers because any number whose digits add to 9 will be found to be exactly divisible by 9. In fact, most of the sacred numbers of ancient time measures and so on will be found to be divisible by 9, in both east and west. Now, neither 365 nor 364 are in themselves divisible by 9, because by themselves they are incomplete, just as man is incomplete without woman and woman without man; but when they are joined together they produce a number which is not only divisible by 9 but is 9 multiplied by itself and by itself again. This is reminiscent of the *hieros gamos* or Sacred Marriage which was such an essential part of the ancient mysteries.

What of the other version of the goddess's name given by Dion Cassius? Why should there be two versions of the name? Do both contain some esoteric meaning? We can only guess at the answers to these questions; but let us see what the name Andraste gives when written in the old Celtic alphabet called Ogham.

In the Ogham characters, the double letter ST is given as one letter; so in Ogham Andraste is a seven-lettered name. The oldest Ogham inscriptions are cut upon the edges of standing stones, though later the alphabet was adapted so that it could be written upon parchment.

The name Andraste requires twenty-two cuts to inscribe it :

A   N   D   R   A   ST   E

As stated at the beginning of this chapter, the proportion of twenty-two divided by seven gives the rough equivalent of *Pi*, the relation of the diameter of a circle to its circumference. This mathematical ratio pervades the whole physical universe. It is part of the basic design of things, as well as having the symbolic meaning previously given, that of the relation of the finite with the infinite.

Thanks to the researches of Professor Thom, we know that the

* In their book *Gematria*, Frederick Bligh Bond and Thomas Lea state that the number 729 'symbolizes the perfect ashlar or cubic stone', which is a significant concept in the lore of Freemasonry.

people of Ancient Britain were very interested in this ratio. They went to a great deal of trouble to design a form of stone circle the shape of which was slightly distorted from the round, so that it gave a relation of diameter to circumference which should be exactly three, the sacred trinity. Admittedly, these stone circles were already very ancient when Queen Boadicea reigned; but the secrets of geometry and what they signified were still very much a part of mystic doctrine, as they have continued to be right down to our own day, for instance in the traditions of Freemasonry.

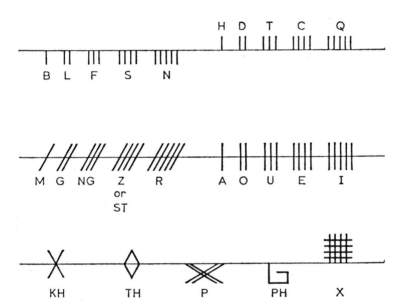

The Ogham Alphabet

Ogham was a sacred Druidic alphabet and would certainly have contained magical secrets. The majority of Ogham inscriptions which have survived are found in Ireland, though such inscriptions also occur in Wales and the Isle of Man. A few have even been found in Hampshire, Cornwall and Devon. An old Irish book known as *The Book of Ballymote* gives various written forms of Ogham. It was compiled in about 1391 by Solomon of Droma and Manus MacDonugh. The book also contains information about the Bardic lore of old Ireland, which was inherited from the Druidic traditions as was the Bardic lore of

Wales.

Lewis Spence, in his book *The Magic Arts in Celtic Britain,* records that there are a number of references in literature to the existence of Druidic books in ancient Ireland. Apparently, St Patrick was personally responsible for the burning of 180 books belonging to the Irish Druids. His example was extensively followed by zealous Christian converts, until the Druidic literature was utterly destroyed, an act which Lewis Spence likens to the senseless destruction of the great library of Alexandria. It is therefore not too fantastic, although admittedly speculative, to look at the Ogham alphabet in search of ancient British religious secrets.

Some old arrangements of the Ogham letters show them set out as a kind of mandala. This was known as the Wheel of Ogham. It will be seen that this arrangement roughly resembles a Celtic cross.

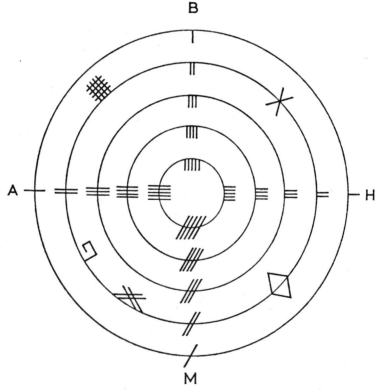

The Wheel of Ogham

To what extent the Druidic lore influenced witchcraft, we do not know, although we are told that there were Druidesses as well as Druids. When the Roman governor Suetonius Paulinus massacred the Druids on the Isle of Anglesey, black-robed women hurled defiance at his soldiers. There are records of true prophecies made in later years by Druidesses to the Roman emperors Alexander Severus, Aurelian and Diocletian. Probably the same thing happened to the Druids as happened to the witches. Those who were not exterminated went underground and preserved their lore in secret.

Certainly, the old Druidic fire festivals of the Celtic year coincide with the Great Sabbats of the witches. Also, the Druids and the witches held a common belief in reincarnation. So there is good reason for witches and pagans in Britain today to regard themselves as the inheritors and perpetuators of the Ogham alphabet.

With the coming of the Angles, Saxons, Jutes and Danes another form of magical writing was introduced to Britain, namely the runic writing used by these people of the north. The runic alphabet was called the futhorc, because its first six letters were F, U, TH, O, R, and K. There were various versions of this alphabet, differing from country to country. Also, the Old Norse runes, common to the Scandinavian peoples during the first six or seven hundred years A.D. were different from the runes of the Viking Age, which lasted from about A.D. 700 to 1050.

The earliest version of the runes consists of twenty-four letters, divided into three groups of eight. These are named after Norse deities : Freya's Eight, Hagal's Eight and Tiu's Eight. Every rune has a dual meaning, outward and inward. Outwardly they indicate things of the material world, such as cattle, a lake, a birch-tree and so on. Inwardly they have a spiritual meaning, such as blessing, life-strength, law.

According to Norse legend, the runes were originally used for spells and magic, and only later descended to the prosaic uses of ordinary writing. The original master of the runes was the god Odin or Woden, just as the use of the Ogham alphabet was supposed to have been originated by the Celtic sun god, Ogma. Like Ogham also, the runes were well adapted to be either cut upon stones or wood or, alternatively, used as written letters.

The word 'rune' is derived from the Old Norse language and means something which is a mystery or a secret. It has also come to mean a spell or a song. The poem which was originally written in runes, has taken its name from the magic letters with which it was inscribed.

Freya's Eight

ᚠ FEOH, cattle or fee

ᚢ UR, yore or ox

ᚦ THORN, THURS, thorn or giant

ᚨ OSS, ASA, god

ᚱ RIT, sunwheel, sun-wain

ᚲ KAON, torch, life-strength

ᚷ GIFU, gift, blessing

ᚹ WUNNA, bliss, Woden

Hagal's Eight

ᚺ HAGAL, hail, health

ᚾ NAUT, need

ᛁ IS, ice

ᛃ YER, year, harvest

ᛇ YR, yewtree

ᛈ PEORTH, paddock, berg

ᛉ AQUIZI, stone axe

ᛋ SIG, sun, winning

Tiu's Eight

ᛏ TIU, the god Tiu

ᛒ BIRCA, birch tree, berg

ᛖ EH, EOH, horse, steed

ᛗ MAN, mankind, world

ᛚ LAGU, lake, water of life, law

ᛜ ING, kin, offspring

ᛟ ODAL, homeland, holding

ᛞ DAG, day

The Runes

The study of the magic and mystery of runes continued in Germany, right down to the present century. Unfortunately, this circumstance served to bring it into disrepute, because it became part of the mystique of the Nazis. The hated SS deliberately wrote their initials on the collars of their uniforms in the runic form of S, because this had the inner meaning of 'victory', the rune *Sig*. Hence, runes have shared the public disfavour of the swastika since World War II. However, both the runes and the swastika were already very ancient long before Hitler appropriated them. One wonders whether perhaps the centuries-old magical potency of these things, which he tried to steal, worked against him in the end.

It seems a great pity that Hitler and his thugs should be able to prevent the study and appreciation of runic lore, which, after all, is part of our heritage as descendants of the Anglo-Saxon race. Perhaps the descriptions and illustrations of the runes contained in this book may reawaken interest in this branch of magic.

The source of our information about Odin and his mastery of the runes is the old Icelandic poem called *The Elder Edda*, of which a good available version is *The Elder Edda: A Selection,* translated by Paul B. Taylor and W. H. Auden. In the section called 'The Words of the High One', Odin tells how he passed through a strange ordeal, hanging nine nights upon a gallows as a sacrificial victim to obtain the knowledge of the runes, which he did not invent but discover, as if it was something that had existed from all time. It may be that the original Odin was not a god but a man, a warrior king who led his people from Asg .i to populate the northern lands; because all our Anglo-Saxon kings were believed to be descended from Odin. Indeed, to be of the blood of Odin was a necessary qualification for kingship in England before the Norman Conquest.

In view of the respect given to practitioners of the magic arts among the Nordic people, it seems strange that so little has been made by the various writers upon the subject, of the contribution of the Anglo-Saxons to the witchcraft tradition. The very word 'witch' is Anglo-Saxon in origin, though authorities differ as to its real derivation so widely as to make that derivation a matter of opinion only.

Modern witches, following Gerald Gardner, have usually associated it with wisdom. A witch, they claim, means a wise person, deriving the word from the same root as 'wit' in the sense of knowing. This derivation, as I showed in my previous book *An A.B.C. of Witchcraft Past and Present*, is at least as old as the time of Dr Henry More (1614–1687). However, some other authorities associate the word 'witch' with the same root as that of the words 'weak' and 'wicked', implying that witches were so called because they were wicked people. Another opinion is that 'witch' is an Anglo-Saxon version of the old Welsh or Celtic word *gwyddon*, the '*dd*' in Welsh being pronounced '*th*'. According to Bardic tradition, the *Gwyddoniad* were the aboriginal 'Wise Ones' who existed in the British Isles before Druidism was organized.

Not being a philologist myself, I will not attempt to say which of the differing authorities is right; though I think the people who are anxious to associate witchcraft with wickedness are not entirely free from bias, whereas they, no doubt, will say the same of those who associate it with wisdom.

We know that Christianity had come to Britain long before the Saxons did. Nevertheless, there must have been some contribution to the pattern of witch beliefs and practices that came from Saxon sources, even if it was only the name 'witch' and the attitude of mind that went with it. In spite of the book-burning attributed to St Patrick, as mentioned above, the Celtic Church was not everywhere on bad terms with the older faiths; whereas the Saxon followers of St Augustine, who owed his allegiance to Rome, were taught that all the old gods were devils. It would follow naturally upon this that the priests and priestesses of all older faiths would be regarded as witches, giving the word a derogatory sense.

For this reason, the use of the old runic and Ogham alphabets was discouraged by the Church. The letters of these old alphabets were associated with pagan magic, so they were eventually completely replaced by the Latin alphabet, the origin of the letters we use today. The process, however, had to be a gradual one. The use of the word 'ye' for 'the', still seen in mock-archaic inscriptions such as 'Ye Olde Englishe Tea Shoppe', is a relic of this changeover. The letter represented by 'y' is not really a 'y' sound at all; it is the old runic letter *thorn*, 'th'.

10

The Working Site

A twisted tree, upon this Hallowe'en,
Rears branches black and bare against the sky,
The air is chill with presences unseen,
And fallen leaves before us drift and fly.

Steep is the hill, and dark the narrow lane,
And wavering our yellow lantern's glow,
As softly tread the footsteps once again,
To keep our tryst and troth of long ago.

Up through the hanging wood to hill-top ring,
The bank and ditch o'ergrown with mighty trees,
There in the gloom the ritual flame we bring,
The witch-fire burning through the centuries.

And as it leaps, unto the pipe's thin sound,
And chanted invocation, deep and low,
All hand in hand, we dance the circle round,
As wheeling stars and turning seasons go.

Then halt, and pass the wine-cup round the flames,
The fire's glow reflected in each heart,
As in the wine we pledge the ancient names :
'The Old Ones! Merry meet and merry part!'

Such is the poem I wrote to describe a secret outdoor meeting
of witches. Its site was a prehistoric earth-work that has a long
tradition as a meeting-place for the old seasonal rituals of the
Sabbats. Although the rite we performed was quite simple, it
raised a wonderful atmosphere and provided an unforgettable
experience for all those who took part.

Unfortunately, such outdoor rituals are seldom a practical
possibility in these days. The countryside is so much more thickly
populated than it used to be, that it is difficult to find a suitable

place which is sufficiently private for such a purpose. Nevertheless, I feel that all covens and individual witches should attempt
at some suitable opportunity to get out of doors and seek communion with the living forces of nature at first hand.

The particular site to which this poem refers has a curious
history. It does not seem to like outsiders. People who have gone
there, moved by idle curiosity, having heard some rumour of its
connection with the Old Religion, have had strange and fright-
ening experiences when they tried to perform some mocked-up
rite for a laugh. Personally, however, I have always felt a sense
of welcome there—so long as one did not take liberties.

If one lives in a fairly open and unspoilt part of the country,
it may be possible to find a suitable site for regular working. *If
you do, however, please leave it unspoilt.* Witches, even more
than most people, should be concerned with the preservation of
our countryside. Be particularly careful with bonfires and lan-
terns, especially if the weather has been dry for any length of
time. Remember, even a carelessly-dropped cigarette can cause
horrifying damage to trees and the habitat of wild creatures; so
never leave any smouldering ashes of a bonfire behind you. If
you have no water available, smother the embers with freshly-
dug earth.

Be careful, too, of stones, especially flints. If these get in or
near your bonfire, they may become so hot that they explode
and send fragments flying dangerously around. They can be
painful to tread on while dancing, too; in fact, it is a good idea
to clear your site carefully in daylight before you actually perform your ritual there. A daylight reconnaissance is really essential, if you have never been to a particular site before.

Apart from the obvious requirement of privacy, there are certain other more subtle factors which may determine the suit-
ability of a working site for witchcraft rituals. The site of an old
pagan religious centre, for instance, would be instinct with power,
just waiting to be re-awakened. There might, indeed, be so
much latent power there that it would be advisable to tread
cautiously until one became sufficiently attuned to the place to
be sure of what one was dealing with. In general, the grisly tales
of 'human sacrifice' and 'unspeakable rites' so often told of our
pagan ancestors are sheer guesswork and exaggeration; but not
always—although they never invented anything so grisly as the
atom bomb. Moreover, power itself can induce fear, without
anything evil being necessarily involved. So get the feel of a site
before you actually use it for working. This is another reason for
the daylight reconnaissance referred to above.

Get a good map of your district and study it well. Clues of place-names may appeal to you or intrigue you, bearing as they often do some reference to the old gods, either Anglo-Saxon or Celtic. For instance, the Ordnance Survey maps for the area around my home town of Brighton, Sussex, glanced over at random show Thundersbarrow Hill, inland on the Downs above Shoreham—evidently related to the old god Thunor, the Anglo-Saxon form of Thor. Near Rusper is Puck's Croft, a place of the fairy folk who were often the old gods in disguise. There are a number of other 'Puck' place-names in Sussex and elsewhere. South-east of Godalming is Hascombe, which means 'witch's valley'. *Hexe* was the old Saxon word for 'witch' and *cwm* is Celtic for '*Valley*', so Saxon and Celt mingled there. The old Roman road of Stane Street runs through Billingshurst, 'the wood of Belin', that Druidic Belenos referred to in the previous chapter. Straight as a die it runs, just as the Romans built it— or did they merely pave an even older track? There is Faygate, just north of St Leonard's Forest, another place-name connected with the fairy folk; and so on. It can be a fascinating and thought-provoking occupation, studying maps; especially when one's study is later supplemented by investigation of the actual countryside.

A man whose discoveries in this connection are now being closely studied and more and more appreciated, is the late Alfred Watkins of Hereford, whose major work *The Old Straight Track* was first published in 1925 and has since been reprinted several times. It was the intuitive observation of Alfred Watkins which led to the rediscovery in our time of the system of alignments criss-crossing our countryside with an invisible network, to which he gave the name of 'leys' (pronounced 'lays', as in the expression 'the lay of the land').

These alignments are marked by prehistoric standing stones and other megalithic monuments, barrows and other earthworks, beacons, moats, mark-stones, very old cross-roads and old churches which are built upon older pagan sites. Notches on the edge of hills which form the skyline, historic old trees and deliberately planted clumps of trees, or those which seem to be such, especially Scotch firs, come into the picture too.

Alfred Watkins realized that his discovery was a fantastic one in several senses of the word; but that it is not a fantasy can be proved by anyone who cares to study the subject—not, however, by merely drawing lines upon maps, though that can be intriguing enough, but by actual research upon the ground, taking in the message of the land itself. This is the idea behind the Chinese art of *feng-shui,* roughly translated 'geomancy', by which for thousands of years the whole landscape of China was regulated as propitious places for building were selected and unpropitious ones avoided. The Chinese had straight tracks, too, which they called 'dragon-paths'; recalling the remarks made previously in Chapter 5 of this book about Chartres Cathedral and the orientation of old churches. The dragon seems to have been a worldwide symbol of invisible energy of a magical kind; magical, that is, to us, though seemingly well understood by those bygone people of east and west whose lore has been all but lost and is today being rediscovered and revalued.

John Michell's work in this connection has already been alluded to. Another very comprehensive book on the subject of leys is *Quicksilver Heritage,* by Paul Screeton, editor of the magazine *The Ley Hunter.* It bears the sub-title 'The Mystic Leys—Their Legacy of Ancient Wisdom', which indicates its scope, not so much providing all the answers as showing the extent of the questions, as it ranges over such subjects as the appearance of elementals on leys or at their convergence, sightings of unidentified flying objects (UFOs) at similar places, and the associated question of the existence of terrestrial zodiacs such as the Great Zodiac of Glastonbury discovered by Mrs Katharine Maltwood.

Alfred Watkins realized that he was going to have a hard time of it to convince the world of the existence of leys, without bringing anything metaphysical into the discussion. So during the lifetime he refrained from emphasizing such aspects of the matter in print, confining himself to proving his theory by field work. According to his son, Allen Watkins, however, Alfred Watkins fully realized that there was a lot more to the ley system than merely a collection of trackways; though even as trackways the leys meant that prehistoric Britain was not just a pathless wilderness. There was thought and organization behind the making of such a system. The maintenance of it had to be handed down from one generation to another, until it became second nature among country folk, even when its original significance had been forgotten. For instance, the planting of a clump of Scotch firs is obviously not prehistoric; yet such clumps of fir trees are a well-recognized ley mark. In this connection one recalls the importance attached to boundaries and landmarks, which was shown in such old ceremonies as 'beating the bounds', whereby the younger generation were shown the place of the landmarks and received a symbolic 'beating' as a practical means of impressing the lesson upon their memories, a custom which in itself might have taken the place of an earlier sacrificial rite.

In No. 18 of *The Ley Hunter* (April, 1971), Allen Watkins published a short but very thought-provoking article, 'The Straight Path In Wisdom Teaching', in which he suggested that the traversing of a ley might actually be a way of initiation by means of the traveller's encounter with the four elements of fire, water, air and earth. One has the plodding on across earth itself, the fording of streams, the clear air on the heights and the beacon hill where the ritual fire was lit. Fire and light have always been connected with inspiration, progress with an upward climb, 'scaling the heights' and so on. For man, the pilgrim of eternity, the metaphor of a journey has often been used to describe his spiritual evolution : John Bunyan wrote his *Pilgrim's Progress*, King Arthur's knights rode forth in quest of the Grail, and William Blake saw himself in the image which he engraved and entitled 'The Traveller Hasteth in the Evening'.

The idea of enhancing one's spiritual advancement by performing a pilgrimage to some holy place is found all over the world and in all ages. People still make pilgrimages to such places as Glastonbury and Walsingham, just as in prehistoric times they followed the ridgeways along the heights of Britain which converged upon the great spiritual centres of Stonehenge and Avebury. Ley lines leading to the old sacred places have also been traced, as mentioned previously in Chapter 5. Old roads often followed the course of a ley, which may have a bearing on the old belief that witches met at crossroads, where in Roman times the statue of Hecate or of Diana Trivia (Diana of the Three Ways) used to be erected. Statues of Hermes were also used as landmarks of boundaries, hence the word 'herm' for a stone pillar. This was originally a simple phallic upright stone; later such stones were sculptured with the head of the god Hermes and a phallus. Hermes or Mercury was the patron of travellers and the messenger of the gods. He was also much involved with the lore of magic, its teaching and preservation.

What, however, is the real nature of the unseen force which flows along the ley paths? If we knew this, we might begin to answer the supplementary question, were the leys mapped out to conduct this power or to show where the power flowed?

That this power is profoundly connected with the life force of the earth seems evident from the system of beliefs which centres around it. Seasonal rituals were celebrated at the old sacred centres, all of which were ley centres. We know that these rituals had as their object the harmonizing of humanity with nature, the uplifting of the mind and spirit and the promotion of fertility in humans, animals and the earth itself. This, at once, gives the so-called 'fertility cult' which is the origin of witchcraft an entirely new status. The old orgiastic rites were not merely a communal letting off steam, nor even just sympathetic magic which worked by a kind of induction, using the means of fertility in humans to arouse that of the earth. They were undoubtedly these things, but also something more, something perhaps even more fundamental, by which people got into sympathetic communion with the profoundest forces of the cosmos.

As mentioned above, Alfred Watkins deliberately played down any occult significance inherent in the ley lines. Yet it is a remarkable fact that the late Dion Fortune brought this aspect of ley hunting into one of her occult novels, *The Goat-Foot God*, which was first published in 1936. As this book was out of print for some years, this fact has been little noticed by the present generation of ley hunters. Now, however, in common with most of Dion Fortune's other books, *The Goat-Foot God* is back in print. The question, therefore, arises, how did Dion Fortune know about the esoteric significance of the leys? She does not use the term 'leys' in *The Goat-Foot God*; but from her description it is evident that this is what she is referring to.

Personally, I feel that, with the exception of *The Mystical Qabalah*, Dion Fortune's works of fiction are more important and informative than her non-fictional books. A pagan inspiration seems to be coming through in her work, which becomes more and more marked towards the end of her life and which is very different from the present-day attitude of the fraternity she founded, the Society of the Inner Light.

Briefly, the story of *The Goat-Foot God* tells of the regeneration of the lives of two people, a man and a woman, by a successful invocation of Pan. At the beginning of the book, they set out to find a place in the country in which to take a house that would be suitable for such an invocation. The woman, an artist called Mona Wilton, has acquired a certain amount of occult knowledge which enables her to advise on where to look. As she tells the man in the book, there are certain places that are more suitable for invoking the Old Gods than others, just as there are some soils that are good for growing rhododendrons and others that will grow roses. They set about finding the right place by studying a map, one which shows not only the towns but also the geological strata of the country. According to Mona Wilton, the best sites are those which are on the chalk.

I have not seen this particular statement made elsewhere. However, it is worth considering. Any place which is on the

The author holding a Witches' Wishing Mirror. This old hand-carved mirror was for many years in the possession of a Cornish family.

Old-time conception of flying witches. An illustration by Sir John Gilbert to *The Lancashire Witches* by Harrison Ainsworth.

Portrait of a modern witch. Patricia Crowther, Priestess of the Sheffield Coven.

"Old George" Pickingill, the master witch of Canewdon, Essex (*picture by courtesy of* Eric Maple).

Distant view of Chanctonbury Ring, the traditional past meeting place of old-time Sussex witches (*photo by* A. W. Stubbs).

A typical example of a blocked-up north door from the fourteenth-century church at Alfriston, Sussex.

Witchcraft implements displayed on an altar: two cloven-hoof candlesticks, the Pentacle, the Bell, the Horn Wine-cup, the Cauldron, the Athame or black-hilted knife, the Crystal, the Cord, the Wand, jar of incense and incense-burner.

Wooden carving of the Horned God. The two faces look towards the Past and the Future. The four horns represent the four winds, the four seasons and so on. The base of the statue bears four coloured stones, symbolising the four elements.

The regalia of the Horned God: a crown or helmet surmounted by actual deer's horns, plus a rough dark-coloured cloak. In olden days this would have been of animal skins.

A modern version of the Green Man, or Foliate Mask. This example is made of painted fibre-glass.

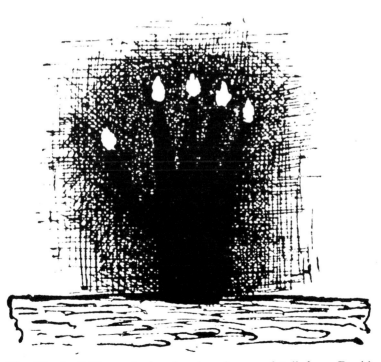

The Hand of Glory. A drawing based on a detail from David Teniers' picture "The Departure for the Sabbat".

The author holding the Sabbat wine-cup, with a holder made from a large cloven hoof.

Demonstrating the invocation of power into a glass ball for purposes of clairvoyance.

The author demonstrating the use of the water-filled cauldron for clairvoyance.

Traditional witch costume of hooded black cloak and broomstick.

chalk in the present day must at some previous date, very long ago, have been beneath the sea, that great primordial elemental mother of all life on this planet. The question of the influence of the actual geological make-up of a particular place is an intriguing one which seems to have been very little explored. However, I find it hard to believe that places on the chalk are the only ones which are suitable for a successful invocation of the ancient powers. It seems more likely to me that each particular place would have its own typical influence. For instance, how about the famous second sight of the Scottish Highlands, which I believe contain some of the oldest rock formations in the British Isles? Or of the many strange stories told about the lonely places of Iceland, which also consists of very old rock formations?

I have not the space here to pursue this particular subject, but point it out as a possible line of future enquiry. We may recall in this connection the remarks about geomancy as practised in ancient China, which was concerned with the actual conformation of the land, the message of the landscape. Also, that spirit of a place which the Romans personified and called the *genius loci*.

Returning to *The Goat-Foot God,* Mona Wilton advises that the great power-centres are very often occupied with Christian edifices in these times; but that where such edifices are built upon ancient pagan sites, as most of our very old cathedrals and churches are, then the older influence will still be there under the surface. (One remembers the altar to Cernunnos that was found beneath Notre Dame in Paris). However, she says, for practical purposes of seclusion and privacy, the lines *between* the power centres, especially when such lines cross chalk soil, are the best.

Dion Fortune, through the mouth of her fictional characters, then proceeds to outline the ley system and to do what other writers upon the subject up to then had, so far as I know, definitely not done; namely, to discuss the strange esoteric power which flows along these lines and which, she says, can be utilized for occult purposes. This, remember, was written back in 1936. Had Dion Fortune somehow drawn information from a body of knowledge that has been secretly handed down in esoteric circles for a very long time?

I myself have encountered a witch coven that possessed some scraps of knowledge that certainly tied in with geomancy and the ley system. They did not, however, refer to leys as such; they called them 'bearings' and regarded certain places as being of more significance than others in an occult sense. I was told that gypsies shared this knowledge and used certain woods and heaths as traditional encampments for this reason.

I wonder if this is the reason behind those strange stories we see in the national press from time to time, of peculiar hauntings in recently built or even perfectly new houses, often upon council estates? Where there seems little, if any, cause for a haunting arising from the previous history of a house, can the ground it is built on have something to do with it, in the sense of somehow attracting psychic activity? This is another question for future researchers.

Reverting to the question of ancient sites and power centres, the great Stonehenge-Avebury complex has already been alluded to, with Avebury as probably the older site of the two. Glastonbury is the great spiritual centre of the West Country, the Avalon of ancient legend. It is a remarkable fact that in our day Glastonbury has come into its own again as a centre of pilgrimage, not only for Christians but for all those who seek spiritual insight. Indeed, I am told that the native inhabitants of Glastonbury have become rather impatient with the influx of hippies. But it is not only wandering eccentrics who seek the spiritual atmosphere of the great Tor. Not exactly secretly, but quietly, Glastonbury has been the centre for followers of the native mystic traditions of Britain for many years. At one time Dion Fortune lived there, and has told its story in her book *Avalon of the Heart*.

There are plenty of excellent guide books to the antiquities of Britain today, which detail our stone circles and other megalithic monuments. Taken in conjunction with the books on ley-hunting already mentioned, no one need be short of data to work on. Not so well known, however, are the locations of the ancient Druidic colleges of Britain, according to an old book entitled *The History of Britain from the Flood to A.D. 700, Compiled from the Various Ancient Records,* by Richard Williams Morgan. My copy of this book was published in 1933 but the author's Introduction is dated 1857.

According to Morgan, the seats of the three Arch-Druids of Britain were Caer Troia, also called Caer Lud (London), Caer Evroc (York) and Caer Lleon (Caerleon). Under the rule of these were the seats of the Chief Druids, which were as follows: Caer Caint (Canterbury); Caer Wyn (Winchester); Caer Municip (St Albans); Caer Sallwg (Old Sarum); Caer Leil (Carlisle); Caer Grawnt (Cambridge); Caer Meini (Manchester); Caer Gwrthegion (Palmcaster); Caer Coel (Colchester); Caer Gorangon (Worcester); Caerleon ar Dwy (Chester); Caer Peris (Porchester); Caer Don (Doncaster); Caer Guoric (Warwick); Caer Meivod (Meivod); Caer Odor (Bristol); Caer Llear (Leicester);

Caer Urnach (Wroxeter); Caer Lleyn (Lincoln); Caer Glou (Gloucester); Caer Cei (Chichester); Caer Ceri (Cirencester); Caer Dwr (Dorchester); Caer Merddin (Carmarthen); Caer Seiont (Carnarvon); Caer Wysc (Exeter); Caer Segont (Silchester); Caer Baddon (Bath). It seems a reasonable supposition that these Druidic seats were not chosen arbitrarily. In our own day, some of them such as Palmcaster and Meivod have sunk into obscurity; but many of the others became the sites of our oldest cathedrals, which recalls the information given in *The Goat-Foot God*. How far back their importance and sanctity actually go is lost in the mists of prehistory. Here is further material for those who wish to redraw the lines of power.

A very curious and little-known place in Britain which I feel should receive mention here is Brimham Rocks, near Harrogate in Yorkshire. Thanks to the writings of authors like Louis Pauwels, Jacques Bergier and George Hunt Williamson, many people today have heard with wonder of the strange rocks of the high Andes, which so resemble various giant figures of gods and animals that they are believed to be the weathered remains of sculptures executed by some long vanished race. Indeed, more British people have heard of the giant sculptures of Marcahuasi than have heard of Brimham Rocks; yet the latter in some cases seem just as convincing as having been at least partially shaped by unknown hands long ages ago.

There are lingering traditions linking Brimham Rocks with the Druids. It has been claimed that on one gigantic rock known as 'The Druid's Idol' the marks of tooling can definitely be seen, especially on the base of the pedestal which supports a great mass of rock on a small pivot. However, less imaginative writers explain all the strange shapes of the rocks by weathering and other natural causes, as they do in the case of the similar sculptures of Marcahuasi.

Certain it is that Brimham Rocks are situated on a plateau which affords a wide view over the surrounding countryside, allowing many landmarks to be seen; a natural ley centre. Perhaps this brief notice of this neglected wonder of Britain may inspire further and more imaginative research than it has received in the past.

It has been for too many years a curious characteristic of the British race that they have admired the mystic traditions of other lands while ignoring and neglecting their own. Today, I am glad to see this viewpoint being reversed and the Mystery Tradition of Britain being appreciated once more. I feel that this is yet another sign of the times, the approaching Aquarian Age.

Slowly, but surely, humanity is rediscovering the Old Gods. People are being compelled to appreciate the value of their relationship with nature. We are learning that we cannot continue to pollute and violate the surface of our earth and to destroy animals and vegetation, without paying the penalty for our callousness. But more than this, the Old Gods themselves are returning actively to human consciousness.

Carl Gustav Jung opened the door to the exploration of the collective unconscious of humanity. His archetypes have been demonstrated to make their appearance in the various religious systems and myths of all ages and countries. Sometimes such archetypal figures are benign, sometimes malignant. They may display either a positive or a negative aspect, which can be an active thing and not by any means merely legendary. Research into Jung's ideas in the realm of psychology is still continuing. But even more striking is the way in which physical science has now caught up with psychology in this respect and even overtaken it, in the presentation of the Gaia Hypothesis.

The propounders of this revolutionary theory of our relationship with the planet Earth are Dr James Lovelock, FRS, and Dr Sidney Epton, who presented their views in the issue of *The New Scientist*, dated 6 February 1975. Briefly, they suggest that the earth is a self-controlling organism, a vast living creature, which is somehow able to regulate the conditions of its own biosphere, so as to enable life to exist and evolve within it. For this fundamental and obviously superhuman power, the novelist William Golding suggested to them the name Gaia, which is the name of the earth goddess of ancient Greece.

Instead of the materialistic scientific view that life arose on earth fortuitously, simply because the conditions happened to be right, the Gaia Hypothesis postulates that life itself defined the material conditions necessary for its survival, brought them about and ensured their continuation, and that this moreover is a continuous living and evolving process which is still going on.

Dr Lovelock and Dr Epton list some of the reasons for their advancement of this theory. For instance, how has the critical temperature of the earth's surface been maintained for millions of years, not becoming either too hot or too cold to support its evolving life? How has the composition of the earth's atmosphere been maintained in a steady state, far from chemical equilibrium? What purposes are served by the presence in the atmosphere of certain trace gases and how did they get there? What really causes climatic changes? These and other questions are discussed by the propounders of the Gaia Hypothesis in scientific terms; but it is their conclusions which vitally interest us here.

We need, they say, to make peace with Gaia, the great Mother Earth, on her terms. We need to stop thinking of our relationship with nature as a battle and begin to think of it as a need for peaceful co-existence, finding ways of entering into harmony with the life-force of our planet. Our survival may, indeed probably does, depend on it.

This planet is our home. Our life and hers are interdependent. It is suggested that the human race on Gaia may be in a sense the equivalent of the central nervous system in the human body. In other words, we need Gaia and Gaia needs us. Otherwise, why would we have been evolved?

When I read this article, I was reminded immediately of the old idea mentioned by Gerald Gardner in Chapter 10 of *Witchcraft Today*, namely that witches in ancient times believed in gods who were not all-powerful. The gods wished well to humanity, they desired the fertility of humans and animals and the realm of all nature; but in order to attain this they needed man's help. The dances, festivals and rituals of the Old Religion were intended to further this aim, the harmonizing of humanity with the life-force of the universe. This is the same aim as that of what the occult philosophers called the Great Work, the union of the Microcosm, the human being, with the Macrocosm, the universe. Such union would surely have to start with entering into sympathetic relationship with our own world, Mother Earth whose children we all are.

When witches today go outdoors to perform their rituals, however simple the rite may be, whether they go as a coven or as individuals, these are things to be mindful of : the communion of the living earth, the inner causes of things, the perception of the realm of form as a veil before the realm of forces. They should bring us to a respect for nature, not in a sentimental way but with a deep feeling of kinship which will manifest itself in attitude and actions.

Witchcraft and Sex Magic

Witchcraft does not need to apologize for involving sex magic. It is other religions which need to apologize for the miseries of puritanical repression they have inflicted on humanity.

We are today in the commencement of a sexual revolution. People are at last beginning to wake up to the fact that they have a right to sexual satisfaction in this life; that they have no need to feel guilty about being human beings. I believe that one of the most important tasks of the Old Religion in our day is to help to nail the Great Lie which humanity has been told for so long: namely, that sex is something which was 'ordained' solely as a means of procreation within 'holy wedlock' and nothing else.

If all that was required was the continuation of the species, then the elaborate complex of sexuality, both physical and psychological, would not have been necessary on the part of nature. There are many organisms in this world, from the amoeba upwards, which procreate by means of simple fission or by virgin birth; but they are all on the lower rungs of the ladder of evolution. The joys and pangs of sexual love are something we have risen towards, not fallen into.

I think, too, that there is a profound truth in the slogan (originated, I believe, by the Young Liberals in this country), 'Make love, not war'. Is it really a coincidence that the hideous events of killing and maiming which have taken place in Northern Ireland within recent years have come to pass in a community which is ruled in a religious sense by anti-sex repression, both Catholic and Protestant? Let us look, too, at other countries where horror and bloodshed abound. How often do we see this accompanied by a sexual ethic which advocates repression?

It is often said today that we live in a violent society. (We always have done, but people are beginning to notice it). What is the root cause of mindless violence? One of the causes, at any rate, is the sheer pressure of natural desire denied its natural satisfaction, especially among the young. In spite of the so-called permissive society, the majority of people of all ages today are not free in a sexual sense. Even when social customs, divorce laws and so on have been relaxed, even when contraception is more freely available than it was before, people are still imprisoned behind the bars of their own minds. They are still in bondage to the false teaching and illusory concepts which they have unquestioningly accepted in their formative years. Moreover, this bondage is often something the people themselves are not conscious of; it applies even to many who regard themselves as enlightened and progressive.

Sheer promiscuity, however, is not the answer to the real sexual needs of anyone. It is quality, not quantity of experience which brings sexual harmony into a person's life. If it were not so, then the happiest and most well-balanced people would be prostitutes and playboys; when, as a matter of fact, they are usually insecure and neurotic.

There is an indefinable magical element about sex, which people have been conscious of ever since the beginning of time. This is why it has always been hedged about with so many rules and regulations by those who have sought rulership over their fellow humans. In particular, the subjugation of woman, the dangerous temptress, has been built into most of the world religions of our day. Yet anthropology and the study of comparative religion and folklore have revealed that long ago the position was reversed. Once upon a time matriarchy, not patriarchy, was the ruling custom of society; descent was traced, not through the father, but through the mother. Religious authority was held not by a high priest, but a high priestess.

Not long ago, admission of women into the priesthood was discouraged by the Church of England on the grounds that priestesses were associated with the orgiastic types of religion. In the Old Religion of witchcraft, however, the priestess still retains her ancient dignity; though I personally consider that neither half of a polarity should be dominant over the other, otherwise the situation is bound to become unbalanced. Working in true polarity is a potent magical operation, because each stimulates and brings out the best in the other. Dion Fortune has written extensively about this question of polarity, on both the physical and the more subtle planes of existence. Most of her work was written back in the 1930s; but while I emphatically disagree with some of her more dogmatic statements, nevertheless her books are still very well worth reading. She could not express herself too frankly, as she had to compromise with the social attitudes of her day; but she clearly recognizes the antiquity of the relationship between sex, religion and magic.

Social attitudes in our own day are sufficiently relaxed for a most significant exhibition to have been held in recent years at the Hayward Gallery in London; an exhibition which in Dion Fortune's time would have resulted in instant prosecution and closure, but in our own was sponsored by the Arts Council of Great Britain. I refer to the exhibition of art associated with the eastern cult of Tantra, held in the autumn of 1971, which has served to awaken a lively interest in Tantric ideas among occultists and other seekers for truth in the western world.

Like witchcraft, Tantra has in the past been associated with 'unspeakable rites', 'nameless orgies' and so on. In fact, one of the earliest writers about Tantra who addressed himself to readers in Britain, W. Ward, whose book *A View of the History, Literature and Mythology of the Hindus* was published in 1822, literally could not bring himself to describe what actually happened at a Vamacharin Tantric circle! He hinted that a naked woman was the object of worship, but added that 'Here things too abominable to enter the ears of man, and impossible to be revealed to a Christian public' were contained in the Tantra Shastras.

It was left to an extraordinary adventurer named Edward Sellon, who was famous for his contribution to the rich field of Victorian pornography, to bring a full description of the material side of Tantric ritual to the west. His book *Annotations Upon the Sacred Writing of the Hindus* appeared, privately printed, in London in 1865. Although materialistic and inadequate, Sellon's presentation of Tantra had considerable influence, notably upon the author and student of Rosicrucian matters, Hargrave Jennings and through him upon the American occultist, Paschal Beverly Randolph, who regarded Jennings as 'one of the master Rosicrucians of England'.

The spiritual side of Tantra was first described in books having any wide degree of publication among English-speaking people by Sir John Woodroffe, who wrote at first under the pen-name of 'Arthur Avalon'. His book *Shakti and Shakta* set out to defend the Tantras from their detractors, both British and Hindu. In it he describes the worship of the pre-Aryan Great Mother Goddess of the ancient East, in terms which are often strongly reminiscent of the practices of European witchcraft, though he shows no signs of being aware of this.

However, in *Shakti and Shakta* we read of the secret circle, often held at midnight, in which men and women worshippers were seated alternately. It was under the direction of a leader, and the object of adoration was a beautiful naked priestess who was regarded as the incarnation of the goddess. A ritual meal was partaken of, which was followed by sexual intercourse as an act of worship to the divinities invoked. This ritual was called the *Panchatattva*, meaning the Five Elements, because the constituents of it symbolized earth, fire, air, water and spirit or *Akasha*. It was also called the *Panchamakara*, or 'Five M's', because each of these constituents according to its name in Sanskrit began with the letter M: wine (*madya*), meat (*mangsa*), fish (*matsya*), grain (*mudra*), and sexual union (*maithuna*). The wine corresponds to the element of fire, the meat to that of air, the fish to water, the grain to earth, and sexual union to spirit.

The word Tantra simply means a treatise, something spread abroad, from the root *tan*, meaning 'to spread'. There are both Buddhist and Hindu Tantras, the earliest surviving complete texts being Buddhist, and dating to about A.D. 600. Scholars differ among themselves as to whether the ideas of the Tantras were originally Buddhist or Hindu; but the truth may well be that they are older than either religion and that both Buddhism and Hinduism have adapted them to their own purposes. The great stronghold of Tantric practice in India is Bengal, while Tantric Buddhism was widely practised in Tibet and is still to be found in the countries which border upon that land.

It is the Tantras which contain the descriptions of the subtle bodies of man and woman, which surround and interpenetrate the physical body. These subtle bodies are a complex network of energies, which contain power centres or *chakras*. The latter are likened to wheels or to flowers, hence they are sometimes called lotuses. The diagrams of the subtle body bear an obvious resemblance to the western mystical diagram of the Tree of Life as depicted in the books of the Cabbala.

The Tantras also contain intricate mystical diagrams called yantras, which are used as objects upon which to concentrate in meditation. The most revered of these is *Sri Yantra*, an intricate arrangement of interlaced triangles. Both the pentagram and the hexagram, widely used by medieval magicians of Europe, appear among the Tantric yantras.

All these mystical diagrams have for centuries been drawn and painted in bright, glowing colours by Tantric devotees, and many beautiful examples of them were on show in the exhibition mentioned above. Exhibited also were many remarkable sculptures showing gods and goddesses united in sexual embrace, as one of the Tantric doctrines is that the universe is the manifestation of the *Lila* or love-play of the god Shiva and the goddess

Shakti. As the material symbols of these two great cosmic principles on the physical plane, the Tantrics revere sculptured representations of the *Lingam* and *Yoni*, the male and female genitals.

A similar idea is represented in a less obvious form in Tantric Buddhism by the two symbols of the *vajra* or 'thunderbolt' and a little bell of similar size hanging among the beads of the Buddhist rosary.

These basic ideas of the great cosmic sacred marriage and its reflection at the human level, of the use of the sexual act as a sacrament and an act of worship, taken in conjunction with the antiquity of Tantric teaching and practice, seem to indicate that what became Tantra in the east became witchcraft in the west. Certainly, the Tantric *chakrapuja*, or circle of worship, bears resemblance to the practices of the witches' Sabbat, both of today and yesterday.

An even more striking reminiscence of the witches' Sabbat is to be found in the stories of the Hindu god Krishna and his moonlight revels with the cow-girls of Brindaban. Among the exhibits at the previously-described exhibition of Tantric art was a painting of the *Rasa Mandala*, or ecstatic round-dance of Krishna and the cow-girls by the light of the full moon in the forest glade. By his magical power, Krishna had provided a male dancing partner for each girl who was the semblance of himself, while his partner was Radha, his favourite beloved. The resemblance to the joyful moonlight revels of witches needs no stressing.

Moreover, Krishna himself bears a remarkable resemblance to the Greek god Pan, as previously mentioned in Chapter 1. Both are manifestations of the Universal Form as described in the famous passage of the *Bhagavad Gita* and often depicted in Indian art. Both are associated with round dances at the full moon and with fertility ceremonies, Pan with the Lupercalia and Krishna with the spring-time Holi festival. Both are musicians, Pan playing the mysterious music of his seven-reeded pipes in the depths of the forest, while Krishna, in the same way, plays upon his flute and enchants all who hear its sound. Both are associated with orgiastic revelry, Pan with the nymphs and Krishna with the Gopis or cow-girls. Both were probably ancient fertility gods, who were adopted into later and more sophisticated pantheons.

The erotic love between Radha and Krishna is a favourite theme of Indian painting and poetry. All of which, it seems to me, makes it very strange that present-day followers of Krishna decry sexual love and devote themselves to celibacy. However, the same puritanism and anti-feminism seem to have swept over the east as they did over the west, giving the whole bent of eastern religion (officially, at any rate) a repressive, anti-sex bias, so that some modern Hindus have actually been ashamed of the erotic glories of their ancient art and the subjugation of women has been elevated to a virtue. The ancient cult of Tantra in its Vamacharin or 'left-hand' form has become more or less secret, its followers having gone underground like the witches did. 'Left-hand' in this sense simply means those circles who celebrate their worship with actual sexual intercourse, and are so called because the woman who represents the goddess sits upon the left hand side of the male worshipper.

Moreover, the actual texts of the Tantras as we have them today have been edited and interpolated by Brahmin and Buddhist copiers, while their English translations, where these are available, have sometimes been what Philip Rawson, the distinguished authority on Tantra, has called 'bowdlerized'. In his informative introduction to the catalogue of the Hayward Gallery exhibition, Philip Rawson has confirmed the antiquity of Tantric ideas which had been previously noted by Sir John Woodroffe. He states that some of the archaic elements of Tantra are as ancient as the palaeolithic caves of Europe, the depicted emblems of which they closely resemble. As we have seen, the witch cult of western Europe can claim to be derived from the same level of antiquity, upon the same evidence.*

Even the artificial phallus, allegedly used by medieval witches and indignantly denounced by churchmen in various early books of penances, makes its appearance in the cult of Tantra. Another of the exhibits at the Hayward Gallery was a *lingam* or sacred phallus carved out of rock crystal and engraved with a representation of the *Sri Yantra*. We are told that it was probably used as an initiation instrument for female followers of the cult. One remembers the accounts recorded from the confessions of European witches of the ice-cold phallus of the Devil, which Margaret Murray speculated could have been an artificial penis used as part of a ritual.

Those Westerners who have derived their ideas of Eastern religion and mysticism from the writings of Madame Blavatsky and other Theosophist authors may well be surprised and even shocked to encounter the beliefs and practices of Tantra. Helena Petrovna Blavatsky was a truly remarkable woman, whose

* Many pictures of objects from this exhibition, together with an excellent summary of the basic ideas of Tantra, will be found in *Tantra: The Indian Cult of Ecstasy* by Philip Rawson (Thames & Hudson, London, 1973).

achievement in arousing the interest of Europeans in the ancient wisdom of the East cannot be denied; but her attitude to sexuality was contemptuously puritanical. Hence the Tantric philosophy could only be dismissed by her as 'phallicism' and 'black magic'. The Tantras are indeed much concerned with magic; but magic is black or white according to the intention of the operator and the way in which its forces are used. The sexual content of the Hebrew Cabbala aroused Madame Blavatsky's dislike, for the same reason.

Moreover, even many Indians came to regard Tantric mysticism with revulsion, when the influence of European education was brought to bear upon them. When Sir John Woodroffe, who was a Justice of the High Court of India at Calcutta in the late nineteenth century, wrote about Tantra, he was in the position of having to defend the ancient Tantric lore and practices against the combined attacks of European missionaries and high-caste Hindus, who were trying to get the cult banned. Hence his books tend to excuse the sexual content of Tantric ritual, while emhasizing the lofty spiritual philosophy behind it.

In our own day, it may well be felt that much less of such excuse is needed. We can see for ourselves the rightness of the claim in the *Mahanirvana Tantra* that the Tantric path is the path of attainment for the men and women of the *Kali Yuga*, or Dark Age, in which we live. We may appreciate the statement made in the Tantras that 'by that by which men fall, by that they rise'. Modern psychology has unmasked the puritan and the prude. It remains for us to find the way of true harmony and happiness in natural things.

It must not be forgotten, however, that not all people are capable of rightly performing Tantric rites, just as not all people are capable of rightly appreciating the rites of witchcraft. There will always be some who, because of their own lack of spiritual evolution, will pervert witchcraft into black magic and crude sensuality, or turn it into a means of exploiting others, just as they would anything else they took up in their unevolved state. They will have to suffer the *karma* they make for themselves and learn by it.

As we have already noted in Chapter 2, the Tantrics recognize this fact of human nature very clearly. They divide humanity into three dispositions or *bhavas*. There is *Pashu-bhava*, or animal disposition, corresponding to *Tamas-guna*, the qualities of grossness and darkness; *Vira-bhava*, or heroic disposition, corresponding to *Rajas-guna*, the qualities of activity, force, fieriness; and *Divya-bhava*, or divine disposition, corresponding to *Sattva-guna*, the qualities of balance, harmony, perfection. The three types of qualities or *gunas* have some analogy with the salt, sulphur and mercury of the alchemists. The fact that Tantric worship is not 'merely an excuse for sex orgies', any more than genuine witchcraft is, although the enemies of both accuse them of being so, is shown by the fact that the Tantrics regard the men and women of *Vira-bhava* and *Divya-bhava* alone as being competent to take part in the *Pancha-tattva*. One of the Tantras, quoted by Sir John Woodroffe in *Shakti and Shakta*, defines *Vira-bhava* thus: 'He is a Hero who has controlled his senses, and is a speaker of truth; who is ever engaged in worship and has sacrificed lust and all other passions.'

The *Pashu*, on the other hand, is the person who is bound, as the word comes from the root *pash*, meaning to bind. There are various descriptions of the bonds, but they are generally enumerated as pity (that is, in a contemptuous, belittling sense, not true compassion), ignorance, shame, family, custom and caste, as well as the cruder forms of greed and dishonesty. It is an interesting footnote to the legend of Krishna already referred to, that when Krishna is said to have stolen the clothes of the bathing Gopi girls and made them approach him naked, he was really removing the bonds of ignorance and all the artificial coverings which are imposed on men and women in this manifested world, which is called in the East *sangsara*, the world of appearance. This incident gives a further meaning to the custom of ritual nudity, which is found in the east as well as the west.

It was not only in the East that the ideas which have come to be called Tantric have been found. Europe, too, had its secret sexual cults in medieval times, other than the obvious one of witchcraft. Omar Garrison, in his book *Tantra: The Yoga of Sex* has noted the occurrence of Tantric ideas among the troubadours of Southern France. These were the singers and poets of courtly love and chivalry, who flourished in the twelfth and thirteenth centuries. In Northern France they were called *trouvères*, both words meaning 'finders', as they were supposed to find old songs and legends and present them in their music and poetry. They were often in bad odour with the Church and were accused of heresy. Ultimately the Pope launched the notorious Albigensian Crusade against the heretical cults of Southern France, extirpating them in circumstances of horrific cruelty. This led to the decline of the troubadours, but not before they had made their mark upon European culture, notably in their exaltation of womanhood and romantic love.

Omar Garrison notes that the troubadours had a special name

for their relationship with a beloved and adored woman. They called it *donnoi*. Examination of troubadour literature makes it clear that *donnoi* was something more than what we generally regard as romantic love. The troubadour literally adored his lady, especially naked, in a way reminiscent of the Tantric adoration of the naked *Yogini* (female practitioner of Yoga). She was his inspiration, from whom he drew his power to sing, play and compose poetry and music, just as the *Yogini* is the *Shakti* or power-giver and incarnation of the goddess to the Tantric, or as the naked priestess is the incarnation of the goddess in the circle of the witches. Nor did the troubadour necessarily desire to consummate his adoration by sexual intercourse. He regarded his lady as the other pole of a working polarity, from whom flowed subtle rejuvenating magnetism—an idea reminiscent of those contained in the writings of Dion Fortune, already referred to.

The source of this undercurrent of ideas of sexual magic is a mysterious one; but the connecting link may be the Sufis. Although contained today within the sphere of Islam, the Sufi mystics maintain that their cult preceded the Islamic faith and goes back to unknown ages. It is, in fact, they say, the secret essence of all religions. Southern France would have been open to the influence of Sufi mysticism through its proximity to Spain, in the days when that country was largely under the rule of the Moors. There was a cult in the Arab world called the Beni Udhra, which taught a peculiar form of sexual magic very similar to that of some Buddhist Tantrics.

These, unlike many of the Tantrics of India, teach a form of magical sexual union wherein the man and woman are united but the man retains control over ejaculation and the flow of semen. Thus, instead of striving for a climax, the couple remain blissfully united, prolonging the act almost indefinitely until the man's erection subsides. A similar practice in the Western world has come to be known as *karezza*, a word borrowed from the Persian language. Among the Beni Udhra, the technique of prolonging the sexual act by the control of emission was known as *imsak*. Among all the practitioners of this form of sex magic, both Eastern and Western, remarkable claims are made for its supposed benefits, both physical and by enabling both partners to attain higher states of consciousness; though it should be said that some sexologists regard *karezza* as harmful.

The techniques by which control is maintained are regarded as among the most important secrets of sexual magic. Briefly, however, judging from the accounts of such things to be found among the sexual literature of the East, they centre around the simultaneous restraint of breathing, thought and semen. Breathing and movement are both slowed down as a climax seems to be imminent, until the crisis is passed. One account says that to distract the mind by fixing it upon mental pictures of peaceful landscapes, lakes and mountains, will restrain it from striving for a climax as in ordinary sexual intercourse. Instead, the minds of both partners will pass into a gentle borderline state, in which psychic and spiritual perception will become possible. Physically, this kind of intercourse is believed to bring about prolonged youthfulness.

Magical sexual intercourse of this kind was believed in and practised from very ancient times, throughout the Eastern world. In China, it became associated with the doctrines of the Yin, the Yang and the Tao, or the cosmic feminine, the cosmic masculine and the perfect balance of the two great principles, the interplay of which is described in the *I Ching*, which is probably the oldest surviving system of divination to be still in actual use. A fascinating novel about China in olden times, based upon the system of sex magic described above, has appeared in recent years; namely, *The Pearly Essence*, by Jonathan Quayne.

To return to the question of the Sufi mystics and their possible connection with the secret sex cults of medieval Europe, it is interesting to note that the supposed centre from which all this curious esoteric lore was diffused, according to the Eastern accounts, is Shambala, the legendary hidden city of Asia where dwell the great adepts in whose hands lie the keys of magic and mysticism. According to one version, Shambala is somewhere near what is now Afghanistan; and Afghanistan is one of the great strongholds of Sufism.

Now, the great culture-hero of Tibet, Padma Sambhava, who brought Tantric Buddhism to that country, is supposed to have arrived there from Shambala in the eighth century A.D., together with his two wives and other followers. In some ways, Padma Sambhava is a Sufi-like figure, with his deliberate defiance of accepted customs and morals, for which some modern writers about him have been impelled almost to apologize. He is a much more colourful character than most saints, either of East or West. His magical powers, his almost shamanistic practices, his wide travels, his relations with women, are all described in detail in surviving stories of him. Moreover, the Buddhism of Tibet makes great use of music and ritual dancing, which the Sufis are famous for also. Considering all these matters, one is compelled to ask whether there may be after all some truth in the legend of one great and ancient centre, perhaps the relic of forgotten prehistoric civilizations, from which the magical and mystical traditions of Europe and Asia have been diffused over a long period of time, by wandering unknown masters like the Sufis and whoever was the real-life original of the Padma Sambhava stories.

Among the most famous, or notorious, practitioners of sex magic in Europe in the twelfth and thirteenth centuries were the Knights Templars. This closed brotherhood of knights, who were extirpated by the powers of Church and State for alleged heresy and sexual immorality, came into contact with Sufis, among the Moslems at the time of the Crusades. The Templars' vast wealth, power and arrogance may well have moved the king of France to proceed against them; but there are some unexplained matters in the history of the Knights Templars, notably a donation of 3,000 gold pieces paid to the Templars by the Syrian branch of the Assassins, or Hashishin as their Arabic name was. The Templars were repeatedly accused of secret collaboration with the Saracens, as well as of such strange matters as worshipping an idol called Baphomet, which they were alleged to regard as being the giver of wealth to the order and of fertility to the earth. In the old church of Saint-Merri in Paris is a sculpture representing a horned and winged demon displaying both male and female characteristics. According to oral tradition this statue depicts the Knights Templars' 'idol', Baphomet.

It seems possible that this old carving was the original inspiration of the well-known engraving of Baphomet by the French occultist, Eliphas Levi. It is really a version of the old concept of the horned god, a fact which recalls the statement made in the charges against the Templars that they regarded Baphomet as being the giver of wealth and fertility. They were also accused of being secretly permitted to indulge in what their opponents regarded as 'all kinds of licentiousness': or as Aleister Crowley put it in much later years: 'Do what thou wilt shall be the whole of the law'.

It is certain that the Knights Templars were a law unto themselves; that their rituals were held in secret; and that they had friendly contacts with the Saracens, to the extent of being influenced by Islamic culture. Even after their suppression in 1307, the Templars were still feared. The story goes that their last Grand Master, Jacques De Molay, just before he was burned at the stake, solemnly cursed both the Pope and the King of France, who had combined to suppress the order, summoning them to appear with him before the tribunal of God before another year had passed; and that within the space of the succeeding year both Pope and King were dead. The curse of the Templars was said to remain throughout the centuries upon the French royal house, a theme which was recently dramatized in a series of historical plays for television called 'The Accursed Kings'.

This mixture of historical mystery, secrecy and magic was a natural inspiration to Aleister Crowley, who took 'Baphomet' as one of his magical names when he became the head of the English branch of the Order of Oriental Templars, or to give it its Latin title, *Ordo Templi Orientis*, abbreviated to O.T.O.

The O.T.O. had been formed in Germany in 1902 by a wealthy German business man named Karl Kellner, in association with three fellow occultists, Theodor Reuss, Franz Hartmann and Heinrich Klein. Kellner professed to have received the secret teachings of sexual magic upon which the order was founded from three oriental adepts, one of whom was an Arab while the other two were Hindu. He claimed that the order was derived from the tradition of the old Knights Templars, who had also used and guarded these secrets. Because the founders of the O.T.O. were all high-ranking Freemasons, the Order had a ritual resembling that of Freemasonry, though with its own interpretation of it. An official manifesto declared that the teaching of sexual magic explained all the symbolism of Freemasonry and of all systems of religion.

When Crowley rose to a position of influence in the O.T.O., he rewrote all the rituals for the English-speaking branch of it in accordance with his own views and the message of his inspired manuscript, *Liber Legis*, the Book of the Law. It is noteworthy that instead of commemorating the murder of Hiram Abiff, as the third degree of orthodox Freemasonry does, the third degree of the O.T.O. commemorates the death of the Sufi martyr, Mansur El-Hallaj, who was executed as a heretic from Islam in A.D. 922.*

The sex magic secrets of the O.T.O. were incorporated not into ritual but into certain teaching papers which were given to initiates upon their admission to the higher degrees. In addition to these Crowley wrote a treatise, *De Arte Magica*, in 1914, with the sub-title *Epistola anno belli universalis ne perdat arcanum scripta* (Written in the year of universal war, that the secret might not be lost). The teaching papers referred to above are to be found within the book edited by Francis King. The secrets, in theory at any rate, are therefore secrets no longer. The question remains, does sex magic of this kind really work?

* See *The Secret Rituals of the O.T.O.*, edited and introduced by Francis King (C. W. Daniel Co., London, 1973).

One writer, at any rate, fervently maintains that it does. This is Louis T. Culling, a follower of the Crowleyan tradition, who is the author of *A Manual of Sex Magick*. Mr Culling also maintains that many alchemical writings are really a disguised form of sex magic instruction, coded so that only initiates would realize their true import, while others imagined them to be concerned with the transmutation of metals, the search for the elixir of life and so on. It will be remembered in this connection that alchemical symbolism also greatly interested the psychologist Carl Gustav Jung, who felt that something more was involved in the complex and often beautifully executed drawings and paintings which illustrated alchemical manuscripts than the search for gold which was allegedly the alchemists' quest.

Crowley and his followers also made use of alchemical terms to describe the operations of sexual magic. The male organ was called the athanor and the female the cucurbite, both names of alchemical vessels. The word 'athanor' is derived from the Arabic *at-tannur*, meaning 'the furnace', with its obvious association with the purest male element, fire. 'Cucurbite' is from the Latin *cucurbita*, meaning 'a gourd', after the original alchemist's vessel used in distilling, which was shaped like a gourd; that is, a containing vessel in which an alchemical transmutation could take place. The semen was called 'the blood of the red lion', from Leo, the fixed sign of fire; while the female secretion which lubricates the vagina at the time of sexual excitement was called 'the gluten of the white eagle', the eagle being the esoteric symbol of Scorpio, the fixed sign of water, the purest feminine element.

The semen was also called 'the serpent' or 'the lion-serpent', the latter being an old Gnostic symbol. It is indeed rather curious that the Gnostics had an emblem of an egg encircled by a serpent as a symbol of universal life, long before modern medicine and microscopy revealed the secrets of the ovum and the spermatozoon.

The mingling of the male and female fluids during sexual intercourse produced what was called 'the first matter', which was believed to be transmuted by ritual and by the concentrated mind-power of the participants into 'the elixir', which was then partaken of and consumed by both as a sacrament. ('Elixir' is again from the Arabic, the words *al-iksir* meaning the Philosopher's Stone, by means of which base metals were turned to gold and wonders accomplished.)

It is this to which Aleister Crowley refers in the cryptic phrases of that chapter in his book *Magick in Theory and Practice*, which is entitled : 'Of the Eucharist and of the Art of Alchemy' :

The highest form of the Eucharist is that in which the Element consecrated is One.

It is one substance and not two, not living and not dead, neither liquid nor solid, neither hot nor cold, neither male nor female. . . .

The highest sacrament, that of One element, is universal in its operation; according to the declared purpose of the work so will the result be. It is a universal Key of all Magick.

This practice is also mentioned in the oldest Buddhist Tantra, the *Hevajra,* which describes how the master administers this sacrament : 'Then with thumb and fourth finger he drops the *bindu* (semen) in the pupil's mouth.' The Tantra called the *Karpuradistotram* also advocates the partaking of the mingled sexual fluids by the male partner in the ritual from the vagina of the female, which is precisely the Ninth Degree Instruction of the O.T.O.* However repugnant sexually inhibited people may feel this practice to be, it is undoubtedly of great antiquity in the realm of magic.

The Ninth Degree O.T.O., probably so enumerated to correspond with the Ninth Sephira, *Yesod,* 'Foundation', which is associated with the genital organs of Adam Kadmon, the universal man of the Cabbalistic system, and with the sphere of the Moon, which rules the sexual fluids, was the essential instruction and central rite of the whole system. But the instruction of the Eighth Degree also contained information about the use of autosexual acts in magic; while Crowley himself, in accordance with his own proclivities, added an Eleventh Degree which was concerned with homosexuality and *coitus per ano,* or as he put it, *per vas nefandum,* 'by the forbidden vessel'. (The Tenth Degree was merely honorary, conferring status upon the Head of the Order.)

By the time Crowley contacted Gerald Gardner, the O.T.O. as a functioning order had practically ceased to exist, except upon paper. Initiation into it consisted of being given the rituals and other papers to read. These were passed on to Gerald Gardner by Crowley while Crowley was resident at Hastings during the last period of his life. Hence, when Gerald Gardner's novel, *High Magic's Aid,* was published in 1949, the author proclaimed himself on the title page to be a member of the O.T.O.; but the only actual O.T.O. sex magic that I ever encountered in the witchcraft rituals as perpetuated by Gerald Gardner was that of the Ninth Degree, and then without the sacramental consumption of the elixir. He regarded the mental concentration and

* *See* the books on Tantra by Omar Garrison and Philip Rawson already referred to.

visualization of the participants, directed upon the object of the rite and reaching its climax during orgasm, to be sufficient.

I have myself, when younger, taken part in rituals of this kind, though performed privately and not in the presence of the rest of the coven; and the end for which they were performed was attained. As always, of course, much depends upon the conditions and the mood of the participants; when these are right, the magic works.

With regard to the morality or otherwise of taking part in such rituals, the witches have a saying : 'The circle of the coven is between the worlds; and what takes place between the worlds is no concern of either world' (or as some versions give it, 'no concern of this world').

As I mentioned in the introduction to this book, Gerald Gardner gave me his original Book of Shadows. At that time, these matters of which I have written in this chapter were kept very secret, as the discussion of such things was much more obscured by prejudice than it is today. Nor were the secret instructions of the O.T.O. available in print, as they are now. I feel that times and circumstances have changed sufficiently for me to be justified in quoting here directly from old Gerald's Book of Shadows, certain passages which were written in code :

It is important to work naked from the start, so it becometh as second nature, and no thought 'I have no clothes' shall ever intrude and take your attention from the work. Also, your skin being so accustomed to unconfinement, when power is given off the flow is more easy and regular. Also, when dancing you are free and unconfined. . . .

And the greatest of all, the touch of the body of your beloved thrills your inmost soul, and so your body gives out its utmost power; and then it is most important of all that there is not the slightest thing to divert the attention, for then the mind must seize and mould the power generated, and redirect it to the desired end with all the force and frenzy of the imagination.

It has been said that no real knowledge may be gained our way, that our practices are such that they can only lead to lust; but this is not really so. Our aim is to gain the inner sight, and we do it the most natural and easy way. Our opponents' aim is ever to prevent man and woman loving, thinking everything that helps or even permits them to love is wicked and vile. To us it is natural, and if it aids the Great Work it is good.

'Tis true that a couple burning with a frenzy for knowledge may go straight to their goal, but the average couple have not this fire. We show them the way, our system of props and aids [i.e., magic ritual]. A couple working with nothing but lust will never attain in any case; but a couple who love each other dearly should already be sleeping together, and the first frenzy of love will have passed, and their souls will already be in sympathy. If the first time or two they do stay a while to worship Aphrodite, 'tis only a day or two lost, and the intense pleasure they obtain only leads them again to the mysteries of Hermes, their souls more attuned to the great search. Once they have pierced the veil they will not look back.

This rite may be used as the greatest of magics if it be done both partners firmly fixing their minds on their object and not thinking of sex at all. That is, you must so firmly fix your mind on your object that sex and all else are naught. You inflame your will to such an extent that you may create a strain on the astral that events happen. . . .

Today, under the influence of such writers as Alan Watts, whose philosophy has had considerable effect, especially upon the younger generation—for instance, his book *Nature, Man and Woman*—a new outlook upon sex is gradually developing, very different from that which prevailed when the above words of Gerald Gardner's were written. Yet in those words we can see the commencement of it. The idea of sensuality has ceased to be opprobrious, except among very 'uptight' people. Instead, its true meaning is being restored : the capacity to respond to the senses, especially the sense of touch; the feel of another person's naked body, the colour of a flower, the music of a waterfall, the flow of air, the earth under one's feet, the slow rhythm of movement, the scent of sandalwood and musk. People can pleasure each other by stroking and caressing, instead of 'the sex act' being something which had to be got over as quickly as possible by striving for a climax. All the universe is a sex act; to take part in sex is to partake of the nature of the universe in its deeper sense, beyond time and form. This is the old philosophy of the Tantras, which is being rediscovered.

Not only witchcraft groups, but many other groups, including those devoted simply to the attainment of better human understanding, are adopting practices incorporating this philosophy. They are exploring the possibilities of 'cool sex', as opposed to 'hot sex' which is genitally centred and organized upon the basis of being something which a man does to a woman and to which she submits. 'Cool sex', on the other hand, involves all of the senses; sexuality is generalized, instead of being urgently concentrated in the genitals and striving for relief. To be relieved of something is to wish to be rid of it and to obtain that wish—

the other side of the coin of Puritanism. 'Cool sex' enjoy sex for its own sake and wishes to prolong its enjoyment.

Among such groups, the Sanskrit word *maithuna* has come to be synonymous with 'cool sex', though it actually means simply sexual intercourse. *Maithuna* neither strives for nor seeks to prevent orgasm, on the part of either the man or the woman. In these days of the Pill, it has no need to; nor does present-day sexology give much support to the old-fashioned theories current among Puritans of East and West about the alleged debilitating effects of the outflowing of semen. Moreover, many sexologists believe that the absorption of the male semen by the woman is actively beneficial to her, quite apart from it fecundating properties; a benefit of which, until the coming of the Pill, women were often deprived.

A favourite attitude for *maithuna* is that which is described among western Tantrics as the Yab-Yum position, while among witches it is known as the Pyramid position. It is particularly adapted for use in a magic circle, where conditions of space sometimes make lying at full length inconvenient; though some witches bring a small couch or mattress into the circle for sexual rites and lay it across the circle from east to west, in front of the altar which is placed in the north and facing south.

The Pyramid position is very similar to that in which the Tibetan Tantric deities are often depicted in statues, hence its alternative name of Yab-Yum. The man takes his place in the circle, either cross-legged or kneeling, whichever he prefers (in the actual Yab-Yum statues, the male is in the so-called lotus posture of yoga, but few Westerners can manage this). Then the woman sits astride him so that his erect penis penetrates her vagina. She twines her legs around him and the couple embrace.

The woman will be the more genitally active partner; but both will caress each other and gaze into each other's eyes until they seem to have become one being. If the man's erection wanes, the woman's body will still contain him. They will experience the true meaning of 'intercourse'—a flowing between. Their interchange of vital energies will create a new aura around them, more potent than either of them individually. Sometimes they will actively embrace, sometimes rest with hands hanging over each other's shoulders, listening to the music of each other's silence, like a tree rooted in the earth while the wind flows through its leaves. There is little need here to give instruction in this kind of intercourse, because instinct will do that better. Nor will there be any need to judge whether success has been attained, because the participants will know by their own feelings the trembling of the veil.

Some general indication, however, of the value of this state may be taken from the fact that one set of participants regard about two hours as the *minimum* time of communion. In that time, the illusion of duality has been transcended by unity. The Two become One. The One becomes Nought—No-thing and All-things.

Apart from the insight behind the veil of matter afforded by this kind of sexual magic, the practice of *maithuna* is said to confer mental and physical benefit upon both partners, and to arouse the latent psychic powers which dwell naturally in us all. It stimulates the responses of all planes of being: spiritual, psychic, mental and physical.

It will be seen from the foregoing how naturally it has followed, in accordance with the evolving trends of the Aquarian Age, that modern witches should adapt the Tantric sexual magic for use in their own private magical circles, instead of the mass seasonal orgies of ancient times. Everything in this world is flowing, as the old Greek philosopher said. Nothing stands still, nor does time go back upon itself; but it proceeds in a spiral, ascending upon itself. The spiral has gone round again, to its ancient place, but higher. What appears to be borrowing from another tradition is really the reuniting of many things which have proceeded from a common source.

What actually is the common source of the magical tradition we do not know; perhaps the legendary city of Shambala is really situated in the universal unconscious of humanity. Perhaps so too is the sunken water city of Atlantis. On the other hand, I have endeavoured in this book to trace some, at least, of the shadowy outlines of the magical path, travelling as it does through the realms of witchcraft, ritual magic, alchemy and mysticism, back to our earliest beginnings in the cave sanctuaries of the Stone Age. Yet I feel that we still have a great deal to learn about our own history and the past of the human race. The witches have a tradition that their craft came from the East; but who knows? If you travel far enough east, you will find yourself back on your own doorstep. 'What is here is elsewhere. What is not here is nowhere.'

WISE AND BLESSED BE.

Liber Umbrarum

A Book of Shadows

Casting the Circle

Preliminary Instruction

The usual rite for casting the circle is as follows, when working indoors. The procedure outdoors will, naturally, be slightly different; but most people will commence their witchcraft working in their own homes.

You will need a small table or chest, to serve as an altar. This should be placed in the middle of the space where you intend to work. Ascertain, with a compass if necessary, the position of the four cardinal points, north, south, east and west, and arrange your altar to be four-square to them, or as close to this as you can reasonably get.

Work by candle-light; but place your candles carefully, so that they are not likely to catch anything on fire (be particularly careful of swirling cloaks or robes, if you are not working in the nude). Ideally, you should have four candles round the room, placed east, south, west and north, and one upon the altar. However, if this is not practicable, then have just two candles upon the altar, or simply one large altar candle, if this gives sufficient light.

The ideal width for a magic circle is nine feet across. The old way to draw it was to get a cord four-and-a-half feet long, with a loop at one end. Then the witch took her black-hilted knife, the athame, and stuck it in the centre of the floor. In olden times, this floor was probably made of hard-packed earth, or of flag-stones with interstices between them large enough to take the blade of a knife. The witch took the cord, slipped the loop over the athame, and proceeded to use the free end of the cord to draw the circle, with the aid of a bit of stick or chalk. Thus automatically she had a nine-foot circle; and she then placed in the centre the small table, box or stool she used as an altar. At the end of the rite, the circle was obliterated to prevent discovery.

Today, we usually have to improvise as best we can. Some people get a roll of plain carpet, on which they paint their circle. When they want to perform a ritual, they simply unroll their carpet on the floor, and roll it up again and put it away when the ritual is over. Others mark out a circle on their carpet with tape or twine. Others cut one out of felt and lay it on the floor, removing it again when they have finished.

Use your own ingenuity; but whatever you do, remember that you must consecrate and visualize the magic circle afresh each time you work. It is your effort and visualization that make a magic circle, not material things like twine or carpet.

Arrange the things you will need upon the altar. These will include your Book of Shadows, a censer or bowl of incense, a bell, the pentacle with its witchcraft symbols, and a small cauldron or a bowl to represent one, which should be half-filled with water. If you use a bowl, it should be black inside, as this makes a useful scrying instrument for clairvoyant vision. There should also be a small platter or bowl of clean earth or sand, to represent the element earth. You will probably also like to have a cup of wine to drink a toast to the Old Gods at some point in the ceremony.

If you do not have an actual censer or thurible to burn incense, then use joss-sticks or incense cones. Burn them in a metal bowl which has been partly filled with sand, so that the joss-sticks can be stuck upright into the sand, or the incense-cones placed upon it. The little oriental brass bowls which can be found in curio and bric-à-brac shops are ideal for this. Have spare incense available, so that it can be replenished as necessary.

None of these articles needs to be large; but they should be of good quality. If you buy second-hand things from curio shops to use in your ritual practice, always clean them well before you use them, to get rid of other influences that may be upon them. A good way to cleanse an article of unwanted influences, as well as cleaning it, is to place it for a while upon freshly dug earth, in bright sunshine. The more important things you use should be consecrated, and a ritual for this is given further on.

Remember, nothing you use for ritual should be used for anything else. Have a box or cupboard for your ritual things, and keep them wrapped up and put away when not in use.

Remember also that when you move in the circle you should move *deosil*, that is, sunwise or to the right. The other direction, *widdershins*, or to the left, is generally regarded as belonging to the realm of sinister, averse magic and cursing. The word 'sinister' literally means 'left' or 'to the left'.

The Ritual

Light the candles and the incense. Then take your ritual weapon, the staff, the sword or the athame, and charge it with the power

of the four elements of life, thus. Standing before the altar, raise up the weapon, and then touch with it the platter of earth and say :
I call Earth to bind my spell.
Wave the weapon in the air, and say :
Air to speed its travel well.
Hold the weapon over the smoke of the incense, and say :
Bright as Fire shall it glow.
Dip the point of the weapon into the cauldron or bowl of water, and say :
Deep as tide of Water flow.
Hold the weapon upright again, and say :
Count the elements four-fold,
In the fifth the spell shall hold.
Now, draw the circle with the magical weapon, tracing over the place where it is marked on the floor. Start at the east, then turn right-handed to the south, then to the west, then to the north, and so back to where you started. As you draw, visualize power pouring from your weapon in a jet of blue flame, and leaving a trail of blue astral fire behind it, so that your circle is a strong thought-form in the realm of the subtler forces. Go around the circle like this three times, chanting this rune :

Black spirits and white,
Red spirits and grey,
Hearken to the rune I say.
Four points of the circle, weave the spell,
East, south, west, north, your tale to tell.
East is red for the break of day,
South is white for the noontide hour,
In the west is twilight grey,
And north is black, for the place of power.
Three times round the circle's cast.
Great ones, spirits from the past,
Witness it and guard it fast.

Then take up the bell, and pass again round the circle, starting at the east. Call upon the Great Ones who have gone before, saying :
I summon, stir and call ye, ye Mighty Ones of the East, the guardian spirits of witchdom, to witness these rites and to guard this circle.
Pass to the south, and say :
I summon, stir and call ye, ye Mighty Ones of the South, the guardian spirits of witchdom, to witness these rites and to guard this circle.

Pass to the west, and say :
I summon, stir and call ye, ye Mighty Ones of the West, the guardian spirits of witchdom, to witness these rites and to guard this circle.
Pass to the north, and say :
I summon, stir and call ye, ye Mighty Ones of the North, the guardian spirits of witchdom, to witness these rites and to guard this circle.
At each invocation, strike a note upon the bell, so that it reverberates, and as the sound dies away, you seem to hear it echoing upon the Inner Planes. The bell should not be loud, but resonant and musical. It may be struck with the back of the athame, if this produces the right note.
Complete the round of the circle to the point where you started (always do this). Then replace the bell upon the altar, and take up the censer of incense. Pass round the circle with it, east, south, west and north as before, and hold up the smoking incense at each quarter, as an offering to the guardian spirits.
The return to the centre of the circle, lift up the censer on high, and say :
In the height and in the deep,
Watch and ward eternal keep.
Replace the censer upon the altar, and strike once upon the bell.
Thus the magic circle is formed, and it is then ready for such rites as you choose, whether of initiation, clairvoyance, travelling in the spirit vision, consecration of weapons or talismans, or whatever work or celebration is to take place.
At the end of the ritual, close the circle by formally thanking the Old Ones for their protection. Do this by taking the censer of incense and offering it up at the four quarters as before, starting at the east and saying :
Guardians of the East, I thank you. Hail and farewell.
Pass to the south, and say :
Guardians of the South, I thank you. Hail and farewell.
Pass to the west, and say :
Guardians of the West, I thank you. Hail and farewell.
Pass to the north, and say :
Guardians of the North, I thank you. Hail and farewell.
Complete the circle back to where you started, and then return to the centre. Lift the censer upwards, and say :
Guardians of the Height, I thank you. Hail and farewell.
Replace the censer on the altar, and say :
Guardians of the Depths, I thank you. Hail and farewell.
Strike once upon the bell, and say :

The Rite is ended.
Then extinguish the altar candles first, before any others.

A Note Upon the Four Elements
The four elements of life, earth, water, air and fire, are considered to have a relationship to the four heavenly quarters, or cardinal points. This depends upon the nature of the four winds, as they affect a particular place. In Britain, a time-honoured attribution is:

East–Air (cold and dry)
South–Fire (warm and dry)
West–Water (warm and wet)
North–Earth (cold and wet)

A great elemental being, or *Deva,* a guardian of each of the four elements, is sometimes associated with each appropriate cardinal point of the circle.

Many practitioners of magic make a mental contact with the appropriate element at each cardinal point of the circle. That is, suppose they are using the elemental attributions given above, they would visualize and attempt to feel and hear rushing wind at the east, great flames of fire at the south, rivers and waterfalls or the sea at the west, and green hills or ploughed fields with their birds and animals at the north.

The fifth element, from which the other four emerge and into which they return, is Spirit, which the Eastern people call *Akasha.*

The colours here given for the cardinal points, namely red for east, white for south, grey for west and black for north, are the traditional colours of 'the four airts', the old Celtic name for the four heavenly quarters. The idea that the north is the place of power is also Celtic, and dates from pre-Christian times. Hence the Christian church was somewhat distrustful of the dangerous pagan powers of the north. The attribution of the colour black to the north derives from the fact that it is the place of midnight, 'the witching hour'.

The Rite of Self-Initiation

Preliminary Instruction
The Rite of Self-Initiation should be performed either on one of the Great Sabbats, or one of the Lesser Sabbats, or on a night of the full moon, or in the time of the waxing moon.

Have the room warm, as you should work in the nude for this ritual, in token of stripping off all inhibitions and frustrations of the past. You may, however, wear such magical jewellery as appeals to you. In particular, a woman should always wear a necklace in the circle, as the goddess of witchcraft, whose living representative she is, wears one in most ancient representations we have of her. Diana of Ephesus, for instance, is shown wearing a necklace of acorns; Adya-Kali, the great mother goddess of the Tantrics of India, is naked, 'clothed in space', save for her jewels and the Garland of Letters, the sacred Sanskrit alphabet, which she wears as a necklace. A man may prefer to wear a lamen; that is, a magical pendant with perhaps his astrological birth-sign upon it, or a symbol such as the ankh cross.

In addition, you may have a cloak to wrap around you when you sit in meditation; but for the more active part of the ritual the cloak should be discarded.

You will need all the things already described in the rite of forming the circle, and also a staff of oak, ash, rowan or thorn wood, preferably one which you have cut yourself on the night of the full moon. The circle is usually drawn with the sword or the athame; but as you have not yet got an athame, in this case you must use the staff. You will also need a small flask of anointing oil. This should always be pure vegetable oil; plain olive oil will do, though you may prefer to use a scented oil such as sandalwood.

The Ritual
Form the magic circle according to the instructions already given. Then stand with arms upraised, facing north, and repeat the Eleven-fold Invocation of the Word of Power, ABRAHADABRA:

> *This is the day, this is the hour,*
> *Cry aloud the Word of Power—*
> *ABRAHADABRA!*
> *By blazing noon or black midnight,*
> *It is my will to seek the light—*
> *ABRAHADABRA!*
> *Be far hence, all things profane,*
> *From the portals of this fane—*
> *ABRAHADABRA!*
> *Eleven-fold the right I claim,*
> *By the virtue of this Name—*
> *ABRAHADABRA!*
> *Faring forth adventurous,*
> *By the pathway perilous—*
> *ABRAHADABRA!*

Fend me from the fear of fear,
By the Voice of the Chief Seer—
ABRAHADABRA!
Show within the darkest night
The Extension of the Light—
ABRAHADABRA!
Great Ones who have gone before,
Speak the Blessing evermore—
ABRAHADABRA!
Here between two worlds am I,
Child of the earth and sky—
ABRAHADABRA!
Deeply do I dare assay
One step on the mystic way—
ABRAHADABRA!
Aid me from the realms above,
Powers of Life and Light and Love—
ABRAHADABRA!

Take the flask of anointing oil and pass it three times through the smoke of the incense. Then perform the three anointings: firstly upon the forehead, in the place of the third eye (that is, in the centre of the forehead, just above the place where the eyebrows meet; known in the eastern tradition as the *Ajna Chakra*). Then upon the breast, over the heart; and lastly upon the genitals. With the first anointing, say: *Let the mind be free.* With the second, say: *Let the heart be free.* With the third, say: *Let the body be free.*

Do the anointing by putting a spot of oil upon your finger, and making with it an X-shaped cross. This is the Rune *gifu*, meaning a gift or blessing. (In ancient times, this rune was carved upon drinking cups, because it was believed to protect people from poison. We still use the X-shape to represent a loving kiss.)

Now kneel before the altar, still facing north, and repeat in a low voice the following Invocation:

By night's dark shade, and by this ritual hour,
Most ancient of the Gods, on you I call.
Remembrance of past lives in me awaken,
That day's delusion no more shall enthrall.

I claim my life, my liberty, my light,
Part of all life that flows eternally.
I am the microcosm of the Whole,
Kindred of star and stone and greenwood tree.

Awake in me the power to do my will,
Kindle within me love's eternal flame.
Accept me as your own, a pagan soul,
O Powers of Life, that did this Cosmos frame.

Pause for a moment in silence, with bowed head. Then change to a comfortable sitting position, cross-legged. Wrap yourself in a cloak, if you wish. Now begin mentally to formulate yourself and the altar as the centre of a mandala. Think to yourself something like this: 'The infinity of the height and the infinity of the depth. The infinity of the east and the infinity of the west. The infinity of the north and the infinity of the south. The circle whose centre is everywhere and whose circumference is nowhere. I and that Centre are One.'

Sit thus with eyes closed, in complete silence and stillness. Clear your mind as far as possible of all thought, even that of trying to achieve a higher state of consciousness. I cannot give you any directions for this, except those of the ancient Tibetan sage, Tilopa: 'Do not imagine, think, analyse, meditate, act; keep the mind in its natural state.'

You may find that the natural state of your mind is something much more wonderful than you knew!

It is in this time that your real self-initiation will take place, if your aspiration is sincere and the other conditions are conducive to it. You may feel yourself to have touched, even if only for a brief moment, upon a higher state of consciousness. You may see some vision in the mind's eye; if so, a description of it should be written down immediately after the ritual is ended, as it is sure to have a meaning, even if this is not immediately apparent.

The length of this period of silence and stillness is up to you. Your own spontaneous feeling will tell you when it is time to end it. When it does, rise up, light fresh incense if necessary, and cense round the circle, deosil, raising the censer at the four quarters.

Then return before the altar, and repeat this Affirmation:

I am unique. There is no one else exactly like me. And yet I am One with the whole of Nature.
I have the right to be what I am. My essential Self is divine and beautiful. I have the right also to be better than I am, that the outer manifestation may be more true to the inner reality.
Beloved Pan, and all the other gods who haunt this place, grant me beauty in the inward soul, and may the outward and the inward life be at one.

Then break into a dance of rejoicing, deosil, round the circle. Let yourself go; clap hands, or shake the sistrum if you have one,

or a tambourine, and chant these words and sounds over and over
again :

O IO PAN!
O IAO!
IA IA ARADIA!
IO EVOHE KERNUNNO!
IO EVOHE DIANA!

(You will find that this chant falls into a natural rhythm. It is
pronounced like this : O ee-oh Pan! O-ee-ah oh! Ee-ah ee-ah
A-rah-dee-ah! Ee-oh ee-voh-ay Ker-nun-no! Ee-oh ee-voh-ay
Di-an-ah!)

Do any steps you like, so long as you enjoy them. Keep it up
until you are out of breath and want to stop. Then drop down in
front of the altar, and lie there until you have got your breath
back, and feel able to rise.

Take the wine, and end the ceremony by drinking a toast to
the Old Gods : 'To the Old Ones! Merry meet, merry part, and
merry meet again !'

Sit for a few minutes more in meditation, if you like, just en-
joying the atmosphere of the circle, the incense and the candlelight,
and the sense of being naked and free. Then close the circle
according to the form already given, by thanking the Old Ones
for their protection, censing with the incense, striking upon the
bell, and extinguishing the altar lights.

A Note Upon the Words of Power
ABRAHADABRA is the true version of the ancient Word of
Power, of which the popular 'Abracadabra!' as used by con-
jurers is just a faint and far-off echo. It is a word of eleven letters, five vowel-sounds and six consonants, signifying the Great
Work, the union of the Microcosm (five, the pentagram), with
the Macrocosm (six, the hexagram). Its Cabbalistic numeration
is 418, and much elucidation of it will be found in *The Qabalah
of Aleister Crowley*. It is the numerical equivalent of *ATh IAO*,
'the essence of IAO'; and also its digits added together, 4+1+8,
add to 13, the witches' number, the Cabbalistic equivalents of
which are *Achad*, 'Unity', and *Ahbah*, 'Love'.

It also contains the meanings of 'the Voice of the Chief Seer'
and 'Speak the Blessing'.

Iao is the ancient magical name of the Supreme God, containing both masculine and feminine elements within Itself.

Pan is the ancient Greek god whose form was universal: *to
Pan*, 'the All'. He was the horned, goat-footed god of nature and

the joy of life. Kernunno is a version of the name 'Cernunnos', the Celtic horned god, similar to Pan, who was worshipped in Western Europe, including Britain, in pre-Christian times.

Aradia is the name of the moon goddess of the witches of Italy. She was described as the daughter of Diana; this probably means simply that she is a later version of the ancient moon goddess Diana, who in the old myths was the secret lover of Pan. Her still-surviving legends were collected by the great American folk-lorist, Charles Godfrey Leland, and published by him under the title of *Aradia: or the Gospel of the Witches*.

There is just a chance that the name 'Aradia' is Celtic in origin, connected with *airidh*, the summer pastures to which the cattle were driven at Beltane (1 May), and from which they returned to winter quarters at Samhain (1 November). The Celts originated in central Europe, and spread south into Italy, as well as westwards to Spain and the British Isles.

IO EVOHE, IO and *IA* are some of the ancient cries or calls used by the ecstatic worshippers in the mystery cults of long ago.

THE RITE OF CONSECRATION

Preliminary Instruction
Having learned how to form a magic circle, and performed the Rite of Self-Initiation, you are now ready to consecrate your working tools and magical weapons.

This work of consecration can be carried out on one of the Ritual Occasions, and is better if it be done so; but if necessary to further your practice of the craft, it can be done at any time.

With regard to the number of the working tools or magical weapons, they can be many or few, as you require. The essential ones, however, are the staff, the athame, the cauldron, the pentacle and the cord; because these represent the four elements of life and the quintessence, or spirit. The staff corresponds to fire, the cauldron to water, the athame to air, the pentacle to earth, and the cord to spirit. The first four, in their essential nature, also correspond to the four suits of the ancient Tarot cards, the wands, the cups, the swords and the disks.

The four elements are also mystic symbols of human life. Fire is the life energy, the element most closely allied to spirit. Water is the feelings and instincts, the emotional life. Air is the mind, and earth is the physical body.

This is why witches and magicians use the magical sword. It is the weapon of air, and represents the power of thought. However, because of the danger of having a magical sword in the times of persecution, and the difficulty of obtaining a specially forged sword, unpolluted by association with war, witches came to use instead the athame, a large black-hilted knife. This could easily be disguised as a simple kitchen knife, especially if the owner was a woman; whereas a sword, in the hands of anyone except a person of rank, would immediately arouse suspicion.

In the same way, a witch's staff or riding-pole, with the end carved, as it often was, in the shape of a phallus, could be disguised with a bunch of twigs to look like a common broomstick. The cauldron was just a cooking-pot, the cord a length of twine or a garter; while the pentacle was made of wax or wood, which in an emergency could be quickly destroyed in the kitchen fire, or else it was a stone which could be buried.

Today, there is less need for the tools of magic to be either disguised or expendable, so they can be somewhat more elaborate if you wish, and openly adorned with magic signs; though simple tools, well cared for, will serve you just as well. It is the power of a magical instrument to create atmosphere, the aura which it bears, that matters.

The pentacle can be painted in red upon a piece of smooth wood, according to the design in the illustration, and finished off with a coat of clear varnish, or it can be engraved upon metal.

The staff you will have already cut, and a good black-hilted knife is not difficult to obtain. There is no need for the knife to be very sharp, but it should be pointed, and capable of practical use for cutting herbs, etc.

If you are lucky, you may find a real old-fashioned 'gypsy-pot', or small three-legged iron cauldron. Otherwise, a black or dark-coloured earthenware bowl will do (other kinds of metal than iron are not really suitable, with the exception of silver, the moon's metal, which is somewhat expensive!)

The cord should be scarlet, the colour of the lifeblood of men and animals, and hence the colour of life. During your ritual working, if it is not being used for anything else, the cord may be worn like a garter, tied round the left leg above the knee.

The Ritual

Form the circle according to the ritual already given. Then take the working tool or weapon to be consecrated, and hold it up with both hands over the altar, saying :

I take and consecrate this—(name the instrument), *in the name of the Old Ones, unto the arts of magic.*

Sprinkle the instrument with a little water from the cauldron,

using a sprinkler of herbs if you wish, and saying :
I purify you with water.
Then hold the instrument in the smoke of the incense, and say :
I consecrate you with fire.
Then repeat the Prayer of Consecration :

> *I conjure you, O form of this instrument, by the Powers of*
> *Life that have created the heavens, the earth and the sea, and*
> *all things which they contain; by the virtues of the heavens,*
> *and of all the stars which rule therein; by the virtues of stones*
> *and herbs; by the virtues of the four elements; and in like*
> *manner by the virtues of the four winds of the air; herein to*
> *receive such consecration that we may obtain by you the*
> *perfect issue of our will. I conjure you to be a strength and*
> *defence against all enemies, visible and invisible, in every work*
> *of magic. So may it be.*

Hold the instrument closely for a few moments, breathe on it,
and will power into it.

The newly-consecrated instrument should, if possible, immediately be made a token use of. Thus, the athame should be
used to draw the circle, the cauldron should be gazed into and
passes with the hands be made over it, as if for scrying, and so on.
If no other token use is convenient, then carry the newly-consecrated object deosil around the circle, lifting it up at the four
quarters.

Explanation of the Pentacle and its Signs
The five-pointed star or pentagram is one of the oldest signs in
the world. It represents, among other meanings, magic itself, the
dominion of the spirit over the four elements of the material
creation.

The circle which encloses it, being without beginning or ending, represents infinity and eternity. Another meaning of the
pentagram is that it bears a rough resemblance to a human figure,
as if standing upright with arms and legs outstretched. Hence the
pentagram in a circle is a symbol of the human being in relation
to the infinite.

The eight-armed figure in the centre of the pentagram represents the Eight Ritual Occasions of the witches' year, four Greater
Sabbats and four Lesser Sabbats. The Greater Sabbats are
Candlemas, May Eve, Lammas and Hallowe'en. The Lesser
Sabbats are the equinoxes and solstices. The eight of this symbol
plus the five of the pentagram makes thirteen, the traditional
number of the witches' coven.

The three X-shaped crosses around the pentagram represent

the three anointings of the initiation ceremony, 'two above and one below'; that is, two above the waist and one below it.

The Pentacle

The two spirals or S-shapes represents the ancient symbol of the twin serpents, the dual forces of positive and negative, *yang* and *yin*, masculine and feminine, that underlie all manifestation.

The symbols on the three upper points of the pentagram are the two crescents of the waxing moon and the waning moon, and the circle of the full moon. Together they represent the primordial goddess of nature, often depicted in triple form as nymph, mother and crone, the three phases of the moon.

The symbols on the two lower points of the pentagram represent the two aspects of the ancient god of the witches. They are conventionalized drawings of a horned head and a skull and crossed bones. The former sign represents the horned god of life and fertility, and the latter the god of death and what lies beyond.

The Full Moon Esbat Rite

Form the circle in the usual manner. Then dance round the circle, deosil, nude if you wish, chanting the words used in the Self-Initiation Ceremony:

O IO PAN!
O IAO!
IA IA ARADIA!
IO EVOHE KERNUNNO!
IO EVOHE DIANA!

Do this in a joyful manner, for as long as you will. Remember, the meaning of the Esbat is rejoicing. The word is derived from the Old French *s'esbattre*, 'to frolic'; so leave your cares behind and rejoice.

Then rest by reclining or sitting cross-legged on the floor in front of the altar. When you feel sufficiently rested, take the winecup and consecrate the wine to drink a toast to the Old Gods.

Stand before the altar, and lift up the athame over the cup, grasping the hilt with both hands. Then say:

As the athame is the male, so the cup is the female, and conjoined they bring blessedness.

Lower the point of the athame into the cup, so that it dips into the wine. Then shake the drops of wine from the athame on to the floor within the circle.

Lay the athame upon the altar and take up the wine-cup. Lift it up and say:

To the Old Ones! Merry meet, merry part!

Take a sip of the wine, and then say: *May we be joined fivefold with the Ancient Ones. With the wine for taste.* (Take another sip of the wine, and then replace the cup upon the altar.) *With the candle for sight. With the incense for smell. With the pentacle for touch.* (Touch the pentacle upon the altar.) *With the bell for hearing.* (Take up the bell and strike a note upon it, listening until the sound dies away.)

This rite is known as the Communion of the Five Senses. When it is completed, light more incense if necessary, and cense around the circle, deosil, lifting up the incense at the four quarters.

Replace the censer upon the altar, and then recite the following Invocation, reading it from your Book of Shadows:

Diana of the rounded moon,
The queen of all enchantments here,
The wind is crying through the trees,
And we invoke thee to appear.

The cares of day departed are,
The realm of night belongs to thee;
And we in love and kinship join
With all things that are wild and free.

As powers of magic round us move,
Now let time's self dissolve and fade.
Here in the place between the worlds
May we be one with nature made.

Thy consort is the Hornèd One,
Whose sevenfold pipes make music sweet.
Old Gods of life and love and light,
Be here as merrily we meet!

For ye the circle's round we tread,
And unto ye the wine we pour;
The sacred Old Ones of this land,
Ye we invoke by ancient lore—

By magic moon and pagan spell,
By all the secrets of the night,
Dreams and desires and mystery,
Borne on the moonbeams' silver light.

Now may we hear, or may we see,
Or may we know within the heart,
A token of true magic made,
Ere from this circle we depart.

Pause—and wait in silence, with eyes closed if you wish. There may come a sound, an outward manifestation, an inner vision, or a message or impression received by the inner mind. Any such should be recorded as soon as possible after the rite has ended.

When your own spontaneous feeling tells you to do so, end the period of silence by bowing towards the altar, and saying :

O goddess-queen of night,
O Hornèd One of might,
In earth and sky and sea
May peace and blessing be!

Now relax and sit or recline upon the floor again, and finish the wine in the cup. Pour some more if you wish, and sit and meditate and enjoy the atmosphere of the circle. You may care to try scrying, or reading the Tarot cards or the I Ching, or some other magical experiment. Or, if you wish, play some appropriate music—anything which you enjoy, and which is conducive to the occasion.

If you are working with another person, your partner in magic, this is the point at which you may, *if you both wish*, make love within the circle, and mentally offer your pleasure as homage to the Old Gods, who are happy to see people happy. (A ritual for initiating others will be given further on.)

If you need to leave the circle and re-enter it for any purpose, say to fetch something, then when you have returned inside re-draw the circle, deosil, with the athame, starting at the east.

If you wish to do any particular magical work, then complete this first, and make love with your partner as the end and consummation of the Esbat.

Close the circle in the usual manner, according to the ritual already given.

Notes
If it is too cold to work comfortably in the nude, or if for any other reason you prefer to be clothed, do not wear your ordinary clothing in the circle. Wear instead a suitable cloak or robe, and sandals or soft slippers. The traditional witches' robes were black, with a hood, something like a monk's robe, the idea being that in the old times of persecution the witches could steal through the shadows to their meeting-place in these robes without being seen. Even if they were seen, one hooded figure looked very much like another, and there was less chance of being recognized. They would, of course, have been going along moonlit country lanes and through woods, rather than along lighted streets as we know them today.

The wine used for the toast may be whatever you prefer.

THE SABBAT RITE

Preliminary Instruction
In the witches' year there are four Great Sabbats and four Lesser Sabbats, so that the year is divided up like a wheel with eight spokes.

The Great Sabbats are Candlemas (2 February), May Eve (30 April), Lammas (1 August), and Hallowe'en (31 October).

The Lesser Sabbats are the spring equinox, the summer solstice, the autumn equinox, and the winter solstice. These are not fixed dates, but vary a little each year, because they represent the times when day and night are equal, and also the longest day and the shortest day. These depend upon astronomical calculations; but the spring equinox is around 21 March, the summer solstice is around 21 June, the autumn equinox is around 21 September, and the winter solstice is around 21 December. The Druids also celebrated these occasions, and to them the winter solstice was known as *Alban Arthan,* the spring equinox as *Alban Eilir,* the summer solstice as *Alban Hefin,* and the autumn equinox as *Alban Elfed.*

Of the Greater Sabbats, May Eve is also known as Walpurgis Night. The name of Beltane, meaning 'bright fire', is also given both to May Eve and the summer solstice, because these dates were anciently celebrated with bonfires. An old name for the winter solstice festival is Yule, a word which has lived on as an alternative to the Christian 'Christmas'.

The Celtic people of Britain and Ireland called Candlemas *Imbolc* or *Oimelc,* May Eve *Beltane,* Lammas *Lughnassadh,* and Hallowe'en *Samhain.* These were the four great festivals of the pagan year, and are frequently referred to in Celtic mythology. (*Samhain* is pronounced *Sav-een.*)

You may, if you wish, decorate the room at each Sabbat with some flowers or branches appropriate to the season. If you have a worthy representation of the Moon Goddess and the Horned God, in the form of either statues or pictures, these too should be displayed somewhere in the room, with candles burning beside or in front of them.

As the Sabbat is a more important occasion than the Esbat, if the two dates should happen to coincide, or to fall so close to each other that it is not practical to celebrate them both, then preference should be given to celebrating the Sabbat.

There are two occasions in the year which are particularly potent for launching a new magical current. These are the spring equinox and the autumn equinox. (*See* Chapter 3.)

The Sabbat of Hallowe'en is particularly suitable for attempts to communicate with the spirits of those who have passed on, as this is the ancient festival of the dead, our ancestors and loved ones who have gone before. It is not, however, a grim occasion to pagans, but a time of cheerful remembrance and goodwill.

At Candlemas we celebrate the first signs of spring. On May Eve, we greet the coming summer. At Lammas, we rejoice at the beginning of the harvest. Hallowe'en is the commencement of winter, and the time when spirits are abroad. The equinoxes and solstices are the astronomical turning-points of the year.

By celebrating these old festivals, all of which can be traced historically to pre-Christian days, we declare our oneness with nature. We are not alienated; we belong here, and all life is one.

The Ritual

Form the circle in the usual manner. Then, standing before the altar, say : *Hail to the Sabbat of*—(give the name of whichever of the Sabbats it is). *Give heed to the Witches' Creed:*

Then recite the Witches' Creed, as follows, reading from your Book of Shadows :

The Witches' Creed

Hear now the words of the witches,
The secrets we hid in the night,
When dark was our destiny's pathway,
That now we bring forth into light.

Mysterious water and fire,
The earth and the wide-ranging air,
By hidden quintessence we know them,
And will and keep silent and dare.

The birth and rebirth of all nature,
The passing of winter and spring,
We share with the life universal,
Rejoice in the magical ring.

Four times in the year the Great Sabbat
Returns, and the witches are seen
At Lammas and Candlemas dancing,
On May Eve and old Hallowe'en.

When day-time and night-time are equal,
When sun is at greatest and least,
The four Lesser Sabbats are summoned,
Again witches gather in feast.

Thirteen silver moons in a year are,
Thirteen is the coven's array.
Thirteen times at Esbat make merry,
For each golden year and a day.

The power was passed down the ages,
Each time between woman and man,
Each century unto the other,
Ere time and the ages began.

When drawn is the magical circle,
By sword or athame of power,
Its compass between the two worlds lies,
In Land of the Shades for that hour.

This world has no right then to know it,
And world of beyond will tell naught.
The oldest of Gods are invoked there,
The Great Work of magic is wrought.

For two are the mystical pillars,
That stand at the gate of the shrine,
And two are the powers of nature,
The forms and the forces divine.

The dark and the light in succession,
The opposites each unto each,
Shown forth as a God and a Goddess:
Of this did our ancestors teach.

By night he's the wild wind's rider,
The Horn'd One, the Lord of the Shades.
By day he's the King of the Woodland,
The dweller in green forest glades.

She is youthful or old as she pleases,
She sails the torn clouds in her barque,
The bright silver lady of midnight,
The crone who weaves spells in the dark.

The master and mistress of magic,
They dwell in the deeps of the mind,
Immortal and ever-renewing,
With power to free or to bind.

So drink the good wine to the Old Gods,
And dance and make love in their praise,
Till Elphame's fair land shall receive us
In peace at the end of our days.

And Do What You Will be the challenge,
So be it in Love that harms none,
For this is the only commandment.
By Magic of old, be it done!

Then take up the pentacle, and pass deosil with it round the circle, holding it up at the four quarters, east, south, west and north, and repeating each time:

> *Eight words the Witches' Creed fulfil:*
> *If it harms none, do what you will!*

Replace the pentacle upon the altar, and strike once upon the bell, listening as the note dies away.

Now perform a slow dance, in silence, deosil three times round the circle, carrying the wand upright as a phallic symbol. On completing the first circuit, touch the platter of earth with the wand, and say: *Life to the earth!* On completing the second circuit, touch the cauldron of water with the wand, and say: *Life to the water!* On completing the third circuit, wave the wand in the air, and say: *Life to the air! Life, luck and love to pagans all!*

Then replace the wand upon the altar, and commence the round dance with the chant, followed by the Communion of the Five Senses, as at the Esbat.

Light more incense if necessary, and cense around the circle deosil, lifting up the incense at the four quarters.

Then perform such magical work as you wish to do, for example, consecration of ritual objects, scrying, divination, or working of spells. End the celebrations with lovemaking in the circle, if you wish, as at the Esbat. Close the circle in the usual manner.

Notes

The above is the basic pattern for the ceremony. Each coven may, and probably will, evolve its own particular variations. A coven will grow from the basis of, firstly, two people, a man and a woman who are partners in magic, and then such friends or relatives as they choose to invite to join them. When the coven has increased to more than the ritual number of thirteen, it should divide and form a new coven, and so on. The original founders will be the priest and priestess of the coven. When a new coven is formed, members will agree among themselves who is to leave the parent coven to form the new one, and they should elect a man and a woman to be the priest and priestess of the new coven. Thus the tradition has been carried on through the ages.

Two other important traditions are, firstly, that initiation into a coven should always be received from a person of the opposite sex; secondly, that the meeting-place of a coven should always be at least three miles from the meeting-place of any other coven, to avoid clashes of interest.

An exception to the first rule, however, is made in the case of one's own children. A father may initiate his son, or a mother her daughter, because your child is in a sense a part of yourself.

With regard to the phallic wand used in the ceremony described above, it was the custom in olden times to carve and round the end of the wand into the rough shape of a phallus, as a symbol of the powers of life and fertility. This shape was often disguised by having a bunch of twigs tied round it, hence the witch's broomstick. Sometimes the phallic appearance of the wand was produced by uprooting a young tree or sapling, and trimming the root into a suitable shape.

Initiation Into The Coven

Preliminary Instruction
All the rituals given so far are designed to be worked either by oneself or in the company of others. But as soon as you enter into partnership with another person, you have the nucleus of a coven. You may decide to remain simply a magical partnership, or go on to recruit other people.

Naturally, the utmost discretion is advisable, if you decide to take the latter course. Remember, you can do more with three people who have genuine enthusiasm and devotion, than you can with a dozen who are just there for a giggle.

Whether or not you decide to come out openly as a witch, or keep your beliefs and practices private, is entirely up to you. No one has the right to dictate to you upon this matter. There are, however, two considerations. One is that freedom of religion is your basic human right; the other is that if you do declare your adherence to witchcraft openly, you have spiked the guns of any blackmailers and bullies who may threaten to 'expose' you.

However, the other extreme of deliberate publicity-seeking generally defeats its own object, as people then cease to take you seriously. It is obviously ridiculous to swear people to preserve 'the secrets of the art', and then perform these so-called 'secret rites' before the cameras of the popular press.

It is also both ridiculous and dishonest to swear people to conceal facts about the Old Religion, such as the names of the Celtic gods of Britain, which they can discover for themselves in the local library. Yet both of these examples of foolishness have been followed by witches since witchcraft came out of hiding in Britain, following the repeal of the Witchcraft Act in 1951.

Your best rules of guidance are those derived from discretion and commonsense. Remember the wise words of Gautama

Buddha, who told his followers to 'take the Self as a lamp', and to 'work out their own salvation with diligence', accepting nothing on authority but only as it complied with their own reason and conscience.

With regard to the expenses of running a coven, these should be fairly shared among the members themselves, by mutual agreement. And if people cannot come to mutual agreement, about this or any other matter, then let the dissidents go off and 'do their own thing'. Do not go into the magic circle with any person with whom you are at enmity. Either be reconciled before you enter the circle, or one or the other of you should leave. Otherwise, your mutual 'bad vibrations' will destroy all magical work.

The founding members of the coven, the priest and priestess, should direct the rites. Which of them takes the leading part is less important than that the ritual should be well carried out. Some people have more practical aptitude for the performance of ritual than others.

Probably the best arrangement, however, is when the ritual actions and speeches are divided between both partners. For instance, the one who has a better speaking voice can be responsible for reading or reciting the invocations, while the other carries out the actions, such as censing round the circle or striking upon the bell. When other people are in the circle, they can repeat some of the ritual in the form of responses, and so on.

When a number of others are in the circle, beside the priest and priestess, they will of course join in the dancing, following behind the leaders. They should always be ranged man and woman alternately around the circle.

The old name given to the male leader was 'the Devil of the coven'; this was probably first bestowed by Christian persecutors, but seems to have been ultimately adopted by the witches themselves. The name probably arose from the fact that on the Sabbats and other important occasions the priest assumed his 'grand array', a costume of animal skins and a horned headdress, so that he really looked like the representative of the Horned God. There is no reason why the priest should not do this today, if he wishes.

The name given to the priestess was 'Queen of Elphame', or 'Queen of the Sabbat'. Elphame is an old word meaning the Land of Faerie, the pagan paradise. The priestess was also called the Maiden of the Coven. She was regarded as the representative of the Moon Goddess.

In addition to the priest and priestess, there was also, especially in larger covens, an Officer, who could be either a man or a woman. It was the Officer's job to attend to the business details, so to speak, and especially to summon people to the meetings.

When members of the Old Religion had acquired many years of experience, they were regarded as Elders. They might be too old to take a very active part in the rites, but they remained in the background and put their knowledge and experience at the disposal of younger folk.

These old names and offices seem quite practical to be continued in the present day. No one should grow too big-headed because they hold some rank in witchcraft; nevertheless, the holders of office are entitled to loyalty and respect. If you cannot respect them, do not elect them. If you do not like the way they do things, then take this book and get out and form your own coven—the more the merrier!

Candidates for initiation to the coven should be in good health both mentally and physically, and of legal adult age, preferably at least twenty-one years of age. Before the initiation, a new witch-name should be chosen for them by mutual agreement. In the case of self-initiation also, a new witch-name should be chosen for oneself.

The Ritual

Form the circle in the usual manner. The candidate should stand in the circle, nude, before the altar, while the priest or the priestess conducts the ceremony. The priest should initiate women candidates, while the priestess should initiate men, in accordance with the old rule that initiation into witchcraft should always pass from one sex to another. If other members of the coven are present, they should take their positions man and woman alternately around the circle.

The initiator should have the Charge of the Coven already written out in red ink upon a new piece of paper. This paper the initiator will read from, and it will then be ceremonially burnt, so the sheet of paper should not be too large or thick. It is written in red, because red is the colour of life, and in olden times magical sigils were frequently written in red as a means of symbolically giving life to them.

As in the ceremony of self-initiation, a small flask of suitable anointing oil will be needed, in order to put the three X-shaped marks upon the candidate.

The initiator commences by reading the Charge of the Coven to the candidate.

Initiator : *This is the Charge of the Coven:*

That you will keep secret what you are asked to keep secret, and never divulge the names or dwelling-place of our people unless by their consent.

That you will learn and try to master the Art Magical; but ever remember the rune: 'What good be tools without the inner light? What good be magic without wisdom-sight?'

That in due course you will strive to find a worthy pupil in magic, to whom in future years you can hand down the knowledge you acquire.

That you will never use the Art Magical merely to impress foolish persons, nor for any wrongful end.

That you will try to help the Craft of the Wise, and hold its honour as you would your own.

That you consider these vows taken before the Elder Gods; and that if you betray this Charge you accept as your just reward that retribution of destiny which overtakes those who basely betray the trust and confidence that others have placed in them. Know that none can escape the fate, be it curse or blessing, which they make for themselves, either in this life or in another life.

Will you answer truly this Charge, and keep it in your heart?

The Candidate should answer, *'I will'*. In the event of the candidate changing his or her mind, and not wishing to accept the Charge, the ritual should be brought to an immediate end, and they should be permitted without argument to leave the circle and depart.

If the candidate answers in the affirmative, then the initiator says: *'Kneel before the altar, place your hand upon this pentacle* (holds pentacle so that candidate can do this) and repeat after me:*"I have heard the Charge and understand it. I swear to abide by it. May the Old Gods witness my words".'*

The initiator replaces the pentacle upon the altar, together with the paper upon which the Charge has been written, and strikes a note upon the bell. Then the paper is taken and burnt in the censer.

Initiator: *As the smoke of this burning arises, so these words can never be revoked. By the earth and moon and sun, in name of magic be it done!*

The initiator then kneels besides the candidate, places his or her right hand on the candidate's head, and the left hand just beneath the candidate's knee as the latter remains kneeling.

Initiator: *Do you vow all between these hands to the Old Gods of witchcraft?*

Candidate: *I do.*

Initiator: *I will the powers of witchcraft into you.*

There is a pause in silence, while the initiator and the candidate kneel together thus, before the altar. This is the ancient traditional posture for the transmission of initiation. It should be held for some moments, until such time as the initiator spontaneously feels it is time to resume the ceremony. Then he or she should arise, and assist the candidate to arise also.

Initiator: *Arise and receive the witches' mark.*

The initiator then takes the flask of anointing oil, and marks the candidate three times with an X-shaped cross (the rune *gifu*, as in the rite of self-initiation), each time taking a spot of oil upon the finger for this purpose. The first mark is placed, as in the rite of self-initiation, in the middle of the forehead, the place of the 'third eye'; the second is placed upon the breast, over the heart; the third is placed upon the genitals. In giving the first mark, the initiator says: *Let the mind be free.* In giving the second, the initiator says: *Let the heart be free.* In giving the third, the initiator says: *Let the body be free. I give you the witch-name of—* (giving the witch-name that was chosen beforehand).

The initiator then embraces the candidate with the kiss of greeting.

Initiator: *I recognize you as a pagan. Be from henceforward as a stone of the ancient circle, standing firmly based and balanced upon earth, yet open to the winds of heaven and enduring through time. Coven's oath, keep troth!*

If others are present, they too should give the candidate the kiss of greeting, or a handshake in the case of men greeting another man. As they do so, each should repeat the words, *Coven's oath, keep troth!*

Then all should join in the round dance with the chant, as before described, followed by the consecration of wine and the Communion of the Five Senses. This may be followed as usual by magical work and/or love-making in the circle. The circle should be closed in the usual manner.

Notes

If the initiation is of one's own first-chosen magical partner, either man or woman, then the rite should certainly be ended by sexual intercourse within the circle; because it is preferable that the partners should be upon the intimate terms of lovers if they want to be able to work real magic together. Apart from this, however, no one should have to take part in love-making in the circle unless they wish to. Moreover, if you choose someone to be your magical partner, then they should know quite clearly from the beginning what is involved. In fact, it is preferable that you should already be either lovers or husband and wife.

Remember, people's bodies are their own. No one has the right, either by force or trickery, to violate them, especially in the name of magic. Remember also, however, that the Great Work of magic is the union of opposites, of which the union of male and female is one form, and that most potent, wherefore it is sometimes called the Great Rite.

In the event of someone who has already performed the rite of self-initiation, as given in this book, later wishing to become a member of someone else's coven, they should still go through this rite of initiation into the coven in full. It will serve the dual purpose of linking them in fellowship with the rest of the coven, and confirming before others what has already been done in private.

The Coven Spell

The coven spell is magical work performed within the circle by the assembled coven. It may be described as a battery of wills, each person visualizing the thing that the coven wishes to bring about, concentrating on it and willing it to happen.

Evidently, therefore, the object of the rite must be decided beforehand, and everyone must agree that it should be made to come to pass. They must be in earnest, and keep their minds all the time upon their objective, while the spell is being performed. The power of thought is a very real and potent force, for good or ill. It can be greatly aided by visualization, either actual or in some symbolic form, of the thing one wants to come about.

The circle is formed in the usual manner, and if the occasion is an Esbat or a Sabbat, the prescribed ritual should be performed, as already given. Then when the time for magical working has arrived, the coven sit cross-legged around the circle, man and woman alternately, and join hands. The leader sits in the centre, with his or her back to the altar, so that the altar light illumines the Book of Shadows and enables it to be read from. The coven should be seated in whatever is the most convenient way, according to the number of people present. If there is enough to make a complete joined circle, so much the better. If not, let them make a semi-circle facing the leader.

If the occasion is not a Sabbat or an Esbat, then there should be some ritual done first, to get the coven into the mood for magical working, and to raise power. Have at least the round dance first, and then the Communion of the Five Senses. It is best also, upon every occasion, to proclaim the object of the rite beforehand, so that everyone has it clear in their mind before sitting down to concentrate as described above.

In order to do this, the leader should pass round the circle, deosil, carrying the phallic wand. The coven form up, man and woman alternately, and follow behind the leader, pacing deliberately round the circle. Starting at the east, the leader lifts up the phallic wand at each of the four quarters, saying each time : *O guardian spirits of witchdom, we work this rite*— (proclaiming what the object of the rite is).

This deliberate pacing of the circle is called 'circumambulating'. It is different from the wild joyousness of the round dance. It is light yet purposeful, rather like a hunter stalking game. Ceremonial magicians, as well as witches, make use of it in their rituals; and Aleister Crowley, in one of his telling phrases, has described it as 'the pace of the tiger who stalks the deer'. It is sometimes performed to the measured beating of a small drum, so that it is half-pacing and half-dancing. Once the purpose of the rite has been proclaimed, the coven may continue pacing round the circle for a while, if the leader wishes, in order to work up more power before sitting down to concentrate in the manner described above.

When they do settle down cross-legged in the circle, they may care to put a burning candle in the centre, to provide a point to concentrate on. A short, heavy candle is best for this, with the light close to the floor. It should be lit before the recitation of the spell commences, and extinguished when the spell ends.

The leader reads the coven spell from the Book of Shadows, and again the measured beating of a small drum may be used to accompany the working, if the leader has an assistant who can do this. Of course, an experienced leader will soon know the spell by heart, and can then accompany himself or herself with drum-beats or hand-clapping. Each time the line : *We chant the coven spell, thus shall it be!* occurs, the whole coven joins in. They should be instructed in this beforehand, so that they know what to do. They will soon start to sway spontaneously to the rhythm of the chant; the whole thing should be performed rhythmically.

The Coven Spell

O ancient ones of heaven, earth and sea,
We chant the coven spell, thus shall it be!
To music of the night-wind blowing free,
We chant the coven spell, thus shall it be!

The owl hoots within the hollow tree,
The black cat runs by night and silently,
The toad beneath the stone dwells secretly.
We chant the coven spell, thus shall it be!

To moon that draws the tides of air and sea,
We chant the coven spell, thus shall it be!
To god that bides beneath the greenwood tree,
We chant the coven spell, thus shall it be!

By witches' garter bound about the knee,
By staff and cauldron and all powers that be,
We will the thing that in our minds we see,
We chant the coven spell, thus shall it be!

(At this point, all sit in silence for a time, concentrating hard and visualizing the thing they want to happen. Then the leader takes up the chant again).

The spell is flowing like the sea,
The spell is growing like the tree,
Like flame that burns and blazes free.
We chant the spell, thus shall it be!
We chant the spell, thus shall it be!
We chant the spell, thus shall it be!
IT IS!

On the second and third repetitions of *We chant the spell, thus shall it be!*, the whole coven joins in; and at the end, everyone cries out loudly *It is!* and claps hands. At this point, you *release* the spell into the astral plane. Let it go, and do not think about it any more at this time, or speculate on how or whether it is working. Otherwise, you will be like a man who plants a seed, and then keeps digging it up again to see whether it is growing or not.

For important or difficult matters, however, the spell may be repeated on three occasions. It is unusual for a spell to be repeated for more than three occasions, though this is sometimes done; but it is generally better to rest the matter if a spell has been done three times, and then take it up again later if necessary.

The circle should, of course, be closed in the usual manner at the end of this working.

The Seven-Pointed Star

The foregoing are the seven basic rituals which make up this Book of Shadows. The number seven has always been a magical and mystical number, in the occult philosophy of both east and west. Ancient India had its Seven Rishis, or wise men, and ancient Greece had its Seven Sages. There were the Seven Wonders of the pre-Christian world, and Christianity has its Seven Sacraments and Seven Deadly Sins, while the number seven occurs very frequently in the Bible. This sacredness of the number seven is taken from pagan sources, as it is found in the famous pagan romance, *The Golden Ass* by Lucius Apuleius, who was a priest of Isis. The story is a parable of his initiation, and he tells how he obtained a vision of the goddess upon the seashore by night, at the time of the full moon: 'Wherefore, shaking off my drowsy sleep I arose with a joyful face, and moved by a great affection to purify myself, I plunged my head seven times into the water of the sea; which number seven is convenable and agreeable to holy and divine things, as the worthy and sage philosopher Pythagoras hath declared.' (William Adlington's translation, 1566.)

There seems to be something basic about the number seven in nature. There are the seven colours of the rainbow, and the seven notes of the musical scale. Western science recognizes seven chief glands in the human body, called the endocrine glands; while Eastern yoga systems speak of the seven *chakras,* or centres of force, in man's subtle body.

Medieval astrology had its seven sacred planets: Saturn, Jupiter, Mars, Sun, Venus, Mercury, and the Moon or Luna. These are the seven *visible* heavenly bodies which make up our solar system, the planets Uranus, Neptune and Pluto not being visible to the naked eye. Strictly speaking, of course, the Sun and Moon are not planets, and are more correctly described as the two luminaries; but the term 'seven sacred planets' was used for convenience. Everything upon earth is under the governance, astrologically speaking, of these seven influences.

This is the reason why we have the seven-day week. Each day is ruled by one of the planets. The Sun rules Sunday, the Moon Monday, Mars Tuesday, Mercury Wednesday, Jupiter Thursday, Venus Friday, and Saturn Saturday. These rulerships go back to the days of ancient Chaldea and Babylon.

Also, in the northern hemisphere, we have the most conspicuous constellation of the night sky, the Plough, or the Great Bear (*Ursa Major*), which points to the North Star, and which consists of a group of seven bright stars.

Occult philosophy connects the number seven with the planes of the universe. There are four planes, corresponding to the four elements; but as each plane above the physical has both a higher and a lower aspect, the planes can be tabulated as seven:

7. Higher Spiritual	} Force : Fire
6. Lower Spiritual	
5. Higher Mental	} Form : Air
4. Lower Mental	
3. Higher Astral	} Force : Water
2. Lower Astral	
1. Physical	Form: Earth

The terms 'higher' and 'lower' in this connection are purely figurative. The planes are not places, but states of consciousness, and they are interpenetrating.

All of these manifold correspondences of the mystic number seven are summed up in the seven-pointed star, which some traditions in Britain regard as the sign of authority in witchcraft. These traditions connect it with seven qualities, which they regard as the seven basic requirements for attainment in magic: humility, respect, trust, kindness, truth, honour and dignity.

The seven-pointed star, therefore, makes a suitable lamen for the leader of the coven to wear. A lamen is an old term for a magical pendant worn round the neck so that it hangs upon the breast over the heart.

It is a notable fact that if the signs of the seven planets are written round the star in the order of their apparent motion, from Saturn the slowest moving to Luna which has the swiftest apparent motion, then by tracing along the lines of the star one sees the order in which the planets rule the days of the week, beginning with Sunday (the Sun), passing to Monday (the Moon), and so on ending with Saturday (Saturn).

The seven-pointed star or heptagram is not a very easy figure to draw quickly; so witches have reason to be grateful to the people who designed Britain's decimal coinage and gave us a seven-sided coin, the fifty pence piece. This provides us with an easy guide to drawing a small seven-pointed figure, from which a larger one can be elaborated. Hence the fifty-pence piece has come to be known in some circles as 'the witches' coin', just as the old twelve-sided threepenny piece was known as 'the astrologers' coin', because it provided the basis of a twelve-pointed figure for the signs of the Zodiac.

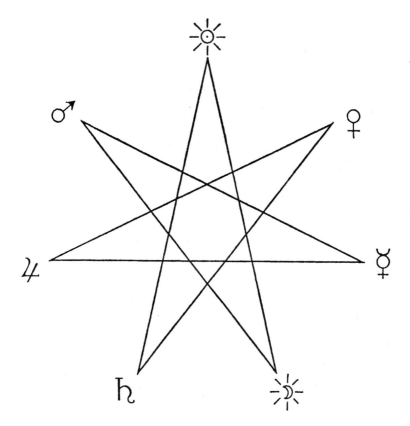

The Seven-Pointed Star

Seven is pre-eminently the sacred and mystical number. Most people are familiar with its popular connotations, such as the seven continents, the seven seas, and so on, and the belief that the seventh child of a seventh child has supernormal powers. But there is an important idea connected with this number which is less well known, and that is its association with the magic circle.

In the magic circle, we have the four quarters, or cardinal points, north, south, east and west, plus the height and depth, above and below. These are the six directions, and the centre of the circle, the place of stillness from which they all radiate, is the seventh.

Moreover, the occult traditions of ancient Egypt, and those of India and Tibet, declared the human being to consist of seven principles; not only the physical body which is apparent to normal sight, but other and more subtle bodies also, together with the mind which animates them. These beliefs were held centuries before the discoveries of modern physics, which have shown us that matter and energy are interchangeable terms, and that what we perceive as 'solid matter' is simply energy manifesting in a particular way.

The Runes Of Andred

The word 'rune' is used by witches in two senses. Firstly, as a rhyme which is recited or chanted during a ritual; secondly, as a letter of a magical alphabet. The Runes of Andred are the letters or signs of a magical alphabet which is named after the goddess Andred, who was worshipped in the area of the great forest called Coed Andred by the ancient British, and Andredsweald by the Saxons. Parts of this forest still remain in the southern counties of England, particularly in Sussex. It was once of great extent, stretching from Hampshire to Kent. This alphabet was originated by a Sussex coven, by whose permission it is reproduced here.

The significance of a magical alphabet is that it compels the writer to concentrate more deeply on what they are writing, because they have to express it in an unfamiliar and strange-looking script. It will be noted that the runes are arranged in two rows of thirteen. When written down in a witch's Book of Shadows, they should always be arranged thus, in order to connect them with the magic of the witches' number thirteen, and also with the 'twin pillars', the powers of male and female.

The way in which the runes are used is this. If the operator wishes to invoke some wished-for thing, they should choose the time of the waxing moon for the work. If instead their desire is to banish something, then the period of the waning moon should be chosen. (*See* Chapter 3.)

Then, taking a new, clean piece of paper or parchment, the operator first draws the appropriate symbol or sigil of the moon, waxing or waning as the case may be. The sigil of the waxing moon is a crescent with the horns pointing to the left. The sigil of the waning moon is a crescent with the horns pointing to the right.

Red ink should be used, in order to give potency to the writing, because red is the colour of life. Beneath the sigil of the moon, the operator writes down their wish, using the magical alphabet.

They must do this when they are alone, and cannot be disturbed; and they must keep the paper secretly, and show it to no one, or

A	=	▽	N	=	⊁
B	=	Ⴓ	O	=	⅂Ⴑ
C	=	Ϛ	P	=	ⴲ
D	=	ↆ	Q	=	▯
E	=	Ⲧ	R	=	ⴕ
F	=	⌐	S	=	Ɛ
G	=	ꝏ	T	=	↓
H	=	Ꞁꞁ	U	=	∩
I	=	Ꞁ	V	=	<
J	=	ⴹ	W	=	ꟽ
K	=	⋋	X	=	⅄
L	=	⏌	Y	=	⋔
M	=	ⴼ	Z	=	Ꝫ

The Runes of Andred

it will lose its power.

Then the writing should be hidden in a special box or a drawer, which should not contain anything else except perhaps some incense or scented herbs appropriate to the wish expressed. Witches of times past often used the little desks or bureaux which had small secret drawers in them, and one of the purposes of these secret drawers was to hide such written spells. A typical piece of furniture of this kind used to be on show in the Museum of Magic and Witchcraft, which was run by the late Gerald B. Gardner at Castletown, Isle of Man. It was among objects lent by an existing coven of witches, and possessed no less than seven secret drawers.

The paper or parchment should be kept thus for a lunar month, and then burnt. That is, when the moon returns to the same phase as it was in when the spell was written; say, so many days after new moon or full moon as the case may be. If the wish has not yet come to pass, the process may be repeated, another paper or parchment being prepared in the same manner, as often persistence and faith are necessary in order for the spell to work.

Each spell should be for one wish only. If the witch wants to work for more than one thing, a separate paper or parchment must be made for each matter.

The Runes of Andred, like other magical alphabets, can also be used for decorative purposes upon ritual objects, such as writing the name of a god or goddess, or some magical motto.

The Spell of the Cord

By the knot of one
The spell's begun.
By the knot of two
It cometh true.
By the knot of three
Thus shall it be.
By the knot of four
'Tis strengthened more
By the knot of five
So may it thrive.
By the knot of six
The spell we fix
By the knot of seven
The stars of heaven.
By the knot of eight
The hand of fate.

By the knot of nine
The thing is mine.

Take a new piece of string, twine or cord. Perform the spell
at midnight, the traditional 'witching hour'. You must be alone,
in a room lit only by candlelight.

Have some incense burning. Get very clearly in your mind
what you wish for. Concentrate on this and try to banish all
other thoughts. Above all, *believe* in what you are doing. Work
with faith in the magic that you do.

Pass the cord through the smoke of the incense, back and
forth, while you whisper the words of your wish. Then begin to
tie the knots, reciting the words of the spell as you do so. Keep
concentrating hard on your wish and picture it coming true.

If you tie the knots in this order, you will find it easier to
space them evenly :

—x—x—x—x—x—x—x—x—x—
1 6 4 7 3 8 5 9 2

That is, first tie a knot at either end of the cord, then a knot
in the middle; then a knot half-way between each end and the
middle, then a knot half-way between each of these knots. This
will give you nine evenly-spaced knots. Practise a little first, if
you wish; but use an old piece of string to practise with, because
the cord you use for the actual spell must be new, one that has
never been used for anything else.

When you have completed the nine knots, pass the cord again
through the smoke of the incense. Then extinguish the candles
and the incense. Go straight to bed, putting the cord under your
pillow. You may have a significant dream, which will tell you
something about your wish.

Carry the knotted cord with you as a talisman; but keep it
hidden. Do not tell anyone else about it, except a fellow witch.
Even then, be discreet. Remember, magic power is concentrated
by silence and dissipated by babbling.

Invocation of the Moon Goddess

Diana, queen of night,
In all your beauty bright,
Shine on us here,
And with your silver beam
Unlock the gates of dream;
Rise bright and clear.
On earth and sky and sea,
Your magic mystery
Its spell shall cast,

Wherever leaf may grow,
Wherever tide may flow,
Till all be past.
O secret queen of power,
At this enchanted hour
We ask your boon.
May fortune's favour fall
Upon true witches all,
O Lady Moon!

INVOCATION OF THE HORNED GOD

By the flame that burneth bright,
O Horned One!
We call thy name into the night,
O Ancient One!
Thee we invoke, by the moon-led sea,
By the standing stone and the twisted tree.
Thee we invoke, where gather thine own,
By the nameless shrine forgotten and lone.
Come where the round of the dance is trod,
Horn and hoof of the goatfoot god!
By moonlit meadow, on dusky hill,
When the haunted wood is hushed and still,
Come to the charm of the chanted prayer,
As the moon bewitches the midnight air.
Evoke thy powers, that potent bide
In shining stream and the secret tide,
In fiery flame by starlight pale,
In shadowy host that rides the gale,
And by the fern-brakes fairy-haunted
Of forests wild and woods enchanted.
Come! O come!
To the heart-beat's drum!
Come to us who gather below
When the broad white moon is climbing slow
Through the stars to the heaven's height.
We hear thy hoofs on the wind of night!
As black tree-branches shake and sigh,
By joy and terror we know thee nigh.
We speak the spell thy power unlocks
At solstice, Sabbat and equinox,
Word of virtue the veil to rend,
From primal dawn to the wide world's end,
Since time began—
The blessing of Pan!

Blessed be all in hearth and hold,
Blessed in all worth more than gold.
Blessed be in strength and love,
Blessed be, where'er we rove.
Vision fade not from our eyes
Of the pagan paradise
Past the gates of death and birth,
Our inheritance of earth.
From our soul the song of spring
Fade not in our wandering.
Our life with all life is one,
By blackest night or noonday sun.
Eldest of gods, on thee we call,
Blessing be on thy creatures all.

Chants and Dances

Here are some additional chants which can be used by the coven to accompany its dancing round the circle. This, incidentally, is the origin of the word 'carol', which originally meant a round dance accompanied by singing. There were carols for May Day as well as Yuletide or Christmas, and the words of some of them are still preserved in English folklore. Here is an example, of unknown age or origin:

Here we come a-piping,
In Springtime and in May;
Green fruit a-ripening,
And Winter fled away.
The Queen she sits upon the strand,
Fair as lily, white as wand;
Seven billows on the sea,
Horses riding fast and free,
And bells beyond the sand.

'The Queen . . . fair as lily, white as wand' is the White Goddess of the moon and of nature, the Lady of the May who is commemorated by the crowning of the May Queen in many a village carnival. The 'horses riding fast and free' are the white horses of Manannan, the old Celtic god of the sea, the white-crested sea-waves. The 'bells beyond the sand' are the sunken bells of Caer Arianrhod, or of the city of Ys, or of lost Lyonesse, or any of the other drowned cities of myth and legend, back to great Atlantis itself.

This is an instance of the way in which folksongs preserve ancient pagan lore. Another example of this is the old folksong 'Green Grow the Rushes-O', of which there are many different versions, including two from Brittany, one of which is said to be Druidical.

May Eve was particularly significant to the Celts, as was November Eve or Hallowe'en, because in pre-Christian times these signified the two halves of the year. The summer half began on May Day and lasted until 1 November, when the winter half began, which lasted round until May Day again. The eve, or night before, was the time of celebration.

According to the beliefs of the Old Religion of the witches, the summer half of the year belongs to the Goddess, and the winter half to the Horned God. Hence the Sabbats of May Eve (or Walpurgis Night) and Hallowe'en are particularly important dates in the witch calendar.

Here, then, are the words of a chant which can be used with the round dance on May Eve :

> *Walpurgis Night, the time is right,*
> *The ancient powers awake.*
> *So dance and sing, around the ring,*
> *And Beltane magic make.*

> Chorus :
> *Walpurgis Night, Walpurgis Night,*
> *Upon the eve of May,*
> *We'll merry meet, and summer greet,*
> *For ever and a day.*

> *New life we see, in flower and tree,*
> *And summer comes again.*
> *Be free and fair, like earth and air,*
> *The sunshine and the rain.*

> Chorus :
> *Walpurgis Night, Walpurgis Night, etc.*

> *As magic fire be our desire*
> *To tread the pagan way,*
> *And our true will find and fulfil,*
> *As dawns a brighter day.*

> Chorus :
> *Walpurgis Night, Walpurgis Night, etc.*

> *The pagan powers this night be ours,*
> *Let all the world be free,*

And sorrow cast into the past,
And future blessed be!

Chorus :
Walpurgis Night, Walpurgis Night, etc.

The following is a similar chant for Hallowe'en. It can be used outdoors round a bonfire, or indoors round an extra large altar candle :

Fire red, summer's dead,
Yet it shall return.
Clear and bright, in the night,
Burn, fire, burn!

Chorus :
Dance the ring, luck to bring,
When the year's a-turning.
Chant the rhyme at Hallows-time,
When the fire's burning.

Fire glow, vision show
Of the heart's desire,
When the spell's chanted well
Of the witching fire.

Chorus :
Dance the ring, luck to bring, etc.

Fire spark, when nights are dark,
Makes our winter's mirth.
Red leaves fall, earth takes all,
Brings them to rebirth.

Chorus :
Dance the ring, luck to bring, etc.

Fire fair, earth and air,
And the heaven's rain,
All blessed be, and so may we,
At Hallows-tide again.

Chorus :
Dance the ring, luck to bring, etc.

Finally, here is a merry chant, which can be used upon almost any occasion. It goes to the tune of the old folksong, 'The Lincoln-shire Poacher' :

Come join the dance, that doth entrance,
And tread the circle's round.
Be of good cheer, that gather here,
Upon this merry ground.

Chorus :
Good luck to we that faithful be,
And hold our craft so dear,
For 'tis our delight of a shiny night,
In the season of the year.
Oh, 'tis our delight of a shiny night,
In the season of the year.

While stars do shine, we pledge the wine
Unto the Gods of old.
Nor shall there fail the witch wassail,
Nor shall their fire grow cold.

Chorus :
Good luck to we that faithful be, etc.

Throughout, about and round about,
By flame that burneth bright,
We'll dance and sing, around the ring,
At witching hour of night.

Chorus :
Good luck to we that faithful be, etc.

HERE ENDS THIS BOOK OF SHADOWS.

Bibliography

Lucius Apuleius, *The Golden Ass,* trans. William Adlington, 1566.
Tantra of the Great Liberation (Mahanirvana Tantra), trans.
Arthur Avalon (Sir John Woodroffe) (Dover Publications, Inc.,
New York, USA, 1972).
The Book of Ballymote, compiled by Solomon of Droma and
Manus MacDonough (Ireland, 1391).
Barddas, Rev. J. Williams Ab Ithel (Welsh MSS. Society, Llan-
dovery and London, 1862).
The Bhagavad Gita. Many translations are available. A notable
one is *The Geeta: The Gospel of the Lord Shri Krishna,* put into
English by Shri Purohit Swami. (Faber, London, 1969).
John Blofeld, *The Book of Change* (Allen & Unwin, London,
1968).
Frederick Bligh Bond and Thomas Lea, *Germatria* (reissue, Re-
search Into Lost Knowledge Organisation, London, 1977).
Janet and Colin Bord, *Mysterious Britain* (Garnstone Press,
London, 1972).
Sir E. A. Wallis Budge, *The Book of the Dead: An English
Translation of the Theban Recension,* (Kegan Paul, London, and
E. P. Dutton, New York, 1938).
Carlos Castaneda, *The Teachings of Don Juan* (Penguin Books,
London, 1970).
Carlos Castaneda, *A Separate Reality* (Penguin Books, London,
1974).
Louis Charpentier, *The Mysteries of Chartres Cathedral* (Re-
search Into Lost Knowledge Organisation, London, 1972).
Ithel Colquhoun, *Sword of Wisdom: MacGregor Mathers and
the Golden Dawn* (Neville Spearman, London, 1975).
The Confessions of Aleister Crowley, ed. John Symonds and
Kenneth Grant (Jonathan Cape, London, 1969).
Aleister Crowley, *The Magical Record of the Beast 666,* ed. John
Symonds and Kenneth Grant (Duckworth, London, 1972).

The Qabalah of Aleister Crowley (Samuel Weiser, New York, 1973).

Aleister Crowley, *De Arte Magica* (The Level Press, San Francisco,USA, N.d.)

Aleister Crowley, *Liber Aleph* (Unicorn Press, Seattle, USA, N.d.)

Aleister Crowley, *Magick in Theory and Practice* (Castle Books, New York, USA, N.d.)

Louis T. Culling, *A Manual of Sex Magick* (Llewellyn Publications, USA, 1971).

T. F. G. Dexter, *Fire Worship in Britain* (Watts & Co., London, 1931).

The Elder Edda: A Selection, trans. Paul B. Taylor and W. H. Auden. (Faber, London, 1969).

Mircea Eliade, *Shamanism: Archaic Techniques of Ecstasy* (Princeton University Press, USA, 1970).

The Equinox, Vol. I, No. 3. (Simkin, Marshall, London, 1910, publication sponsored by Aleister Crowley).

The Tibetan Book of the Dead, ed. W. Y. Evans-Wentz (Oxford University Press, London, 1957).

Tibetan Yoga and Secret Doctrines, ed. W. Y. Evans-Wentz (Oxford University Press, London, 1973).

C. L'Estrange Ewen, *Witchcraft and Demonianism* (Heath Cranton, London, 1933).

Dion Fortune, *The Sea Priestess* (published by the Author, London, 1938).

Dion Fortune, *The Goat-Foot God* (Aquarian Press, London, 1971).

Dion Fortune, *The Mystical Qabalah* (Williams & Norgate, London, 1935).

Dion Fortune, *Avalon of the Heart* (Aquarian Press, London, 1971).

Gerald B. Gardner, *High Magic's Aid* (*Scire*) (Michael Houghton, London, 1949).

Gerald B. Gardner, *Witchcraft Today* (Riders, London, 1954).

Gerald B. Gardner, *The Meaning of Witchcraft* (Aquarian Press, London, 1959).

Omar Garrison, *Tantra: The Yoga of Sex* (Academy Editions, London, 1974).

Robert Graves, *The White Goddess* (Faber, London, 1961).

Michael J. Harner, *Hallucinogens and Shamanism* (Oxford University Press, London and New York, 1973).

Jacquetta Hawkes, *A Guide to the Prehistoric and Roman Monuments in England and Wales* (Sphere Books, London, 1973).

Gerald S. Hawkins, *Beyond Stonehenge* (Hutchinson, London, 1973).

Ellic Howe, *The Magicians of the Golden Dawn* (Routledge & Kegan Paul, London, 1972).

Thomas Ingoldsby, (R. H. Barham), *The Ingoldsby Legends* (Richard Bentley & Son, London, 1887).

Man and his Symbols, ed. Carl Gustav Jung (Aldus Books, London, 1964).

Francis King, *Ritual Magic in England* (Neville Spearman, London, 1970).

Francis King, *Sexuality, Magic and Perversion* (New English Library, London, 1972).

The Secret Rituals of the O.T.O., ed. and introd. Francis King (C. W. Daniel Co., London, 1973).

Richard Payne Knight and Thomas Wright, *Two Essays on the Worship of Priapus* (privately printed, London, 1865).

Rudolf Koch, *The Book of Signs* (Dover Publications, USA, N.d.).

Charles Godfrey Leland, *Gypsy Sorcery and Fortune-Telling* (University Books, New York, 1962).

Charles Godfrey Leland, *Aradia:* or the Gospel of the Witches, (David Nutt, London, 1899).

Lord Lytton, *The Coming Race* (Routledge, London, 1874).

Eric Maple, *The Dark World of Witches* (Robert Hale, London, 1962).

The Key of Solomon the King, trans. S. Liddell MacGregor Mathers (George Redway, London, 1889).

John Michell, *The View Over Atlantis* (Abacus Books, London, 1975).

Richard Williams Morgan, *The History of Britain* (Marshall Press, London, 1933).

Margaret Alice Murray, *The God of the Witches* (Sampson, Low, London, 1931).

G. F. Northall, *English Folk Rhymes* (Kegan Paul, London, 1892).

Sheila Ostrander and Lynn Schroeder, *Psychic Discoveries behind the Iron Curtain* (Prentice-Hall, USA, 1970).

Jill Purce, *The Mystic Spiral* (Thames & Hudson, London, 1975).

Jonathan Quayne, *The Pearly Essence* (Mayflower Books, London, 1969).

Philip Rawson, *Tantra* (Catalogue of Exhibition at the Hayward Gallery, London, 1971, Arts Council of Great Britain).

Philip Rawson, *Tantra: The Indian Cult of Ecstasy* (Thames & Hudson, London, 1973).

The Golden Dawn, ed. Israel Regardie. (Hazel Hills Corporation, Wisconsin, USA, 1969).

Israel Regardie, *The Tree of Life* (Samuel Weiser, New York, 1972).

Wilhelm Reich, *The Function of the Orgasm* (Panther Books, London, 1968).

Frederick W. Robins, *The Smith: The Traditions and Lore of an Ancient Craft* (Riders, London, 1953).

Paul Screeton, *Quicksilver Heritage* (Thorsons, Wellingborough, 1974).

Edward Sellon, *Annotations Upon the Sacred Writings of the Hindus* (privately printed, London, 1865).

Idries Shah, *Oriental Magic* (Paladin Books, London, 1973).

Lewis Spence, *The Magic Arts in Celtic Britain* (Riders, London, 1946).

Lewis Spence, *Encyclopaedia of Occultism* (Citadel Press, USA, 1974).

The Sepher Yetzirah, trans. Knut Stenring (Riders, London, 1923).

William Stirling, *The Canon* (Garnstone Press, London, 1974).

Montague Summers, *History of Witchcraft and Demonology* (Kegan Paul, London, 1926).

Alexander Thom, *Megalithic Lunar Observatories* (Oxford University Press, London, 1971).

Doreen Valiente, *Where Witchcraft Lives* (Aquarian Press, London, 1962).

Doreen Valiente, *An A.B.C. of Witchcraft Past and Present* (Robert Hale, London, and St Martins Press, New York, 1973).

M. Volin and N. Phelan, *Sex and Yoga* (Sphere Books, London, 1968).

Erich Von Daniken, *Chariots of the Gods* (Corgi Books, London, 1971).

Erich Von Daniken, *In Search of Ancient Gods* (Souvenir Press, London, 1974).

Benjamin Walker, *Sex and the Supernatural* (Macdonald Unit 75, London, 1970).

Alfred Watkins, *The Old Straight Track* (Garnstone Press, London, 1970).

Alan Watts, *Nature, Man and Woman* (Wildwood House, London, 1973).

E. M. Wishaw, *Atlantis in Andalucia* (Riders, London, 1929).

George Hunt Williamson, *Road in the Sky* (Neville Spearman, London, 1965).

Sir John Woodroffe (Arthur Avalon), *Shakti and Shakta* (Luzac & Co., London, 1918).

Periodicals :
Daily Mirror, 14 June 1975.
'The Straight Path in Wisdom Teaching' by Allen Watkins, *The Ley Hunter*, No. 18, April, 1971.
'The Quest for Gaia' by Dr James Lovelock and Dr Sidney Epton. *The New Scientist*, 6 February, 1975.
The Wiccan, Nos. 40, 41 and 42.

Of the books listed here, I would like to mention briefly some which are in my opinion particularly helpful to the student of present-day witchcraft and paganism. Janet and Colin Bord's *Mysterious Britain* gives a good outline of things to be seen which are illustrative of Britain's mysterious past. It also indicates some of the lines of enquiry which are being followed to reveal more of our hidden and lost traditions.

Louis T. Culling's *A Manual of Sex Magick*, though written in a popular and even rather naïve style, nevertheless gives real information upon this subject, which Mr Culling was the first person in modern times to publish in plain words. (Incidentally, my own book *Natural Magic* also contains a chapter entitled 'Magic of Sex').

The researches of Mr L'Estrange Ewen into the recorded history of British witchcraft are detailed and extremely valuable.

The occult novels of Dion Fortune are both entertaining and full of practical esoteric knowledge. They were mostly written in the 1930s and tend to reproduce the idiom of that period; but their value is lasting. *The Sea Priestess* contains some fine invocations in verse to the goddess of the moon.

Gerald B. Gardner's *Witchcraft Today* has become a classic and been several times reprinted. It is a basic source book.

Charles Godfrey Leland wrote of witches and gypsies with real sympathy and insight. His books reveal first-hand knowledge of the subjects he devoted his life to studying. He was the first president of the Gypsy Lore Society and one of America's greatest collectors of folklore. His publication of *Aradia: or The Gospel of the Witches* in 1899 was a landmark in the history of modern witchcraft. (This book is now available in several reprinted editions.)

Margaret Murray's books, too, have become classics. In addition to *The God of the Witches*, I would add her other volume, *The Witch Cult in Western Europe*, as being indispensable to the serious student of this subject. Both are available in various paperback editions.

John Michell is a remarkably original writer about Britain's prehistoric culture, whose books are imaginative yet carefully researched. His *View Over Atlantis* genuinely deserves that over-worked adjective 'epoch-making'.

Philip Rawson is the outstanding present-day writer upon the Tantric traditions of the East. He has succeeded in popularizing this subject without losing its profundity, by no means an easy task.

Israel Regardie is the writer to whom we owe the unfolding of the knowledge of the Order of the Golden Dawn, with its revelation of the practical magical techniques of the western tradition. Occult students are also greatly indebted to Francis King for his researches into the history of Western occultism, though naturally I differ from his opinions about witchcraft.

Paul Screeton and John Michell continue the pioneer work of Alfred Watkins into the ley-line system and its mysterious energies. Not everyone will accept these theories; but they reveal many intriguing possibilities. Another notable pioneer of research into borderline energies is the late T. C. Lethbridge, who has written a whole series of books on this subject.

There are of course many other useful and important books for the student to discover. These notes are written in the hope of providing the beginner with some guidance in the collection of an occult library.

One final word of attribution. The words contained in the 'Affirmation' of the Self-Initiation Ritual in *Liber Umbrarum*, beginning 'Beloved Pan, and all the other gods who haunt this place . . .' are adapted from a prayer used by Socrates, as given at the end of the *Phaedrus* of Plato, which was written in Athens in the fourth century B.C.

Index